SUCCESS

at Key Stage 3
Science

Eileen Ramsden, David Applin and Jim Breithaupt

with Tony Buzan

Hodder & Stoughton

A MEMBER OF THE HODDER HEADLINE GROUP

Key to symbols

As you read through this book you will notice the following symbols. They will help you find your way around the book more quickly.

 shows a handy hint to help you remember something

 shows a short list of key facts

 means remember!!!

 says 'can you explain?'

 gives worked examples to help you with calculations and equations

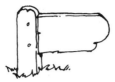 points you to other parts of the book where related topics are explained

 (and ★ in previews) shows the extra topics you'll need if you're ambitious and aiming at level 7

ISBN 0 340 725109

First published 1998
Impression number   10 9 8 7 6 5 4 3 2 1
Year   2002 2001 2000 1999 1998

The 'Teach Yourself' name and logo are registered trade marks of Hodder & Stoughton Ltd.

Copyright © 1998 Eileen Ramsden, David Applin and Jim Breithaupt
Introduction ('Shortcuts to success') © 1998 Tony Buzan

Designed and produced by Gecko Ltd, Bicester, Oxon
Printed in Great Britain for Hodder & Stoughton Educational, a division of Hodder Headline Plc, 338 Euston Road, London NW1 3BH by Scotprint Ltd, Musselburgh, Scotland.

Mind Maps: Peter Bull and Chris Rothero
Illustrations: Peter Bull, Karen Donnelly, Sarah Jowsey, Mike Parsons, John Plumb, Chris Rothero and Tokay Ltd.

Cover design: Amanda Hawkes
Cover illustration: Paul Bateman

Contents

Tackling each topic

★ Make a copy of the table below and fill in the topic titles.
★ Do the Test yourself questions at the beginning of each topic.
★ Look at the Answers section and mark your answers.
★ Enter your mark for the test in the grid.
★ Work through the topic. Draw a Mind Map.
★ Now do the Round-up questions.
★ Look at the Answers section and mark your answers.
★ Enter your mark in the grid.
★ Are you pleased with your marks? If not, come back to this topic at a later date and try again.
★ Enter your new scores in the grid. Have you improved?

Topic	Test yourself			Round-up		
	Score 1	Score 2	Score 3	Score 1	Score 2	Score 3

Shortcuts to success

Would you like your homework to be fun and a lot easier? Would you like to be able to remember things better? Would you like to read faster and understand more? To find out how, read the next three pages and follow the suggestions throughout this book.

Your *amazing* brain

Your brain is like a super, *super*, SUPER computer. The world's best computers have only a few thousand chips. Your brain has brain cells – 12 *million* MILLION of them! This means you are a genius just waiting to discover yourself! All you have to do is learn how to get those brain cells working together, and you'll not only do better at school, you'll do your homework more quickly and therefore have more free time too.

Your *magnificent* 'Memory Muscle'

Your memory is like a muscle. If you don't use it, it will grow weaker and weaker, but if you do keep it exercised, it will grow stronger and stronger.

Here are four tips for improving your Memory Muscle:

1 Work for between 20 and 40 minutes at a time, and *then take a break*

The break allows your Memory Muscle to rest and lets the information sink in. This also makes your Memory Muscle stronger for your next learning session.

2 Go back over your work

If you wait for a little while after you have been learning something, and you then look back at it later, you'll catch your brain at the top of the memory wave and remember even more.

3 Make connections

Your Memory Muscle becomes stronger when it can link things together. You can use your brain's amazing power to conjure up a huge number of pictures and ideas at once to help you to remember information. Join the separate facts together in some way to make a picture, for example on a Mind Map, and they'll come back to you all together, in a flash!

4 Think BIG

Your Memory Muscle gets stronger if what it is trying to remember is special in some way, so 'think big' and make what you are learning brightly coloured, funny, peculiar, special.

Your new *magic* learning formula – The Mind Map

When people go on holidays or journeys they take maps to give them a general picture of where they are going and to help them find their way around when they get there. It is exactly the same with your memory and schoolwork. If you have a 'map' of what you have to cover, everything is easier.

The Mind Map is a very special map. It helps you to find your way around a subject easily and quickly because it mirrors the way your brain works. Use it for organising your work both at school and at home, for taking notes and planning your homework.

The Mind Maps in this book

Below you will see a Mind Map on rocks.

In the centre of this Mind Map is a picture of the rock cycle, which summarises the theme of the topic. Coming out from this there are five branches, each one covering an important part of the topic.

You see how easy it is! You have summarised an entire topic on just one page, and this is now firmly logged in your brain, for you to get at whenever you want! If you look at this Mind Map five times over the next five months, the information it contains will be in your brain for many, many years to come.

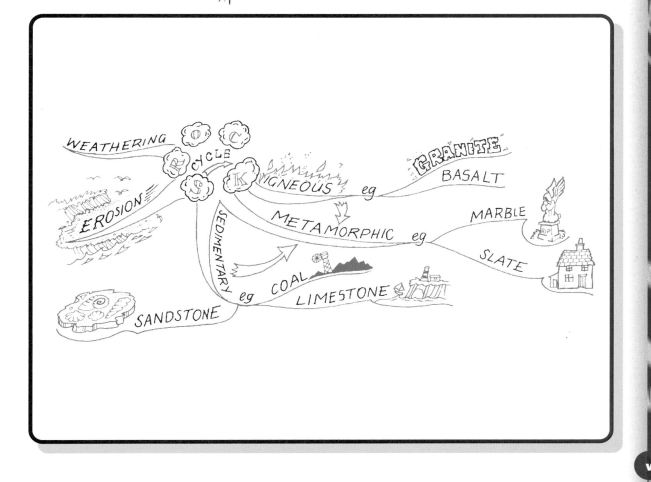

How to read a Mind Map

1. Begin in the centre, the focus of your topic.

2. The words/images attached to the centre are like chapter headings: read them next.

3. Always read out from the centre, in every direction (even on the left-hand side, where you will have to read from right to left, instead of the usual left to right).

How to draw a Mind Map

1. Start in the middle of the page with the page turned sideways. This gives your brain the maximum width for its thoughts.

2. Always start by drawing a small picture or symbol. Why? Because a picture is worth a thousand words to your brain. And try to use at least three colours, as colour helps your memory even more.

3. Write or draw your ideas on coloured branching lines connected to your central image. These key symbols and words are the headings for your topic.

4. Then add facts, further items and ideas by drawing more, smaller, branches on to the main branches, just like a tree.

5. Always print your word clearly on its line. Use only one word per line.

6. To link ideas and thoughts on different branches, use arrows, colours, underlining, and boxes.

Make life *easy* for your brain

When you start on a new book or topic there are several things you can do to help get your brain 'on line' faster:

1. **Quickly scan through the whole book or topic,** as you would do if you were in a shop deciding whether or not to buy a book or magazine. This gives your brain *control*.

2. **Think of what you already know about the subject.** You'll often find it's a lot more than you first thought. A good way of doing this is to do a quick Mind Map of *everything you know* about the subject after you have skimmed through it.

3. **Ask 'who?' 'what?' 'why?' 'where?' 'when?' and 'how?' questions about the topic.** Questions help your brain fish the knowledge out.

4. **Have another quick scan through.** Look at the diagrams, pictures and illustrations, and also at the beginnings and ends of sections – often most information is contained at the beginnings and ends.

5. **Build up a Mind Map.** This helps your brain to organise and remember information as you go.

6. **Mark up any difficult bits and move on.** Your brain *will* be able to solve the problems when you come back to them a little while later – much like saving the difficult bits of a jigsaw puzzle till last. They all fall into place in the end.

7. **Have a final scan.** Look through the book or topic quickly one more time. This will lodge it permanently in your memory banks.

And finally...

1. *Have fun while you learn* – people who enjoy what they are doing understand and remember it more.

2. *Use your teachers* as resource centres. Ask them for help with specific topics and with more general advice on how you can improve your all-round performance.

3. *Personalise your* **Success at Key Stage 3 Science** by underlining and highlighting, by adding notes and pictures. Allow your brain to have a conversation with it!

Your brain is an amazing piece of equipment. The more you understand and use it, the more it will repay you. I wish you and your brain every success.

Tony Buzan

Matter

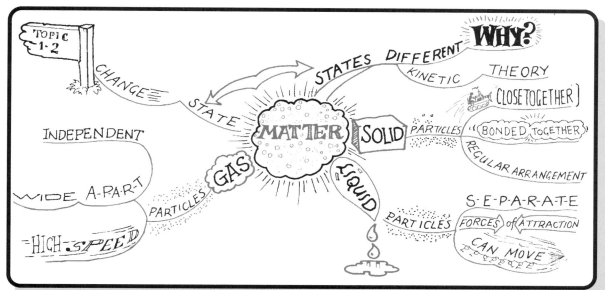

What does 'classifying' mean?

It means 'sorting out', you bird brain!

TOPIC 1·2

preview

At the end of this section you will be able to:
- **describe the states of matter and changes of state**
- **understand and apply the kinetic theory of matter**

Test yourself

1 Name the three chief states of matter. [3]
2 What is the difference between evaporation and boiling? [2]
3 How can you tell when a liquid is boiling? [1]
4 Explain the difference between 'heavy' and 'dense'. [2]

5 Why do crystals have a regular shape? [2]
6 What happens to the heat energy that is supplied to a solid to make it melt? [1]
7 One litre of water forms 1333 litres of steam. Explain the big difference in volume. [2]
8 Explain why a spoonful of salt can flavour a whole pan of soup. [1]

1.1 Solids, liquids and gases

Everything in the universe consists of matter. There are three chief **states of matter**: solids, liquids and gases. Their characteristics are shown in the table.

	volume	shape	effect of heating
solid	fixed	definite	expands slightly
liquid	fixed	flows – changes shape to fit the shape of the container	expands
gas	changes – it always fills the container	changes to fit the shape of the container	expands greatly (gases have much lower densities than solids and liquids)

Characteristics of solids, liquids and gases

1.2 Change of state

Matter can change from one state into another, as shown in the diagram.

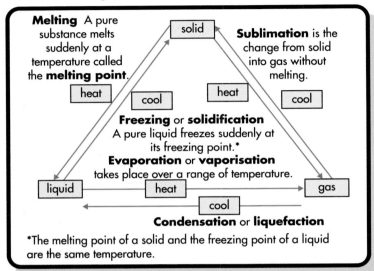

Melting A pure substance melts suddenly at a temperature called the **melting point**.

heat | cool

Sublimation is the change from solid into gas without melting.

heat | cool

Freezing or **solidification** A pure liquid freezes suddenly at its freezing point.*

Evaporation or **vaporisation** takes place over a range of temperature.

liquid | heat | gas

cool

Condensation or **liquefaction**

*The melting point of a solid and the freezing point of a liquid are the same temperature.

Change of state

1.3 Describing matter

* **Density:** Density = $\dfrac{\text{mass}}{\text{volume}}$

  For example 1 cm³ of gold weighs 19 g; the density of gold is 19 g/cm³
* **Compressibility:** Gases can be compressed (squeezed into a smaller volume) much more than liquids or solids. An increase in pressure from 1 atmosphere to 2 atmospheres halves the volume of a gas (provided the temperature stays the same).
* **Ease of flow:** Gases flow readily. A gas diffuses (spreads out) to occupy all the space available to it. Liquids flow. Some liquids flow slowly; they are **viscous** (like treacle). Solids do not flow.
* **Melting point:** Solids melt on heating. Impure solids melt gradually over a range of temperature. A pure solid melts suddenly at a temperature called the melting point. The temperature remains steady at the melting point as long as there is some solid left.
* **Boiling point:** A mixture of liquids boils over a range of temperature. A pure liquid boils suddenly when the temperature reaches its boiling point. The temperature stays at the boiling point of the liquid as long as there is some liquid left.

* **Conductivity:**
  Thermal: metals and alloys (mixtures of metals) conduct heat. Thermal insulators do not conduct heat. **Electrical:** metals and alloys and graphite conduct electricity. Non-conductors or electrical insulators do not conduct electricity.

1.4 Matter in motion

'Kinetic' means 'moving' in Greek. According to **the kinetic theory of matter**, all forms of matter are made up of small particles (atoms, molecules and charged particles called ions). These particles are in constant motion. The kinetic theory explains the differences between solids, liquids and gases and changes between them.

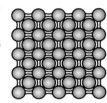

In a solid the particles are close together. This is why solids are dense. Chemical bonds hold the particles in a regular three-dimensional structure. The particles can vibrate, but they cannot leave the structure.

When the solid is heated, the particles gain energy. They may vibrate so much that they break away from the structure and move about. When this happens, the solid has melted.

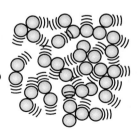

In a liquid the particles are not much further apart than in a solid. They are free to move about. This is why a liquid flows easily and has no fixed shape. There are weak forces of attraction between particles. When a liquid is heated some particles gain enough energy to break away from the other particles and become a gas.

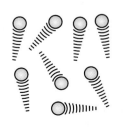

Most of a gas is space. Particles move at high speed through the space. There are almost no forces of attraction between them. When a volume of liquid vaporises it forms a much larger volume of gas because the particles are much further apart in a gas. Particles of gas collide with the container. This is the cause of the pressure that a gas exerts.

1.5 What does the kinetic theory explain?

Dissolving of a solid

When a solid dissolves, particles of solid separate from the others and spread out through the solvent. A solution is formed.

Diffusion of a gas

When a gas enters a container (e.g. a balloon), particles of gas move through the container until the gas has spread evenly through all the space available.

Evaporation or vaporisation

There are forces of attraction between the molecules in a liquid. Some molecules have a more than average amount of energy and are able to break away from the attraction of other molecules – that is, to become a gas. Losing these energetic molecules makes the average energy of the molecules that remain lower than before: the liquid has cooled.

round-up

How much have you improved? Look up your score on page 41.

1 Why must you heat a solid to make it melt? [2]
2 What type of solids conduct **(i)** heat **(ii)** electricity? [2]
3 Why do gases have much lower densities than solids and liquids? [1]
4 Describe what happens to the particles when a solid dissolves. [2]
5 When the pressure on a gas is increased, the gas contracts. Why does this happen? [2]
6 Look at the table.

Substance	Melting point in °C	Boiling point in °C
A	−220	−188
B	−101	−34
C	−7	59
D	114	184

(a) In which state (solid, liquid, gas) are A, B, C and D at room temperature (20 °C)? **(b)** At a certain temperature, the particles of C are close together but randomly arranged. Is C a solid, liquid or gas? **(c)** Substance A is at room temperature. How would you describe the arrangement of particles? [8]
7 What happens to particles of a gas when a balloon containing the gas is heated? [4]
8 Kim is wearing her favourite perfume, Nice Spice. Explain why people can smell her perfume from some feet away. [3]

9 Uncle Johnny uses an aftershave lotion. When he dabs it on, it cools his skin. Explain how the lotion produces this cooling effect. [2]
10 The graph below shows the rise in temperature when a solid is heated.
(a) What name is given to the temperature T1?
(b) Why does the temperature stay the same at B although the solid is being heated?
(c) What has happened at C? [3]

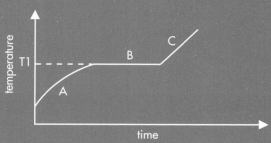

11 The figure below shows the rise in temperature when a liquid is heated.
(a) What name is given to the temperature T2? **(b)** Why does the temperature stay the same at E although the liquid is being heated? **(c)** What has happened at F? [3]

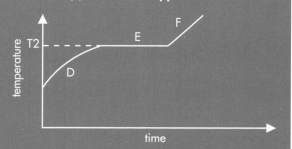

Elements

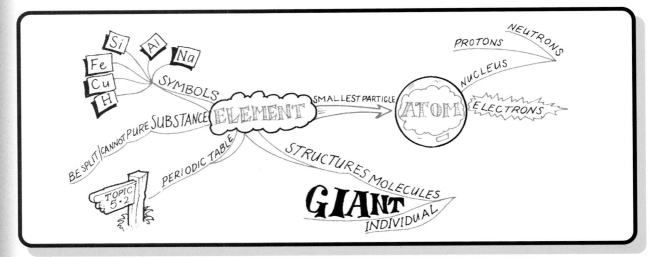

preview

At the end of this topic you will be able to:

- explain what an element is
- describe some elements
- say how protons, neutrons and electrons are arranged in an atom
- ★ describe the structures of some elements

How much do you already know?

Test yourself

1 Explain what is meant by 'an element'. [2]
2 Mention three elements. Give one use for each of them. [6]
3 An atom is made of charged particles called protons and electrons. Why is an atom uncharged? [1]
4 What is meant by **(a)** the atomic number or proton number? **(b)** the mass number of an element? [2]

5 An atom of potassium has mass number 39 and atomic number (proton number) 19. What is **(a)** the number of electrons? **(b)** the number of neutrons? [2]

2.1 What is an element?

There are 92 elements that occur naturally in the Earth's crust. They are all different. The thing that they have in common is that, no matter what you do to it, you can never split an element into simpler substances. You can make more complex substances from elements by combining them. You cannot make anything simpler from an element.

ELEMENTARY, MY DEAR WATSON!

BY ELEMENTARY, DO YOU MEAN SIMPLE, HOLMES?

IT'S THE SAME THING IN CHEMISTRY, WATSON. AN <u>ELEMENTARY</u> SUBSTANCE, AN <u>ELEMENT</u>, IS A <u>SIMPLE</u> SUBSTANCE—WHATEVER YOU DO, YOU CAN'T SPLIT IT UP INTO SIMPLER SUBSTANCES.

Here are some examples of important elements.

Gold: people died for it

During the Gold Rush in the USA in 1850, thousands of people made their way to Alaska. In winter the temperature in Alaska is between 0 °C and −30 °C. Many miners made their fortunes, but many more perished in the search for gold.

Diamond: a brilliant element

Diamonds are 'for ever' because diamond is the hardest naturally occurring substance. The amazing sparkle and fire of a diamond comes from its ability to split light into different colours and reflect them.

Copper: Bronze Age element

Stone age people discovered bronze, an alloy (mixture) of the elements copper and tin. The knives and arrowheads that they made out of bronze revolutionised their lives. The Bronze Age was born.

Iron: revolutionary element

It was iron that made the industrial revolution possible. Our technology uses machines made of iron and steel (which is an alloy of iron). Buildings, cars, trains, railways and ships depend on steel.

Chlorine: killer and life-saver

During the First World War, British and French soldiers saw a great green cloud rolling along the ground towards them. It was chlorine, a poisonous dense green gas. It left a trail of dead soldiers behind it. But chlorine has another side. It has saved more lives than any other chemical because it is able to kill bacteria. The water industry treats our water supply with chlorine to make it safe to drink.

Silicon: element of the computer age

The use of computers has been made possible by the silicon chip. Silicon is a semiconductor (with behaviour between that of a conductor of electricity and a non-conductor). An electronic circuit can be built onto the surface of a tiny silicon chip.

SURFING THE NET – THANKS TO SILICON!

Aluminium: wonder metal

The statue of Eros in Piccadilly Circus in London has stood for a century without corroding. It is made of an aluminium alloy. Freedom from corrosion is the reason why aluminium is used in doors and window frames, food packaging and saucepans. Its low density is the reason why aluminium is used to make aeroplanes and small boats.

2.2 What are elements made of?

According to the atomic theory, solids, liquids and gases are all made up of enormous numbers of minute particles. A British chemist called John Dalton succeeded in getting this idea accepted. In 1808 Dalton wrote that all forms of matter consist of atoms, minute particles that cannot be split up. In some elements a number of atoms combine to form a more complex particle called a molecule. For example, oxygen molecules consist of two atoms.

The atom is the smallest particle of an element that can take part in a chemical reaction. A molecule is the smallest particle of an element that can exist independently.

2.3 What are atoms made of?

At the beginning of the twentieth century scientists found experimental evidence that atoms are composed of smaller particles: **protons, neutrons** and **electrons**.

Protons have a positive charge of +1 unit. Electrons have a negative charge of −1 unit. Neutrons are uncharged. The number of protons in an atom equals the number of electrons, so the whole atom is uncharged. The mass of the atom depends chiefly on the protons and neutrons. Electrons have very little mass.

FACTS

The nucleus occupies a tiny volume in the centre of the atom. It consists of protons and neutrons.

The electrons occupy the space surrounding the nucleus. They repel the electrons of neighbouring atoms. The electrons are in constant motion, moving round the nucleus in circular paths called orbitals.

The arrangement of particles in the atom

2.4 Symbols of elements

Every element has its own **symbol**. The symbol is a letter or two letters which stand for one atom of the element – for example the symbol for sulphur is S, the symbol for aluminium is Al. Sometimes the symbol is taken from the Latin name for the element – for example iron is Fe (for *ferrum*), lead Pb (for *plumbum*).

2.5 Structures of elements

In metallic elements the atoms are held together by strong chemical bonds in a **giant molecule**. Some non-metallic elements also consist of giant molecules, millions of atoms bonded together in a crystalline structure. Examples are diamond (a form of the element carbon) and silicon (of silicon chips fame). Other non-metallic elements consist of small individual molecules, for example oxygen consists of O_2 molecules.

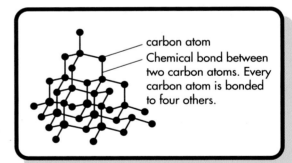

carbon atom
Chemical bond between two carbon atoms. Every carbon atom is bonded to four others.

The structure of diamond

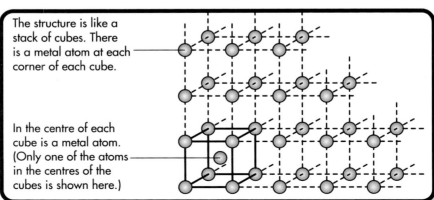

The structure is like a stack of cubes. There is a metal atom at each corner of each cube.

In the centre of each cube is a metal atom. (Only one of the atoms in the centres of the cubes is shown here.)

A small part of a metal

2.6 The periodic table

The periodic table lists all the elements in order of increasing atomic number (the number of protons in the atomic nucleus).

THE PERIODIC TABLE
Page 14.

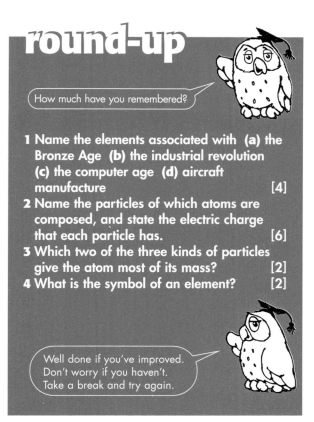

round-up

How much have you remembered?

1 Name the elements associated with **(a)** the Bronze Age **(b)** the industrial revolution **(c)** the computer age **(d)** aircraft manufacture [4]

2 Name the particles of which atoms are composed, and state the electric charge that each particle has. [6]

3 Which two of the three kinds of particles give the atom most of its mass? [2]

4 What is the symbol of an element? [2]

Well done if you've improved. Don't worry if you haven't. Take a break and try again.

Compounds

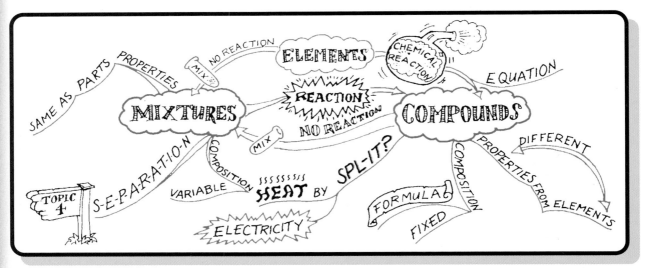

I find formulas fantastic!

preview

At the end of this topic you will:
- **know what a compound is**
- **know what the formula of a compound is**
- **know the differences between a mixture and a compound**

How much do you already know?

Test yourself

1 Explain the difference between an element and a compound. [3]
2 Name two methods that can be used to split a compound into elements. [2]
3 Give the number of atoms in **(a)** H_2O
   (b) H_2SO_4 [2]

3.1 What is a compound?

Two or more elements may combine – join together chemically. When they combine a compound is formed. A compound contains its elements in fixed proportions, for example magnesium oxide always contains 60% magnesium and 40% oxygen by mass.

A **compound** is a pure substance that consists of two or more elements. These are chemically combined in fixed proportions by mass.

FACTS

Some compounds can be **synthesised** (made) from their elements. For example

★ Magnesium burns in oxygen to form magnesium oxide.
★ Hot copper combines with chlorine to form copper chloride.
★ Hydrogen burns in oxygen (or in air) to form water.

Chemical bonds

When we say that elements combine, we mean that atoms of the elements have been joined by **chemical bonds**. In a piece of magnesium, the metal atoms are joined to one another by chemical bonds. An oxygen molecule consists of two atoms of oxygen joined by a chemical bond.

When magnesium and oxygen react, the chemical bonds break. New bonds form between magnesium atoms and oxygen atoms in the new substance, magnesium oxide. During a chemical reaction, existing chemical bonds break and new chemical bonds are made.

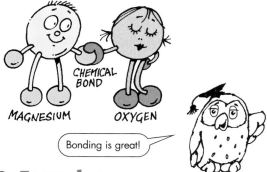

Bonding is great!

3.2 Formulas

Every compound has a **formula**. The formula contains the symbols of the elements present and some numbers. The numbers give the ratio in which the atoms of different elements are present.

A molecule of water contains two hydrogen atoms and one oxygen atom, giving the formula H_2O.

A single molecule of H_2O

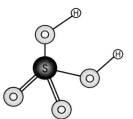

A single molecule of H_2SO_4

A molecule of sulphuric acid contains two hydrogen atoms, one sulphur atom and four oxygen atoms, giving it the formula H_2SO_4.

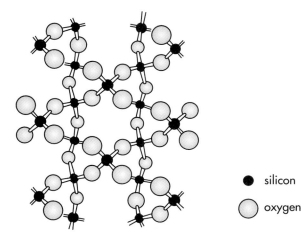

● silicon
○ oxygen

SiO_2, a giant molecule

Silica (the main component of sand) consists of giant molecules with two oxygen atoms for every silicon atom, giving the formula SiO_2.

Formula	Chemical
Water	H_2O
Carbon monoxide	CO
Sodium hydroxide	$NaOH$
Carbon dioxide	CO_2
Hydrochloric acid	HCl
Sulphur dioxide	SO_2
Sulphuric acid	H_2SO_4
Ammonia	NH_3
Nitric acid	HNO_3
Calcium oxide	CaO
Sodium chloride	$NaCl$
Calcium carbonate	$CaCO_3$
Sodium carbonate	Na_2CO_3
Calcium hydroxide	$Ca(OH)_2$
Sodium sulphate	Na_2SO_4
Calcium chloride	$CaCl_2$
Copper oxide	CuO
Magnesium oxide	MgO
Copper sulphate	$CuSO_4$
Magnesium chloride	$MgCl_2$
Copper sulphate crystals	$CuSO_4 \cdot 5H_2O$
Aluminium chloride	$AlCl_3$

The formulas of some common chemicals

Notice the names. The ending -ide means that there are two elements in the compound – e.g. calcium chloride. The ending -ate means that the compound contains oxygen – e.g. copper sulphate.

Hints & Tips

3.3 Splitting up compounds

Many compounds can be **decomposed** – split up into their elements or into simpler compounds

★ by heat – this is **thermal decomposition** (for example, silver oxide splits up into silver and oxygen when heated)
★ by a direct electric current – by **electrolysis** (for example, water is split up by a direct electric current into hydrogen and oxygen).

Learn more about splitting up compounds on page 28.

3.4 Compounds and mixtures

A compound is different from a mixture of elements,
as you can see in the table.

Mixtures	Compounds
No chemical change takes place when a mixture is made	When a compound is made a chemical reaction takes place. Heat is taken in or given out
A mixture has the same properties (characteristics and behaviour) as its parts	A compound has a new set of properties – it does not behave in the same way as the substances from which it was made
A mixture can be separated into its parts by methods such as those described in Topic 4, e.g. distillation	A compound can be split into its elements or into simpler compounds only by a chemical reaction
TOPIC 4 Page 11. A mixture can contain its parts in any proportions. A mixture of iron and sulphur may contain anything from less than 1% to more than 99% iron	A compound contains its elements in fixed proportions by mass – e.g. iron sulphide always contains 63.6% by mass of iron and 36.4 % by mass of sulphur

Differences between mixtures and compounds

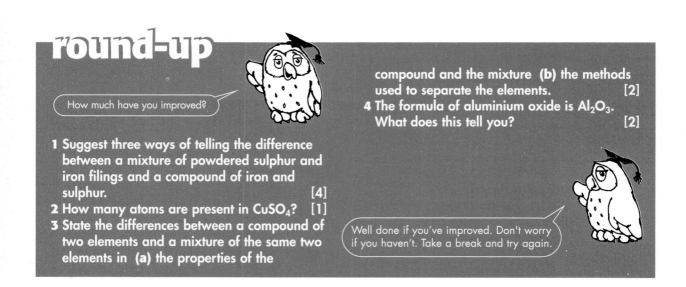

round-up

How much have you improved?

1 Suggest three ways of telling the difference between a mixture of powdered sulphur and iron filings and a compound of iron and sulphur. [4]
2 How many atoms are present in $CuSO_4$? [1]
3 State the differences between a compound of two elements and a mixture of the same two elements in (a) the properties of the compound and the mixture (b) the methods used to separate the elements. [2]
4 The formula of aluminium oxide is Al_2O_3. What does this tell you? [2]

Well done if you've improved. Don't worry if you haven't. Take a break and try again.

Mixtures

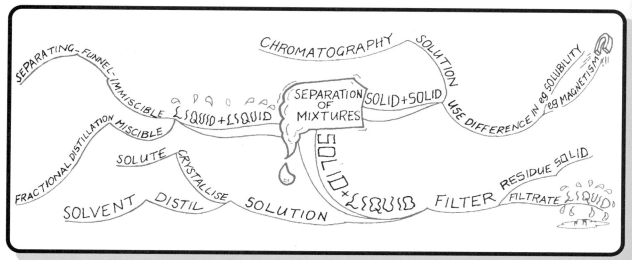

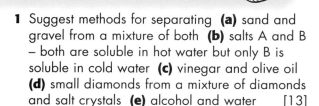

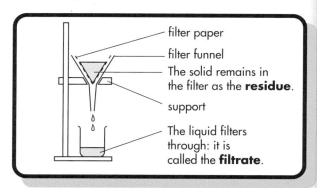

preview

At the end of this topic you will be able to:
- **describe methods for separating substances from mixtures**

It's easy. I did all this in the lab.

How much do you already know?

Test yourself

1 Suggest methods for separating **(a)** sand and gravel from a mixture of both **(b)** salts A and B – both are soluble in hot water but only B is soluble in cold water **(c)** vinegar and olive oil **(d)** small diamonds from a mixture of diamonds and salt crystals **(e)** alcohol and water   [13]

4.1 Earth provides us with mixtures

All the materials we use must come from the Earth's crust and atmosphere. Few of the raw materials we use are found in a pure state in the Earth's crust. We have to find methods for separating the substances we want from a mixture. Some of these methods are shown in the table on page 12.

4.2 Separating two solids, one soluble and one insoluble

Add a **solvent**, e.g. water. Stir to dissolve one solid in the solvent. Filter as shown in the figure below. The insoluble solid is left on the filter paper. The soluble solid is in solution. It is obtained by evaporating the filtrate until it crystallises.

— filter paper
— filter funnel
— The solid remains in the filter as the **residue**.
— support
— The liquid filters through: it is called the **filtrate**.

Filtration

11

Mixture	Type of mixture	Method of separation
Solid + solid	**1** Solid mixture	**1** Use a difference in properties – e.g. solubility or magnetic properties
	2 Two solids in a solution	**2** Use chromatography
Solid + liquid	**1** Mixture	**1** Filter
	2 Solution	**2** Crystallise to obtain the solid Distil to obtain the liquid
Liquid + liquid	**1** Immiscible (separate into two layers – e.g. oil and water)	**1** Use a separating funnel
	2 Miscible (do not separate)	**2** Use fractional distillation

Separating pure substances from mixtures

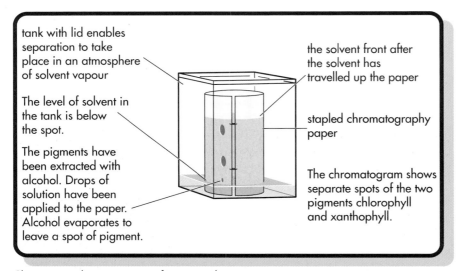

tank with lid enables separation to take place in an atmosphere of solvent vapour

the solvent front after the solvent has travelled up the paper

The level of solvent in the tank is below the spot.

stapled chromatography paper

The pigments have been extracted with alcohol. Drops of solution have been applied to the paper. Alcohol evaporates to leave a spot of pigment.

The chromatogram shows separate spots of the two pigments chlorophyll and xanthophyll.

Chromatography on an extract from green leaves

4.3 Separating substances by chromatography

The figure shows chromatography on a solution of the pigments in green leaves. The solvent is alcohol. It carries the pigments through a strip of **chromatography paper**. The reason why the pigments separate is that they travel at different speeds, like runners in a race.

thermometer records boiling point of liquid

condenser

distillation flask

water out

anti-bumping granules assist smooth boiling

cold water in

heat

beaker

distillate

A laboratory distillation apparatus

4.4 Distillation separates solvent from solution

Heat the solution in the **distillation** apparatus shown. The solvent distils over. It is collected as the **distillate**. The solute (the dissolved substance) remains in the distillation flask.

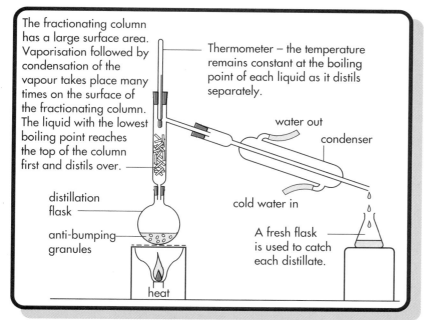

The fractionating column has a large surface area. Vaporisation followed by condensation of the vapour takes place many times on the surface of the fractionating column. The liquid with the lowest boiling point reaches the top of the column first and distils over.

Thermometer – the temperature remains constant at the boiling point of each liquid as it distils separately.

water out

condenser

distillation flask

anti-bumping granules

cold water in

A fresh flask is used to catch each distillate.

heat

Fractional distillation

4.5 Fractional distillation of a solution of two liquids

Heat the mixture in the fractional distillation apparatus shown in the figure. The liquids distil over in order of boiling points. In the example shown, alcohol (ethanol) has the lower boiling point (78 °C) and distils over first. When all the alcohol has distilled the flask is changed. The temperature rises until water distils at 100 °C.

round-up

How much have you learnt?

1 A recycling centre has a collection of empty steel cans and aluminium cans. Can you suggest a method of separating the steel cans from the aluminium cans? [2]

2 Mandy has been set a problem. She is given a mixture of powdered glass and salt crystals. How can she obtain pure salt crystals from the mixture? [3]

3 A mixture contains the salts C and D. Both are insoluble in water but only C is soluble in alcohol. Suggest a method you could use to obtain C and D. Mention any safety precautions that would be needed. [5]

4 The manufacturer Tinto has a patent on three pigments A, B and C. A rival firm Coloro has brought out the pigments P1 and P2. Tinto suspects that Coloro is using Tinto's pigments. The works chemist obtains a chromatogram of all five pigments. The results of her analysis are shown in the figure. What conclusions can you draw? [2]

P1   P2   A   B   C

Chromatogram of pigments A, B, C, P1 and P2

5 Miss Arah receives a 'poison pen' letter. She suspects that one of her neighbours, Mr Brown, Mrs White, Miss Green or Miss Black, is the writer. The police chemist runs chromatograms on the inks from the suspects' pens and compares them with the poison pen letter. Who is guilty? [1]

Miss Arah's letter   Mr Brown's   Mrs White's   Miss Green's   Miss Black's

Chromatograms of the inks from the pens

Metals and non-metals

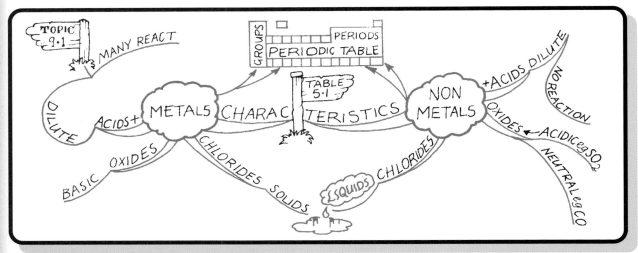

preview

At the end of this topic you will:
- **know the differences between elements which are metals and those which are non-metals**
- ★ **know how elements are arranged in the periodic table**

How much do you already know?

Test yourself

1 Explain what is meant by 'an element'. [2]
2 A is a shiny element that is used to make saucepans. Is A a metal or a non-metal? Explain your answer. [3]
3 B is an element that is used to make electric cables. Is B a metal or a non-metal? Explain your answer. [3]
4 When the element Y is dropped into hydrochloric acid, the acid fizzes. Is Y a metal or a non-metal? Explain your answer. [3]

5.1 Classifying elements

There are 92 elements that occur naturally on Earth. As more and more elements were discovered and more was found out about them it became important to sort them out – to classify them. The first step was to divide them into metallic and non-metallic elements. You can see some of the differences between metals and non-metals in the table on the next page.

5.2 The periodic table

In 1866 a chemist called John Newlands took classification further. He arranged all the elements in order of the masses of their atoms. He noticed a pattern – similar elements appeared at regular intervals.

Lithium, sodium and potassium are similar elements. Sodium followed lithium after an interval of seven elements. Potassium followed seven elements after sodium. Taking the elements in order of atomic masses, Newlands arranged them in rows, called **periods**. Starting a new row every eight elements, he found that similar elements fell into vertical columns, which he called **groups**. A Russian chemist called Dmitri Mendeleev carried on Newlands' work. Mendeleev's classification of elements is known as the **periodic table**. In the periodic table the elements are arranged in order of their atomic numbers (proton numbers), rather than atomic masses.

Metallic elements	Non-metallic elements
PHYSICAL PROPERTIES	PHYSICAL PROPERTIES
Solids except for mercury	Solids and gases, except for bromine (which is a liquid)
Dense, hard	Most of the solid elements are softer than metals – diamond is exceptional
Shiny when the surface is smooth	Dull, except diamond and iodine
A metal does not break when its shape is changed. It can be hammered flat or stretched into wire form	Many are brittle: they break when a force is applied
Conduct heat	Are poor thermal conductors
Are good conductors of electricity	Are poor electrical conductors, except for graphite. Some, e.g. silicon, are semiconductors
Are sonorous: they make a pleasing sound when struck	Are not sonorous
CHEMICAL PROPERTIES	CHEMICAL PROPERTIES
Many react with dilute acids to form hydrogen and a salt	Do not react with dilute acids
Form basic oxides and hydroxides, e.g. NaOH, CaO	Form acidic oxides – e.g. CO_2, SO_2 – or neutral oxides – e.g. CO, NO
The chlorides are crystalline solids, e.g. NaCl	The chlorides are liquids with low boiling points, e.g. CCl_4

Characteristics of metallic and non-metallic elements

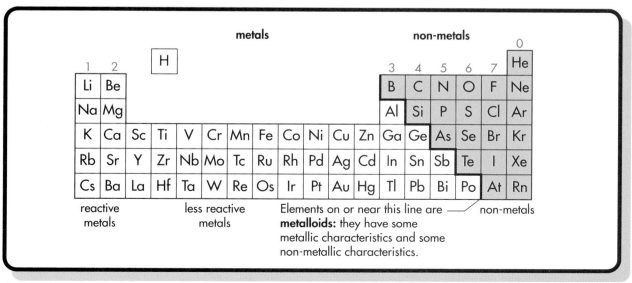

The periodic table

round-up

How much can you remember?
Check out your score on page 42.

1 The element P conducts electricity. Is P metallic or non-metallic? [2]

2 The element R forms an acidic oxide, RO_2. Is R metallic or non-metallic? [1]

3 The element E forms a crystalline chloride ECl_2. Is E metallic or non-metallic? [1]

4 The oxide QO_2 is basic. is Q metallic or non-metallic? [1]

5 List four physical properties in which sulphur (a non-metal) and copper (a metal) differ. [4]

6 Give three chemical properties that classify zinc as a metallic element. [3]

7 In which area of the periodic table are **(a)** the metallic elements? **(b)** the non-metallic elements? [2]

Well done if you've improved. Don't worry if you haven't. Take a break and try again.

Physical changes

6

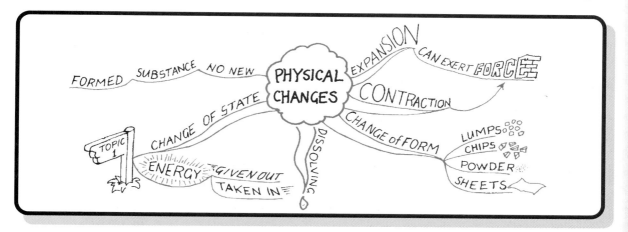

preview

At the end of this topic you will:

- **understand the difference between a physical change and a chemical change**
- ★ **understand solubility curves**

How much do you already know?

Test yourself

1 Divide the following into physical changes and chemical changes. Give reasons for your choices. **(a)** Smashing a glass vase into a hundred pieces **(b)** Breaking an egg **(c)** Boiling an egg **(d)** Evaporating water **(e)** Heating copper sulphate crystals [10]

2 Why does wax have to be heated before it melts? [2]

3 Which of the following is *always* true of a physical change? **(a)** It is easily reversed. **(b)** No heat is given out. **(c)** No heat is taken in. **(d)** No new substance is formed. **(e)** There is no change in appearance. [1]

4 **(a)** Explain what is meant by the statement 'The solubility of potassium nitrate is 35 g per 100 g of water at 25 °C'. **(b)** Why is the temperature stated? [3]

6.1 Change of state

When ice is heated, it simply melts to form water. It changes from the solid state into the liquid state. The change is reversed by cooling.

CHEMICAL CHANGE Pages 18 and 24.

A change of state is one type of **physical change**. No new substance is formed.

Energy: A change of state involves taking in energy or giving out energy.

★ Ice must be heated to melt it. Forces of attraction hold water molecules together in the solid state. Heat energy is needed to separate them. When water freezes, heat is given out. Molecules come together, forces of attraction are set up, and energy is given out.

$$\text{ice} + \text{heat} \underset{\text{freezing}}{\overset{\text{melting}}{\rightleftarrows}} \text{water}$$

★ When liquid water is heated it vaporises. Forces of attraction exist between molecules in the liquid state. Heat energy is needed to separate them. When water vapour condenses to form liquid water, heat is given out. Molecules come together, forces of attraction are set up, and energy is given out.

$$\text{water} + \text{heat} \underset{\text{condensation}}{\overset{\text{vaporisation}}{\rightleftarrows}} \text{water vapour}$$

●Changing materials

17

★ Energy is needed to break chemical bonds. **FACTS**
★ Energy is needed to separate molecules against forces of attraction.
★ When chemical bonds are made, energy is given out.
★ When separate molecules come together, energy is given out.

Test your grasp

Have you had an injection lately? When the nurse dabbed alcohol on your skin, did it feel really cool? Did this have anything to do with a change of state?

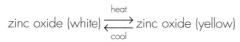

Alcohol vaporises easily. It takes heat from your skin to do so, making your skin feel cool.

Answer

6.2 Change of form

Some physical changes involve a change in form without a change in state.

★ A lump of aluminium can be rolled out into aluminium foil (used for baking etc.). This is a physical change. No new substance has been made.
★ A lump of marble can be used to make part of a building. If it is smashed into hundreds of marble chips for you to experiment with in the laboratory, it is still marble. No chemical change has happened. There is no change in mass: a 1 kg lump of marble gives 1 kg of chips.
★ When zinc oxide is heated, it turns from white to yellow. On cooling it turns back to white.

$$\text{zinc oxide (white)} \underset{cool}{\overset{heat}{\rightleftarrows}} \text{zinc oxide (yellow)}$$

A physical change

No permanent change has occurred. One form of zinc oxide has changed into another but this change is easily reversed. There is no change in mass. The mass of yellow zinc oxide is the same as the mass of white zinc oxide. This is a physical change.

6.3 Chemical changes

Heating copper sulphate

When you heat crystals of copper sulphate steam comes out of the test tube and a white solid is left in the test tube. A chemical reaction has occurred to give two substances which are different from the one you started with. In a chemical reaction, new substances (or one new substance) are formed.

$$\text{blue copper sulphate crystals} + \text{heat} \rightarrow \text{steam} + \text{white copper sulphate powder}$$

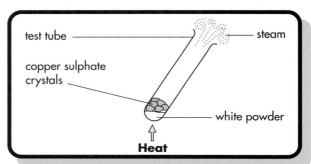

Heating copper sulphate crystals

This chemical reaction can easily be reversed. If the white copper sulphate is allowed to cool and a few drops of water are added, the blue colour returns and heat is given out.

$$\text{white copper sulphate} + \text{water} \rightarrow \text{blue copper sulphate} + \text{heat}$$

The mass of white copper sulphate is less than the mass of blue crystals. This tells you that a chemical change has occurred. If you condensed all the steam and weighed it, you would find that

$$\text{mass of white copper sulphate} + \text{steam} = \text{mass of blue copper sulphate crystals}$$

The reason is that copper sulphate crystals are a compound of copper sulphate and water with the formula $CuSO_4 \cdot 5H_2O$. It is called copper sulphate-5-water. The water is called **water of crystallisation**. It gives the crystals their shape and their colour. Heating drives off the water of crystallisation, and the crystals become a white powder, of formula $CuSO_4$. This is called anhydrous (without water) copper sulphate.

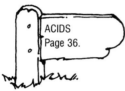

copper sulphate-5-water (blue crystals) $\rightarrow$ anhydrous copper sulphate (white powder) + water

Heating copper carbonate

When you heat copper carbonate, the green solid turns into a black solid. The black solid behaves quite differently from copper carbonate. It does not fizz when put into dilute acid as copper carbonate does. The mass of black solid formed is less than the mass of copper carbonate you started with because a gas was given off. The chemical reaction that has occurred is:

ACIDS
Page 36.

copper carbonate $\rightarrow$ copper oxide + carbon dioxide

If you collected the carbon dioxide and weighed it, you would find that

$$\text{mass of copper carbonate} = \text{mass of copper oxide} + \text{mass of carbon dioxide}$$

A wise old owl like me can tell a physical change from a chemical change. Can you?

when water freezes can exert pressure. After water trickles into a crack in a rock, the temperature may drop and the water may freeze. It expands as it does so, and widens the crack. After many years of freezing and thawing, the rock will break. This is one way in which rock is weathered.

WEATHERING
Page 22.

Solids

Solids expand on heating. This is why there are gaps between adjoining sections of motorway bridges. In hot weather the metal sections expand and, without these gaps, the force exerted by the expanding metal sections would make them buckle.

Gases

When they are heated, gases expand by a large fraction of their volume. When the air inside a hot air balloon is heated, it expands and becomes less dense than the surrounding air – and the balloon rises.

KINETIC THEORY
Page 2.

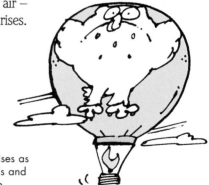

A hot air balloon rises as the air in it expands and becomes less dense

6.4 Expansion and contraction

Liquids

When water is cooled it contracts and its density increases. At 4°C it reaches its maximum density. When it cools from 4°C to 0°C and freezes, its density decreases; it expands. This is why ice floats on top of liquid water. The expansion that occurs

6.5 Solutions

A **solute** dissolves in a **solvent** to form a **solution**. Dissolving is a physical change. A **saturated solution** contains the maximum amount of solute at a stated temperature. If you see some undissolved solute at the bottom of the container, you know that the solution is saturated.

Solubility = mass of solute dissolved by 100 g of solvent at a stated temperature.

Solubility increases with temperature. A graph of solubility against temperature is called a solubility curve – some are shown in the figure.

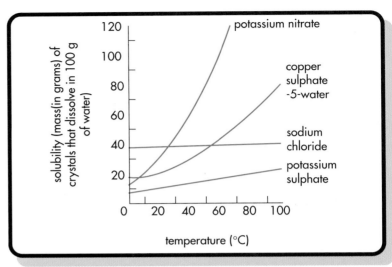

Some solubility curves

round-up

How much have you improved? Look up your score on page 43

1 Are these physical or chemical changes?
(a) A puddle of water evaporates. **(b)** Lumps of rock salt are broken up to make salt for spreading on the roads in winter.
(c) Limestone is heated in a kiln. [3]

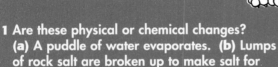
EVAPORATION
Pages 2 and 3.

2 A type of hand warmer contains a mass of sodium ethanoate crystals. The hand warmer is put into the microwave oven to melt the crystals. Later, as the liquid crystallises, heat is given out. Why does this happen? [4]

3 Georgie weighs a mass of iron filings on a petri dish. She places it on a windowsill. After two weeks, Georgie finds that the iron filings have changed colour and the mass of iron filings plus the petri dish has increased. What does this tell her about the change that has occurred? [2]

4 Look at the solubility curve above.
(a) What is the solubility of potassium sulphate at 80 °C?
(b) (i) What mass of copper sulphate-5-water will dissolve in 100 g of water at 100 °C?
(ii) What happens when the solution is cooled to 50 °C?
(c) What is the solubility of potassium nitrate **(i)** at 60 °C? **(ii)** at 20 °C?
(d) A solution of potassium nitrate is saturated at 60 °C. A 100 g sample of the solution is cooled from 60 °C to 20 °C. What mass of crystals will form? [6]

Well done if you've improved. Don't worry if you haven't. Take a break and try again.

Rocks

Do you know the Earth is 4.5 billion years old? Lots of time for geological changes to happen!

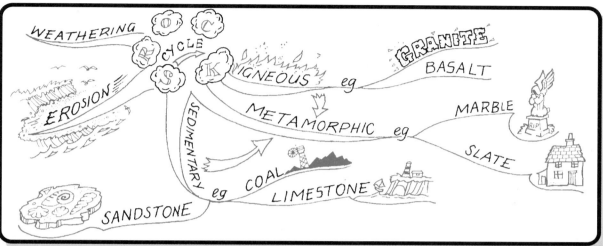

WEATHERING CYCLE

EROSION

IGNEOUS eg

GRANITE

BASALT

METAMORPHIC eg

MARBLE

SEDIMENTARY eg

COAL

LIMESTONE

SLATE

SANDSTONE

RIP

preview

At the end of this topic you will:
- **know how different types of rock take part in the rock cycle**
- **understand how the landscape is formed**

How much do you already know?

Test yourself

1 Name the type of rock that is formed **(a)** when lava solidifies **(b)** by the action of pressure on solid particles **(c)** by the action of heat and pressure on types **(a)** and **(b)**. [3]
2 Name an example of each of the three types of rock. [3]
3 Name the gradual processes which convert rocks slowly into other rocks. [1]
4 Name two weathering agents which act on rocks and shape the landscape. [2]

7.1 Types of rock

The study of rocks is called **geology**. Rocks change very slowly by **geological changes**, which take millions of years.

Igneous rocks

Deep below the surface of the Earth is molten rock, called **magma**. Magma can cool and crystallise to form **igneous** rocks. Often the cooling is slow and large crystals are formed. Sometimes magma is forced out as **lava** in a volcanic eruption (see the figure on the rock cycle). When lava crystallises, it forms igneous rocks on the Earth's surface. Often lava cools quickly to form small crystals.

Igneous rocks:
- ★ appearance: interlocking crystals of different colours; no layers can be seen
- ★ e.g. basalt, formed when lava solidifies above ground
- ★ e.g. granite, formed when magma solidifies below ground
- ★ e.g. pumice, formed from a foam of lava and volcanic gases

FACTS

Sedimentary rocks

The rocks on the Earth's surface are worn down by **weathering**. Then particles of rock are **eroded** – carried away – by winds, ice and rivers. In the end they settle as a **sediment**. A bed of sediment can form on a sea shore, at the bottom of an ocean or in a desert. As more material is laid on top, pressure builds up. The pressure turns the sediment into a **sedimentary** rock. These rocks may contain fossils if dead plants or animals were squashed between layers of sediment as the rocks formed. Fossils are used to date rocks. If a rock contains the marks of creatures which were alive 250 million years ago, the rock must be 250 million years old.

Sedimentary rocks include:
★ limestone, formed from the shells of dead animals
★ coal, formed from the remains of dead plants
★ sandstone, formed by pressure on grains of sand

Metamorphic rocks

Igneous rocks and sedimentary rocks change at high temperatures or high pressures. They change into **metamorphic** rocks:

★ appearance: crystalline, often with bands of different types
★ e.g. marble, formed from limestone at high temperature
★ e.g. slate, formed from clay, mud and shale at high pressure, splits into layers

7.2 The rock cycle

The geological changes that occur between igneous rocks, sedimentary rocks and metamorphic rocks are called the **rock cycle** (see the figure). Changes occur very slowly over millions of years.

7.3 The landscape

Rocks are slowly broken down into smaller particles by **physical forces**, such as the wind. They are also attacked in **chemical reactions**. Both types of process are called **weathering**. When rocks are broken down into particles and then the particles are carried away, for example by the wind, the process is called **erosion**. Weathering and erosion change the rocks and shape the landscape.

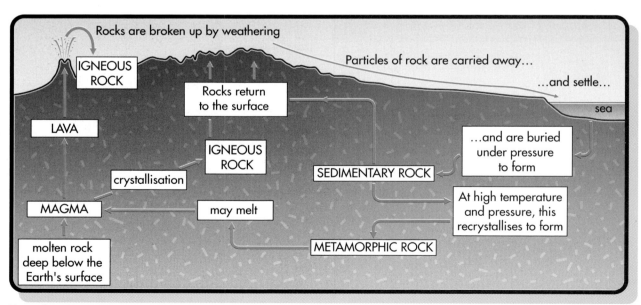

The rock cycle

Weathering by rain water

★ **Freezing:** Water may enter a crack in a rock. When water freezes, it expands and opens the crack wider.

★ **Dissolving:** Some rocks contain salts, which dissolve slightly in rain water.

★ **Reacting:** Other rocks, such as limestone, react chemically with the rain water because it is weakly acidic.

Erosion

★ Rain water can wash away surface soil.

★ When rocks are broken down, rivers and streams carry particles away.

★ The sea can wear away cliffs, creating caves and rock arches.

★ Wind blows away particles, especially in desert areas.

round-up

How much can you remember? Work out your score on page 43.

1 Suggest a method by which a geologist might find the age of a sedimentary rock. [2]

2 State two conditions necessary for changing sedimentary rocks into metamorphic rocks. [2]

3 Say whether each of the rocks in the table is igneous, sedimentary or metamorphic. [5]

Rock	Description
A	Crystalline with black and brown bands
B	Interlocked crystals of different colours
C	A mass of small grains
D	Breaks readily into layers
E	Marks of shells can be seen in it

4 Suggest three ways in which rain may weather rock. [3]

5 Name three agents that erode the landscape. [3]

Well done if you've improved. Don't worry if you haven't. Take a break and try again.

Chemical reactions

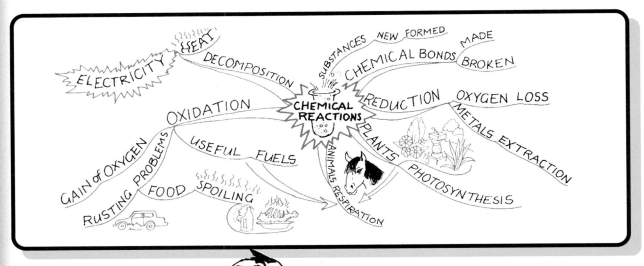

8

At last! My favourite topic!

preview

At the end of this topic you will:
- **understand what happens in a chemical reaction**
- **be able to write word equations**
- **understand oxidation, reduction, decomposition and ★ electrolysis**
- **know about fuels and energy changes in chemical reactions**
- **understand rusting**

How much do you already know?

Test yourself

1 Which one of the following is always true of a chemical reaction? **(a)** Heat is given out. **(b)** Heat is taken in. **(c)** A new substance is formed. **(d)** There is a change in colour. [1]
2 Write word equations for the following reactions: **(a)** iron and sulphur combine to form iron sulphide **(b)** sodium and chlorine react to form sodium chloride **(c)** zinc reacts with sulphuric acid to form hydrogen and zinc sulphate **(d)** sulphur burns in air to form sulphur dioxide (e) calcium carbonate decomposes to form calcium oxide and carbon dioxide. [5]
3 Give one example each of chemical reactions that occur in **(a)** plants **(b)** animals **(c)** car engines. [3]
4 Which substance is oxidised and which is reduced?

  a) carbon + steam $\rightarrow$ carbon monoxide + hydrogen [2]

  b) zinc oxide + carbon $\rightarrow$ zinc + carbon monoxide [2]

  c) iron oxide + aluminium $\rightarrow$ iron + aluminium oxide [2]

  d) hydrogen + tungsten oxide $\rightarrow$ tungsten + water [2]
5 Give examples of oxidation reactions which are **(a)** useful **(b)** a nuisance. [2]

8.1 What is a chemical reaction?

A mixture is formed when substances are simply mixed together. This is different from a chemical reaction. In a **chemical reaction**, substances are changed into new substances.

It is easy to understand this if you have done experiments in the lab. For example, when you heat a mixture of iron and sulphur, you obtain a

MIXTURES
Page 10.

new substance. This substance differs from the mixture you started with in many ways. It is a **compound** of iron and sulphur, called iron sulphide. A chemical reaction has occurred. The elements iron and sulphur have combined to form the compound iron sulphide.

In chemical reactions, the **chemical bonds** that join atoms together are broken and new chemical bonds are formed between atoms. When iron reacts with sulphur, the bonds that join iron atoms to other iron atoms are broken, and the bonds that join sulphur atoms to other sulphur atoms are broken. New bonds are formed joining iron atoms and sulphur atoms in the compound iron sulphide.

★ The substances we start with in a chemical reaction are called the **reactants**.
★ The substances formed in the reaction are called the **products**.

In this reaction, iron and sulphur are the reactants. Iron sulphide is the product.

8.2 Word equations

A **word equation** tells a story. It tells what chemicals take part in a chemical reaction and what new substances are formed. Have you burned magnesium ribbon? The chemical reaction that happens is described by the word equation:

magnesium + oxygen → magnesium oxide
the reactants   the product

The arrow stands for 'form'.

I REMEMBER BURNING MAGNESIUM RIBBON

In the reaction of iron and sulphur,

iron + sulphur → iron sulphide

8.3 What happens to mass?

When a chemical reaction happens, no matter is destroyed, and no matter is created. No mass is lost or gained.

Total mass of reactants = Total mass of products

Sometimes it is difficult to believe this. When you see a piece of wood burn away, you might imagine that mass has been destroyed. But if you could weigh the carbon dioxide and water vapour produced, you would see that no mass has been lost.

wood + oxygen   →   carbon dioxide + water
mass of wood   =   mass of carbon dioxide
  + oxygen   and water

8.4 How fast does a chemical reaction happen?

Some chemical reactions happen very quickly. When sticks of dynamite are set off to blast a rock face, the explosion happens very fast. Other chemical reactions happen slowly. A car takes several years to rust. A bottle of milk takes a few days to turn sour.

There are ways of making chemical reactions take place more quickly or more slowly.

★ **Temperature:** Milk keeps longer in the fridge because the reactions that turn it sour have been slowed down. Iron rusts more quickly in warm, tropical countries.
★ **Powders and lumps:** A powdered solid reacts faster than lumps of the same solid. Acids attack limestone rocks. They react much faster with small chips of limestone.
★ **Concentration:** Metals react with acids. A concentrated acid reacts faster than a dilute solution of the same acid. (A concentrated acid contains more acid and less water than the same volume of a dilute acid.)
★ **Catalysts:** Some reactions take place faster when a catalyst is present. An example is photosynthesis. Chlorophyll in plant leaves acts as a catalyst, helping the reaction along.

Take a short break before going on to oxidation and reduction

8.5 Oxidation reactions

Metals

When sparklers burn and give out light, a chemical reaction is taking place. The product of the reaction is a blue–black solid, iron oxide.

iron + oxygen → iron oxide

We say that iron has been **oxidised** – it has gained oxygen. A reaction in which oxygen is added to a substance is an **oxidation** reaction. Oxidation takes place much more slowly when iron is exposed to damp air. The product is different – it is the iron oxide called rust. Other metals also form oxides in air.

Oxidising iron

Non-metals

Non-metallic elements can also be oxidised. One of the causes of atmospheric pollution is the oxidation of sulphur and sulphur compounds in fuels to sulphur dioxide.

sulphur + oxygen → sulphur dioxide

This reaction is not always a nuisance. For example, it is the first step in the manufacture of sulphuric acid.

Test for oxygen

Substances burn much faster in oxygen than in air. A wooden splint that you have lit and then almost blown out bursts into flame in oxygen. Oxygen relights a glowing splint. This is a test for oxygen.

Compounds

Many compounds can be oxidised. Sugars are carbohydrates, compounds of carbon, hydrogen and oxygen. Oxidation takes place in the cells of animals and plants. The energy released provides the cells with the energy which they need to live. The process is called **respiration**.

RESPIRATION
Page 104.

sugar + oxygen → carbon dioxide + water + energy

Food

Oxidation is a problem with many foods that contain fats and oils.

★ Milk turns sour because fats and oils in milk are oxidised to unpleasant-smelling compounds, e.g. lactic acid.
★ The fats in butter are oxidised to the acids which give rancid butter its smell.
★ Fish oils are easily oxidised. This is why fish is quick to develop a nasty smell.
★ Nuts, bacon and potato crisps are packed in an atmosphere of nitrogen. If there is no oxygen in the packet the food keeps fresh longer.
★ Some foods are protected by food additives. If you spot the E number E320 or E321 on a label, you will know that anti-oxidants are present.

OXIDATION CAN BE A REAL NUISANCE!

★ If a bottle of wine is left open, the alcohol in the wine is oxidised by the air to ethanoic acid. This is the acid in vinegar. We want a sour taste in vinegar, but it won't do for wine. Wine-makers take care to bottle and cork wine to prevent air from entering.

Sometimes oxidation is wanted. Vinegar manufacturers trickle wine through a bed of wood shavings to help the air to reach it.

Oxidation for warmth and transport

  Fuels

Our way of life depends on the combustion of fuels such as coal, oil and natural gas. Without them our transport and our industries would come to a full stop. The vital reaction here is oxidation. These fuels are hydrocarbons, compounds of hydrogen and carbon. When they are oxidised to carbon dioxide and water, energy is released.

hydrocarbon + oxygen $\rightarrow$ carbon dioxide + water   Energy released

When oxidation gives out energy we call it **combustion**. The oxidation of fuels such as petrol is combustion.

When combustion is accompanied by a flame we call it **burning**. You can burn sugar in the laboratory, but the combustion of sugar is also taking place inside your body. Respiration is the series of combustion reactions which release energy gradually inside the cells.

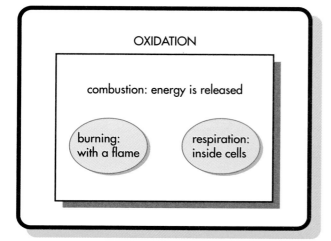

OXIDATION

combustion: energy is released

burning: with a flame   respiration: inside cells

I've changed my mind about oxidation. It keeps me warm and gives me the energy to fly.

8.6 Reduction reactions

We could not manage without metals. We need metals to make the machines which manufacture all our precious possessions. We need metals to make our cars, trains, planes, ships and all other means of transport.

METALS
Page 32.

Fortunately for us, the Earth's crust has plenty of metals. The snag is that they are not free metals – they are present in compounds. Chemistry has to come to the rescue with a method for extracting metals from their compounds. The method is **reduction**.

Carbon can take oxygen away from some metals, such as copper and lead. A reaction which takes oxygen away from a substance is called a reduction reaction. Carbon reduces lead oxide to lead. Lead oxide oxidises carbon to carbon dioxide.

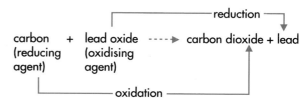

carbon + lead oxide ----> carbon dioxide + lead
(reducing agent) (oxidising agent)

Reduction is the opposite of oxidation. In this reaction,

★ Carbon has gained oxygen: carbon has been oxidised.
★ Carbon is a **reducing agent**.
★ Lead oxide has lost oxygen: lead oxide has been reduced.
★ Lead oxide is an **oxidising agent**.
★ Oxidation and reduction are occurring together: Since oxidation never occurs without reduction, it is better to call these reactions **oxidation-reduction reactions**.

Carbon will not reduce all metal oxides. It will reduce zinc oxide and iron oxide at high temperatures. It will not reduce calcium oxide and the oxides of other very reactive metals.

A useful reduction

Aluminium is a more reactive metal than iron. (Aluminium is above iron in the reactivity series).

REACTIVITY SERIES Page 33.

The following reaction takes place when iron oxide and aluminium are heated:

aluminium + iron oxide → iron + aluminium oxide

The reaction is called the **thermit reaction**. It gives out so much heat that the iron formed is molten.

Reduction mends railway line!

Recently a gap appeared in the rails of the Great Northern Railway. Technician Bob Fixit succeeded in closing the gap with molten iron. Bob made the molten iron on the spot by an amazing chemical reaction. He mixed iron oxide with aluminium powder and lit a fuse. The two metals fought for oxygen. Iron lost. The winner was aluminium. So much heat was given out in the fight that the metal formed was red hot molten iron. It poured into the gap in the lines and welded the broken ends together. Congratulated on his success, Bob said modestly 'I only used the thermit reaction.'

Remember
★ Oxidation = gain of oxygen.
★ Reduction = loss of oxygen.
★ An oxidising agent gives oxygen.
★ A reducing agent accepts oxygen.
★ Oxidation and reduction occur together in oxidation-reduction reactions.

8.7 Splitting up compounds

Thermal decomposition

Some compounds can be decomposed (split up) by heat. The reaction is called **thermal decomposition**. An important example of this is the thermal decomposition of calcium carbonate.

A carbonate is a compound that contains a metal, carbon and oxygen.

Calcium carbonate is quarried as limestone, marble and chalk. In industry, limestone (calcium carbonate) is heated in a furnace, called a lime kiln, at 1000 °C. It decomposes:

calcium carbonate → calcium oxide + carbon dioxide

This reaction is important for agriculture and the building industry:

★ Calcium oxide, CaO, reacts with water to form calcium hydroxide, $Ca(OH)_2$. Calcium hydroxide is spread on soils that are too acidic to grow crops. It neutralises excess acidity and makes the soil more fertile.

ACIDS AND BASES Page 36.

★ Cement is made by heating limestone and clay in a kiln.
★ Mortar is made from cement and sand.
★ Concrete is made from cement, sand, gravel and water.

TAKE A BREAK

Environmental matters

Cement, mortar and concrete are very important building materials. The limestone used in making them is obtained by open-cast quarrying (taking it from the surface). This leaves scars on the countryside. When work in a quarry finishes, the firm responsible has to restore the landscape as far as possible.

Electrolysis

When a direct electric current is passed through some compounds they decompose. This type of reaction is called **electrolysis**. The substance must be molten or in solution. Examples are:

Lead bromide (molten) $\rightarrow$ lead + bromine

Copper chloride (solution) $\rightarrow$ copper + chlorine

Sodium chloride (molten) $\rightarrow$ sodium + chlorine

But the products of electrolysis are not always as easy to predict. For example, sodium chloride solution gives hydrogen and chlorine.

Acids, bases and salts can be electrolysed. Other compounds cannot be electrolysed.

8.8 Energy changes in chemical reactions

When chemical changes take place, heat changes occur.

* Reactions that give out heat are **exothermic** (exo = out).
* Reactions that take in heat are **endothermic**.

Combustion

Coal is a mixture of carbon and hydrocarbons (compounds of hydrogen and carbon). When coal burns in plenty of air,

carbon + oxygen $\rightarrow$ carbon dioxide ⟨Heat is given out⟩

hydrocarbon + oxygen $\rightarrow$ carbon dioxide + water

⟨Heat is given out⟩

We use natural gas (or North Sea gas) in Bunsen burners and to heat our homes. It consists mainly of the hydrocarbon methane, CH_4. When it burns,

methane (CH_4) + oxygen $\rightarrow$ carbon dioxide + water

⟨Heat is given out⟩

Vehicle engines burn petrol and diesel fuel. Aeroplane engines burn kerosene. All these fuels are hydrocarbons. They are all obtained from petroleum oil by fractional distillation. They all burn to form carbon dioxide and water.

Energy changes in plants and animals

The chemical changes that take place in living things are of the same types as the reactions that take place in the laboratory.

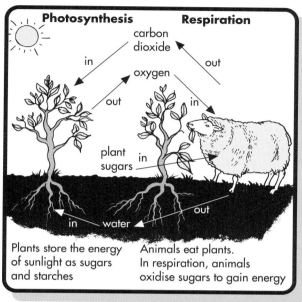

Chemical reactions in plants and animals

Respiration

During respiration sugars are oxidised:

sugar + oxygen $\rightarrow$ carbon dioxide + water + ⟨energy⟩

Respiration takes place in animals and plants. It is exothermic. The energy which is given out is needed to keep plants and animals alive.

RESPIRATION
Pages 26 and 104.

Photosynthesis

During photosynthesis, sugars are made. The energy needed to make the reaction happen is taken in by the plant in the form of sunlight. The energy is converted into the energy of chemical bonds in sugars.

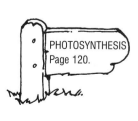

PHOTOSYNTHESIS
Page 120.

carbon dioxide + water + energy $\xrightarrow{\text{chlorophyll}}$ glucose + oxygen

(from the air) (from the soil) (sunlight) (a sugar)

8.9 Pollution from fuels

Tragedy strikes caravanners

The weather turned cold one night when the Smiths were taking a half-term holiday in their caravan. They shut the windows and left the paraffin heater on during the night. In the morning the whole family lay dead in the caravan. Investigators are looking into the cause of the tragedy.

Test your grasp

What happened in the Smiths' caravan?

Answer

The windows were shut so there was not a lot of air inside the caravan. The paraffin heater did not have enough oxygen, and the fuel burned to form carbon monoxide, which is poisonous.

Hydrocarbons burn in plenty of air to form the harmless products carbon dioxide and water. However, if there is a poor supply of air, combustion products include unburnt hydrocarbons, carbon and the poisonous gas carbon monoxide. Cars idling in traffic jams produce carbon monoxide. There is not enough to kill motorists but enough to give headaches to quite a few of them.

Smoke, dust and grit are produced when hydrocarbon fuels burn. They create dirty air and fall on to buildings, plants and clothing.

Most hydrocarbon fuels contain sulphur. When the fuel burns, sulphur dioxide is formed. It is an unpleasant gas with a choking smell. People with breathing difficulties are very much at risk from sulphur dioxide.

Oxides of nitrogen are present in the exhaust gases of cars and factories. Together with sulphur dioxide they drift into the upper atmosphere. There they react with water to form nitric acid and sulphuric acid. This comes to earth as acid rain.

8.10 Rusting of iron and steel

Oxidation can be a nuisance. Millions of pounds are spent each year on replacing rusty iron. Iron rusts when it is attacked by water and air and acid. The carbon dioxide in the air provides enough acidity. If the water contains salts, rusting takes place more rapidly. In a warm climate, rusting is faster than in cooler climates.

The table on page 31 lists some of the methods that are used to protect iron against rusting.

Carbon dioxide
Water vapour
Carbon monoxide
Unburnt petrol vapour
Nitrogen monoxide
Sulphur dioxide
Lead vapour

Your car and pollution

Method	Where it is used	Comment
1 A coat of paint	Large objects, e.g. ships and bridges	If the paint is scratched, the iron beneath it starts to rust.
2 A film of oil or grease	Moving parts of machinery	The moving part must be kept oiled.
3 A coat of metal		
Chromium plating	Trim on cars, cycle handlebars, taps	Applied by electroplating, decorative as well as protective.
Galvanised iron (dipped in molten zinc and lifted out)	Galvanised steel girders are used in buildings	Even if the layer of zinc is scratched, the iron underneath does not rust. Zinc cannot be used for food cans because zinc and its compounds are poisonous.
Tin plating	Food cans	If the layer of tin is scratched, the iron beneath it rusts.
4 Stainless steel	Cutlery, car accessories	Stainless steel is an alloy of iron, carbon and chromium. It does not rust.

Preventing rust

round-up

How much have you remembered?

1 (a) Give an example of an oxidation of foods which benefits us. **(b)** Give two examples of oxidation of foods which we try to slow down. [3]

2 Name the reducing agent in the following reactions:

a) carbon monoxide + iron oxide → carbon dioxide + iron [1]

b) copper oxide + hydrogen → copper + water [1]

c) carbon + lead oxide → lead + carbon monoxide [1]

3 In each of these reactions, state what is oxidised

a) aluminium + iron oxide → iron + aluminium oxide [1]

b) tin sulphide + oxygen → tin oxide + sulphur dioxide [1]

c) tin oxide + carbon → tin + carbon monoxide [1]

4 Which method of preventing rust is used for each of the following? **(a)** food cans **(b)** bicycle chains **(c)** wheel hubs **(d)** bridges **(e)** galvanised iron railings [5]

5 (a) Name the important chemical reaction that takes place in plants and takes in energy. **(b)** Write a word equation for the reaction. [3]

Well done if you've improved. Don't worry if you haven't. Take a break and try again.

Metals

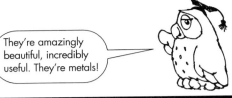

They're amazingly beautiful, incredibly useful. They're metals!

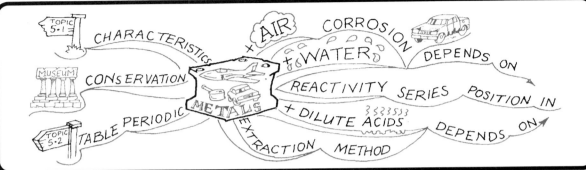

preview

At the end of this topic you will:

- **know the chemical reactions of metals**
- ★**understand displacement reactions**
- **understand the reactivity series of metals**
- **know how metals are obtained from their compounds**
- **understand why recycling of metals is important**

How much do you already know?

Test yourself

1 Name one metal that must be kept out of contact with the air. [1]
2 Name two metals that burn in air to form oxides. [2]
3 Name two metals that do not react when heated in air. [2]
4 Name one metal that reacts with cold water and say what products are formed. [3]
5 What products are formed when zinc reacts with hydrochloric acid? [2]
6 Name one metal that becomes coated with a film of oxide on exposure to the air. [1]
7 What is the reactivity series of metals? [1]

9.1 The chemical reactions of metals

With air

Most metals combine with oxygen in the air to form a surface film of metal oxide. This reaction is called **tarnishing**. Gold and platinum do not tarnish in air. Sodium reacts so vigorously with oxygen that it has to be kept under oil in a stoppered bottle to prevent air from reaching it. Aluminium rapidly forms a surface layer of aluminium oxide. The layer of aluminium oxide protects aluminium from further chemical attack.

Can you put these metals in order?

This is one reason why aluminium is such a useful metal. It can be used for door frames and window frames because it is not attacked by the weather.

With water

In the reaction

metal + water → hydrogen + metal oxide

* ★ sodium reacts vigorously with cold water,
* ★ magnesium reacts slowly with cold water but rapidly with steam,
* ★ iron reacts slowly with cold water as it rusts,
* ★ copper does not react with water.

With acids

In the reaction

metal + acid → hydrogen + metal salt

the metal displaces hydrogen from the acid. Some acids give up their hydrogen more readily than others. Acids that readily give hydrogen are called **strong acids**. Acids that react slowly to give hydrogen are called **weak acids**. Some metals react faster than others with acids. By comparing the reactions of the same acid with different metals you can put metals in order. You can draw up a **reactivity series of metals** from the most reactive to the least reactive.

Metal	Symbol	
Potassium	K	
Sodium	Na	
Calcium	Ca	The reactivity of
Magnesium	Mg	the metal
Aluminium	Al	with air,
Zinc	Zn	with water,
Iron	Fe	with acids
Tin	Sn	increases from
Lead	Pb	the bottom to
Copper	Cu	the top of the
Silver	Ag	series.
Mercury	Hg	
Gold	Au	

Part of the reactivity series of metals

Displacement reactions

When you hear that A is a more reactive metal than B, you know that A is more ready to react with other elements than B is. If A is more reactive than B, then A will displace B from a compound of B. The figure shows an example.

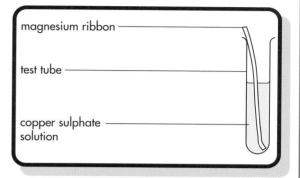

magnesium ribbon

test tube

copper sulphate solution

Magnesium is above copper in the reactivity series. The blue colour of copper sulphate solution fades, and a reddish brown solid appears in the test tube. The reaction is:

magnesium + copper sulphate → copper + magnesium sulphate

Test your grasp

(a) Zinc is more reactive than copper. What happens when you drop a piece of zinc into a solution of copper sulphate? (b) Zinc is less reactive than magnesium. What happens when you drop a piece of zinc into a solution of magnesium sulphate? (c) Look back at Section 8.6 'A useful reduction'. Is the reaction a displacement reaction?

(a) Zinc displaces copper. The blue colour of the copper sulphate solution fades. A reddish brown solid, copper, appears. (b) Nothing happens. (c) Yes, aluminium displaces iron from iron oxide.

Answer

9.2 Making predictions from the reactivity series

Copy and complete these word equations. Use your knowledge of the reactivity series shown in the table to predict what will happen. If there is no reaction, write 'no reaction'.

a) zinc + silver nitrate solution $\rightarrow$
b) gold + copper sulphate solution $\rightarrow$
c) tin + zinc sulphate solution $\rightarrow$
d) tin + copper sulphate solution $\rightarrow$
e) zinc + tin chloride solution $\rightarrow$
f) zinc + copper sulphate solution $\rightarrow$
g) copper + silver nitrate solution $\rightarrow$
h) aluminium + mercury oxide $\rightarrow$
i) potassium + aluminium oxide $\rightarrow$
j) zinc + calcium oxide $\rightarrow$

9.3 How metals are extracted from compounds

A reactive metal readily combines with other elements to form compounds. Unreactive metals, such as gold and silver, are found as the free, uncombined elements. You would not expect to find reactive metals as the free elements because they react with air and water to form compounds.

Very reactive metals, such as sodium, are difficult to extract from their compounds. Metals in the middle of the reactivity series, such as iron and zinc, are not difficult to extract from their compounds. Here are some examples:

★ Zinc is mined as zinc sulphide. The first step is heating in air:

zinc sulphide + oxygen $\rightarrow$ zinc oxide + sulphur dioxide

Then zinc oxide is reduced by heating with carbon:

zinc oxide + carbon $\rightarrow$ zinc + carbon monoxide

★ Tungsten is mined as tungsten oxide. The metal is needed for making the filaments of electric light bulbs. Hydrogen is used to reduce tungsten oxide:

tungsten oxide + hydrogen $\rightarrow$ tungsten + water

★ Iron is mined as iron oxide. The metal is extracted in a blast furnace. Iron oxide, coke (carbon) and limestone are tipped in. Coke is oxidised to carbon monoxide. This reduces iron oxide to iron:

iron oxide + carbon monoxide $\rightarrow$ iron + carbon dioxide

The higher a metal is in the reactivity series

★ the more ready it is to form compounds and
★ the more difficult it is to split up its compounds.

9.4 Conservation

The Earth has vast resources of metals. Unfortunately we are using them up faster and faster as technology spreads. We don't want to run out of metals. It makes sense to collect scrap metals and recycle them. As well as saving metals, recycling saves fuel. It takes ten times more electricity to extract aluminium from its ore than to recycle used aluminium. There is an advantage to the environment too. Less mining means less devastation of the landscape.

Don't throw that can away! Recycle it!

round-up

How much have you learned?
Look up your score on page 44.

1 Give a reason why **(a)** gold is used for filling teeth **(b)** copper is used for water pipes **(c)** silver is used for jewellery **(d)** mercury is used in dental amalgams **(e)** aluminium is used for saucepans. [6]

2 Q, R and S are metals. Q will displace R from the salt R sulphate. Q will not displace S from S sulphate. Which is the correct order of reactivity? **(a)** Q > R > S **(b)** Q > S > R **(c)** R > S > Q **(d)** R > Q > S **(e)** S > Q > R **(f)** S > R > Q [1]

3 You are given a mixture of zinc powder and copper powder. How could you obtain copper from the mixture? [4]

4 Nickel and cobalt are metals. Describe an experiment you could do to find out which is the more reactive of the two metals. [2]

5 The following metals are listed in order of reactivity, with the most reactive first:
Na Mg Al Zn Fe Pb Cu Hg Au
Name one metal which **(a)** occurs as the free element in the Earth's crust **(b)** reacts rapidly with cold water **(c)** reacts with steam but not with cold water **(d)** reacts with dilute acids at a moderate speed **(e)** reacts dangerously fast with dilute acids **(f)** does not react with water but displaces lead from lead(II) nitrate solution [6]

6 Copy and complete the following word equations. If no reaction occurs, write 'no reaction'.
a) copper + oxygen →
b) aluminium + iron oxide →
c) iron + aluminium oxide →
d) zinc + silver nitrate solution → [6]

7 The table shows percentages of some metals which are recycled in the UK.

Metal	aluminium	zinc	iron	tin	lead	copper
%	28	30	50	30	56	19

(a) Explain what 'recycling of metals' means.
(b) Why is aluminium easy to recycle?
(c) How can iron be separated from other metals for recycling? **(d)** Name two aluminium objects and two iron objects which could be recycled. [10]

8 Refer to the reactivity series on page 33. Fill in the table with a ✓ for 'reaction' and a ✗ for 'no reaction'. [16]

Metal	Metal salt solution			
	Copper chloride	**Iron chloride**	**Zinc chloride**	**Magnesium chloride**
Copper				
Iron				
Zinc				
Magnesium				

Don't worry if you couldn't get everything right – take a break and have another go.

9 Four metals W, X, Y and Z were taken. Each metal was placed in turn in solutions of the nitrates of the other metals.
W displaced Z
X displaced W
X displaced Z
Y displaced X
(a) List the four metals in order of reactivity.
(b) Explain why you have chosen this order. [7]

Acids and bases

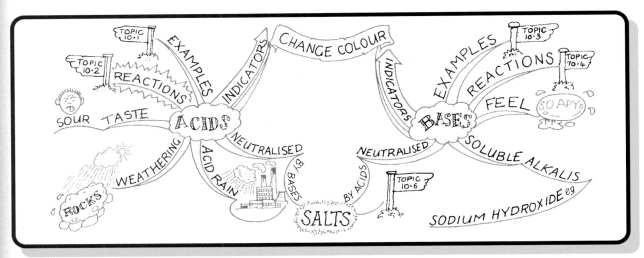

preview

At the end of this topic you will:
- **know the typical reactions of acids and bases**
- **understand pH and indicators**
- **know the uses of some salts**
- **understand acid rain**
- ★**understand chemical weathering of rocks**

I seem to have just flown through the chemical topics. This is the last one. Tough!

Test yourself

1 Say whether the substances listed are strongly acidic (SA), weakly acidic (WA), strongly basic (SB), weakly basic (WB) or neutral (N).
   (a) battery acid, pH 0 **(b)** rain water, pH 6.5
   (c) blood, pH 7.4 **(d)** sea water, pH 8.5
   (e) cabbage juice, pH 5.0 **(f)** saliva, pH 7.0
   (g) washing soda, pH 11.5   [7]
2 You are given two bottles labelled X and Y. One is an acid and the other is an alkali. Describe two tests you could do to find out which is which.   [6]
3 Name: **(a)** a strong acid present in your stomach **(b)** a base present in indigestion tablets **(c)** a weak acid present in fruits **(d)** a base used to neutralise excess acidity in soils.   [4]

10.1 Where are acids found?

The following are strong acids:

- ★ Hydrochloric acid, which occurs in the stomach, where it helps digestion.
- ★ Nitric acid, used in the production of fertilisers and explosives.
- ★ Sulphuric acid, used in car batteries and in the production of fertilisers.

The following are weak acids:

- ★ Carbonic acid, present in fizzy drinks.
- ★ Citric acid, present in lemons and other citrus fruits.
- ★ Ethanoic acid, in vinegar
- ★ Lactic acid, in sour milk

10.2 What do acids do?

An acid is a substance which contains hydrogen that can be replaced by a metal. Some reactions of acids are shown in the figure.

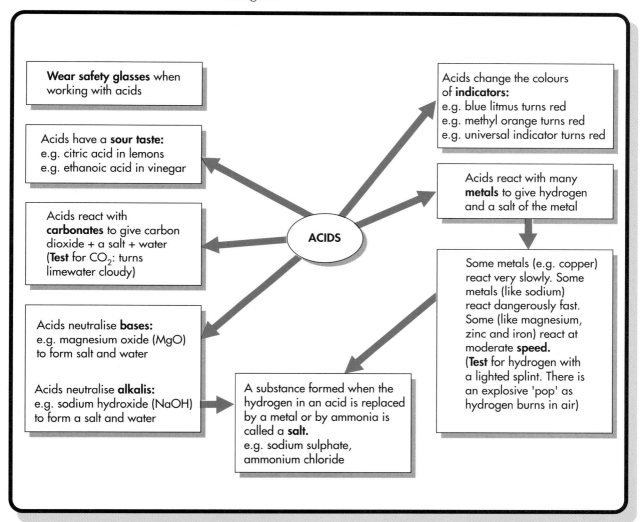

Acids

10.3 Where do you find bases?

The following are strong bases:
★ Calcium hydroxide is commonly called 'slaked lime'. It is used to treat soil which is too acidic to grow crops.
★ Calcium oxide is commonly called 'quicklime'. It is used in the manufacture of cement and concrete.
★ Magnesium hydroxide is used in anti-acid indigestion tablets.

★ Sodium hydroxide is a common laboratory chemical. It is used in soap manufacture and as a degreasing agent.
★ The weak base ammonia is used in household cleaning fluids. It works as a degreasing agent. Another use for ammonia is making ammonium salts to be used as fertilisers.

10.4 What do bases do?

Bases react with acids. This reaction leads to the definition of a base.

A base is a substance that reacts with an acid to form a salt and water as the only products.

For example,

| sodium hydroxide | + | hydrochloric acid | → | sodium chloride | + water |

| base | + | acid | → | salt | + water |

A soluble base is called an **alkali.** Sodium hydroxide, NaOH, is a **strong base** and a strong alkali. Ammonia is a **weak base.**

The reaction

acid + base → salt + water

is called **neutralisation.**

Wear safety glasses when working with bases

Bases change the colours of **indicators:**
red litmus ---→ blue
universal indicator ---→ blue in strong base
universal indicator ---→ violet in weak base

BASES:
e.g. sodium hydroxide (NaOH) a strong base
e.g. ammonia (NH_3) a weak base

Bases have a 'soapy feel'. This is because they turn some of the oil in your skin into soap. Because of this reaction, bases are used as **degreasing agents,** for example as oven cleaners. The base sodium hydroxide is boiled with fats to convert them into **soaps** (an industrial process)

Definition of a base:
A base is a substance that reacts with an acid to form a salt and water only
e.g. magnesium oxide + hydrochloric acid ---→ magnesium chloride + water

Bases **neutralise acids,** such as hydrochloric acid or sulphuric acid, to form water and a salt, such as sodium chloride or sodium sulphate

An **alkali** is a soluble base – for example sodium hydroxide.

10.5 Indicators

There are substances which change colour when an acid is added or when a base is added. They are called **indicators**. Some examples are shown in the table.

Indicator	Acidic colour	Neutral colour	Alkaline colour
Litmus	Red	Purple	Blue
Phenolphthalein	Colourless	Colourless	Red
Methyl orange	Red	Orange	Yellow

Indicators

Universal indicator can distinguish between strong and weak bases, as the figure below shows.

	strongly acidic			weakly acidic			neutral		weakly alkaline		strongly alkaline			
pH	0	1	2	3	4	5	6	7	8	9	10	11	12	13	14
	red		orange		yellow		green	blue			violet				

The colour of universal indicator in solutions of different pH

10.6 Some useful salts

★ Washing soda is used as an ingredient of washing powders. It is sodium carbonate-10-water, $Na_2CO_3 \cdot 10H_2O$

★ Baking soda is added to flour. It decomposes at the oven temperature to give carbon dioxide and steam, which make bread and cakes rise. It is sodium hydrogencarbonate, formula $NaHCO_3$.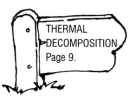

THERMAL DECOMPOSITION Page 9.

★ Plaster of Paris, when mixed with water, sets to form a strong 'plaster cast'. It is calcium sulphate-$\frac{1}{2}$-water, $CaSO_4 \cdot \frac{1}{2}H_2O$.

★ Silver bromide, AgBr, is used in black and white photographic film.

★ 'Iron tablets', which people take for anaemia, contain iron(II) sulphate-7-water, $FeSO_4 \cdot 7H_2O$.

★ 'Barium meals' show up well on X-rays and reveal the position of a stomach ulcer. They contain barium sulphate, $BaSO_4$.

★ Fungicides protect potatoes and grapes from attack by fungi. They contain copper sulphate, $CuSO_4$.

★ Fluoride toothpastes harden tooth enamel. They contain calcium fluoride, CaF_2.

★ NPK fertilisers contain salts: ammonium salts to provide nitrogen (N), phosphates to provide phosphorus (P) and potassium salts as a source of potassium (K).

10.7 Acids and pollution

Acids can be a severe nuisance. Sulphur dioxide (SO_2) and nitrogen dioxide (NO_2) are produced by power plants and factories. Tall chimneys take the gases up into the air, where they may be caught by the wind and taken far away. The gases react with water vapour and oxygen in the atmosphere to form a dilute solution of sulphuric acid and nitric acid. In time, the water vapour with its acid content becomes captured by a cloud. Finally it falls as **acid rain** or **acid snow**. This may turn up days later and hundreds of miles away.

There are many bad effects of acid rain:

★ Lake water becomes acidic, killing fish and plants.

★ Acid rain washes salts out of top soil. Some of these salts are nutrients. As a result, crops and trees are stunted. In some regions, part of the acidity is neutralised by limestone rocks. Such regions suffer less badly from acid rain.

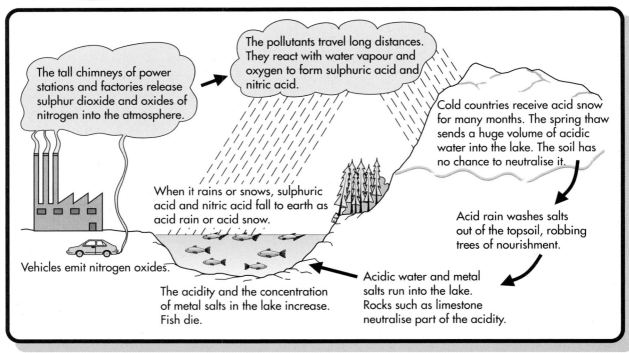

Acid rain: its source and its effect on lake water

★ Many building materials are attacked by acids. Metals suffer, e.g. iron and steel. Limestone, concrete and cement all contain carbonates which are attacked by acids.

What can be done?

Sulphur dioxide

Members of the European Community (EC) have agreed to make a 65% cut in their emission of sulphur dioxide by 2003. Much of the cut will have to come from power stations. They are installing equipment for removing sulphur dioxide from the exhaust gases.

Oxides of nitrogen

The catalytic converters which are now fitted in the exhausts of cars turn nitrogen oxides into harmless nitrogen. Unleaded petrol must be used because lead compounds stop the catalyst working.

10.8 Chemical weathering

Many building materials contain carbonates. These are weathered by rainwater.

WEATHERING
Page 22.

Even in the absence of pollution, rainwater is weakly acidic. This is because carbon dioxide in the air dissolves in rainwater to form a solution of the weak acid carbonic acid.

round-up

How much have you learned?

1 The pH values of some solutions are given. Say whether each is **A** acidic, **B** alkaline or **C** neutral. **(a)** stomach digestive fluid pH 1 **(b)** bath cleaner pH 8 **(c)** lemon juice pH 3 **(d)** distilled water pH 7 **(e)** oven cleaner pH 12 **(f)** sea water pH 8 **(g)** rain water pH 6 [7]

2 A treatment for a bee sting is to dab it with sodium hydrogencarbonate solution. For a wasp sting, vinegar is recommended. What does this tell you about bee stings and wasp stings? [2]

3 You have two bottles of colourless liquids. The labels have come off. One label reads 'Hydrochloric acid'. The other reads 'Citric acid'. What test could you do to tell which acid is which? [3]

4 Complete the following word equations:
a) zinc + sulphuric acid
→ _____ sulphate + _____ [2]

b) magnesium oxide + sulphuric acid
→ _____ sulphate + _____ [2]
c) calcium carbonate + hydrochloric acid
→ calcium _____ + _____ + _____ [3]
d) potassium hydroxide + hydrochloric acid
→ _____ chloride + _____ [2]

5 The following pairs of substances react to form salts. In each reaction, name the salt and say what else is formed.
a) sodium hydroxide + sulphuric acid → [2]
b) zinc + hydrochloric acid → [2]
c) copper oxide + sulphuric acid → [2]
d) calcium carbonate + hydrochloric acid → [3]

6 Sweden has tackled the problem of acid rain by spraying tonnes of calcium hydroxide into acid lakes. Explain how this helps to cure the problem. [2]

7 A geologist collects some samples of rock and tests them. She drops dilute hydrochloric acid onto one sample. It fizzes. What does this tell her about the rock? [1]

Answers

Topic 1 Matter

Test yourself
1 Solid, liquid, gas. (3✓)
2 Evaporation takes place over a range of temperature. (✓) Boiling takes place at a certain temperature. (✓)
3 Bubbles of vapour appear in the body of the liquid. (✓)
4 'Heavy' means high mass. (✓) 'Dense' means high ratio: mass/volume. (✓)
5 Crystals consist of a regular arrangement of particles. (✓) As a result the crystal has a regular shape with regular faces. (✓)
6 The particles which constitute the solid gain enough energy to break free from the attractive forces (✓) between particles which maintain the solid structure and move independently. (✓)
7 In a gas, e.g. steam, the molecules are very much further apart (✓) than in a liquid. (✓)

8 Particles (✓) of salt dissolve (✓) and spread out (✓) through the soup.
Total = 17 marks

Round-up
1 The particles are joined by chemical bonds. (✓) Heat energy breaks the bonds. (✓)
2 **(i)** Metals. (✓) **(ii)** Metals. (✓)
3 *Either:* most of a gas is space *or:* the molecules are far apart. (✓)
4 Particles split off from the solid (✓) and spread through the liquid. (✓)
5 There is so much space between the molecules of a gas (✓) that it is easy for them to move closer together (✓) when the pressure is increased.
6 **a)** A g, B g, C l, D s. (4✓) **b)** l. (✓) **c)** Far apart, random arrangement, moving. (3✓)
7 The gas molecules gain energy (✓), move faster (✓), exert more pressure on the balloon (✓) so that it might burst. (✓)

8 The liquid vaporises. (✓) A gas diffuses (✓) to occupy the whole of the room. (✓)
9 Liquids need energy to vaporise. (✓) Aftershave takes the energy it needs from the skin. (✓)
10 a) Melting point. (✓) **b)** The heat is used in separating particles of the solid while the solid melts, not in raising the temperature. (✓) **c)** All the solid has melted and the temperature is rising as the liquid is heated. (✓)
11 a) Boiling point. (✓) **b)** The heat is used in separating particles of the liquid while the liquid boils, not in raising the temperature. (✓) **c)** All the liquid has vaporised and the temperature is rising as heating continues. (✓)

Total = 32 marks

Topic 2 Elements

Test yourself

1 An element is a pure substance (✓) that cannot be split up into simpler substances. (✓)
2 See section 2.1. (6✓)
3 Number of protons = number of electrons. (✓)
4 a) Number of protons. (✓) **b)** Number of protons + number of neutrons. (✓)
5 a) 19. (✓) **b)** 20. (✓)

Total = 13 marks

Round-up

1 a) Copper. (✓) **b)** Iron. (✓) **c)** Silicon. (✓) **d)** Aluminium. (✓)
2 Protons, positive (2✓); electrons, negative (2✓); neutrons, uncharged. (2✓)
3 Protons and neutrons. (2✓)
4 A letter or two letters (✓) which stand for one atom (✓) of an element.

Total = 14 marks

Topic 3 Compounds

Test yourself

1 An element cannot be split up into simpler substances. (✓) A compound can be split up into elements (✓) or simpler compounds. (✓)
2 Heating (✓), electricity. (✓)
3 a) 3. (✓) **b)** 7. (✓)

Total = 7 marks

Round-up

1 Appearance: the mixture looks like a mixture of yellow sulphur and grey iron. (✓) The compound is grey–black. (✓) Magnetism: the iron in the mixture is magnetic. (✓) The compound is non-magnetic. (✓) (Alternatively: reaction with acid. Iron + acid → hydrogen. Iron sulphide + acid → hydrogen sulphide.)
2 6. (✓)

3 a) The mixture has the same properties as its parts. (✓) The compound has new properties. (✓) **b)** A mixture is separated by physical methods. (✓) (see Topic 4). A compound is split up by a chemical reaction (✓), e.g. heating. (✓)
4 Aluminium oxide contains aluminium and oxygen. (✓) There are 2 aluminium atoms for every 3 oxygen atoms. (✓)

Total = 7 marks

Topic 4 Methods of separation

Test yourself

1 a) Use a coarse sieve to hold back the gravel and let sand through. (✓) **b)** Dissolve the mixture of A and B in hot water. (✓) Cool. (✓) Filter to obtain A. (✓) Evaporate the solution to obtain B. (✓) **c)** Use a separating funnel. (✓) Olive oil forms a layer on top of vinegar. (✓) **d)** Stir with warm water (✓) to dissolve the salt. (✓) Filter (✓) to obtain the diamonds. (✓) **e)** Fractional distillation. (✓)

Total = 13 marks

Round-up

1 Use a magnet (✓) to attract the steel cans but not the aluminium cans. (✓)
2 Stir the mixture with warm water. (✓) Salt dissolves. (✓) Filter. (✓) Evaporate the filtrate (the solution). (✓) Salt crystallises. (✓)
3 Stir the mixture of C and D with alcohol. (✓) Filter. (✓) The residue is D. (✓) Evaporate the solution (✓) to obtain C. (✓) Alcohol is flammable: (✓) evaporate over a water bath. (✓)
4 The chromatogram shows that P1 contains A and C, (✓) while P2 contains A and B. (✓)
5 Miss Green. (✓)

Total = 17 marks

Topic 5 Metals and non-metals

Test yourself

1 A pure substance (✓) that cannot be split up into simpler substances. (✓)
2 Metal. (✓) Metals can be worked into different shapes, e.g. saucepans. (✓) Few non-metals are shiny. (✓)
3 Metal. (✓) Metals conduct electricity. (✓) Although graphite also conducts electricity, it cannot be made into cables. (✓)
4 Metal. Metals displace hydrogen from acids. (✓) Non-metals do not. (✓)

Total = 10 marks

Round-up

1 P is a metal (✓) or graphite. (✓)
2 R is non-metallic. (✓)
3 Metallic. (✓)

4 Metallic. (✓)
5 Four out of the five. Copper is shiny, sulphur is dull. (✓) Copper conducts heat (✓) and electricity, (✓) sulphur does not. Copper can be hammered, sulphur is brittle. (✓) Copper is sonorous, sulphur is not sonorous. (✓)
6 Reacts with dilute acids. (✓) Oxide is basic. (✓) Chloride is solid. (✓)
7 **a)** Left-hand side. (✓) **b)** Right-hand side. (✓)

Total = 14 marks

Topic 6 Physical changes

Test yourself

1 **a)** Physical; no new substance is made. (2✓)
   b) Physical; no new substance is made. (2✓)
   c) Chemical; substances are changed into new substances. (2✓) **d)** Physical; water to water vapour is a change of state. (2✓) **e)** Chemical; new substances are formed. (2✓)
2 In the solid, bonds hold the particles in a regular structure. (✓) Heat must be supplied to give them enough energy to break out of their positions in the solid structure. (✓)
3 d. (✓)
4 **a)** The maximum mass (✓) of potassium chlorate that will dissolve (✓) in 100 g of water at 25 °C is 35 g. **b)** Solubility changes with temperature. (✓)

Total = 16 marks

Round-up

1 **a)** Physical. (✓) **b)** Physical. (✓) **c)** Chemical. (✓)
2 Heat breaks bonds (✓) and the crystals melt. (✓) When the bonds form again, (✓) the liquid crystallises (✓) and gives out heat.
3 A chemical reaction has occurred. (✓) The gain in mass means that iron has combined with something to form a compound of iron. (✓)
4 **a)** 20 g/100 g water. (2✓) **b) (i)** 80 g (✓) **(ii)** 50 g crystallise (✓) because the solubility is 30 g/100 g. **c) (i)** 105 g/100 g (✓) **(ii)** 30 g/100 g. (✓)
   d) 75 g. (✓)

Total = 16 marks

Topic 7 Rocks

Test yourself

1 **a)** Igneous. (✓) **b)** Sedimentary. (✓)
   c) Metamorphic. (✓)
2 **a)** Examples: basalt or granite or pumice. (✓)
   b) Examples: sandstone or limestone. (✓)
   c) Examples: marble or slate. (✓)
3 Rock cycle. (✓)
4 Examples: rain, wind. (2✓)

Total = 9 marks

Round-up

1 Look for fossils in the rock, (✓) and date the fossils. (✓)
2 High temperature, (✓) high pressure. (✓)
3 A metamorphic, B igneous, C sedimentary, D metamorphic, E sedimentary. (5✓)
4 For example, freezing in a crack, expanding and widening the crack; (✓) dissolving salts out of rocks; (✓) reacting chemically with rocks. (✓)
5 Three of e.g. rain, rivers, sea, wind. (3✓)

Total = 13 marks

Topic 8

Test yourself

1 c. (✓)
2 **a)** iron + sulphur → iron sulphide. (✓)
   b) sodium + chlorine → sodium chloride. (✓)
   c) zinc + sulphuric acid → hydrogen + zinc sulphate. (✓)
   d) sulphur + oxygen → sulphur dioxide. (✓)
3 **a)** e.g. photosynthesis. (✓) **b)** e.g. respiration. (✓)
   c) e.g. combustion. (✓)
4 **a)** Carbon oxidised, (✓) water (steam) reduced. (✓)
   b) Carbon oxidised, (✓) zinc oxide reduced. (✓)
   c) Aluminium oxidised, (✓) iron oxide reduced. (✓)
   d) Hydrogen oxidised, (✓) tungsten oxide reduced. (✓)
5 **a)** e.g. respiration, combustion of fuels etc. (✓)
   b) e.g. spoiling of foods, rusting etc. (✓)

Total = 19 marks

Round-up

1 **a)** Respiration. (✓) **b)** Two of e.g. milk turning sour, fats turning rancid, fish going bad, wine turning sour. (2✓)
2 **a)** Carbon monoxide. (✓) **b)** Hydrogen. (✓)
   c) Carbon. (✓)
3 **a)** Aluminium. (✓) **b)** Tin sulphide. (✓)
   c) Carbon. (✓)
4 **a)** Tin plate. (✓) **b)** Oil. (✓) **c)** Chromium plate. (✓) **d)** Paint, (✓) zinc plate. (✓)
5 Photosynthesis. (✓)
   carbon dioxide + water → glucose (or sugar) + oxygen. (2✓)

Total = 17 marks

Topic 9 Metals

Test yourself

1 Sodium/potassium. (✓)
2 Sodium/magnesium/zinc/iron. (2✓)
3 Gold, platinum. (2✓)
4 Sodium/potassium; (✓) hydrogen (✓) + sodium hydroxide/potassium hydroxide. (✓)
5 Zinc chloride + hydrogen. (2✓)

6 Aluminium. (✓)

7 A list of metals (✓) which places them in order of reactivity. (✓)

Total = 13 marks

9.2 Predictions

a) zinc + silver nitrate solution
→ silver + zinc nitrate solution

b) gold + copper sulphate solution → no reaction

c) tin + zinc sulphate solution → no reaction

d) tin + copper sulphate solution
→ copper + tin sulphate solution

e) zinc + tin chloride solution
→ tin + zinc chloride solution

f) zinc + copper sulphate solution
→ copper + zinc sulphate solution

g) copper + silver nitrate solution
→ silver + copper nitrate solution

h) aluminium + mercury oxide
→ mercury + aluminium oxide

i) potassium + aluminium oxide
→ aluminium + potassium oxide

j) zinc + calcium oxide → no reaction

Round-up

1 a) Gold does not react with foods or mouth fluids. (✓)
b) Copper does not react with water. (✓)
c) Silver is a beautiful metal (✓) which does not corrode in air. (✓) **d)** Mercury is a liquid. (✓)
e) Aluminium does not corrode. (✓)

2 e. (✓)

3 Add dilute hydrochloric acid (or dilute sulphuric acid). (✓) Zinc will react. (✓) Filter. (✓) The residue is copper. (✓)

4 *Either:* Add dilute acid. (✓) Which metal gives off hydrogen faster? (✓) *Or:* Find out whether nickel displaces cobalt from a solution of a cobalt salt (✓) or cobalt displaces nickel from a solution of a nickel salt. (✓)

5 a) Gold. (✓) **b)** Sodium. (✓) **c)** Zinc or iron. (✓)
d) Magnesium, zinc, iron. (✓) **e)** Sodium. (✓)
f) Zinc, iron. (A protective layer of aluminium oxide stops aluminium from reacting.) (✓)

6 a) copper + oxygen → copper oxide. (✓)
b) aluminium + iron oxide
→ iron + aluminium oxide. (2✓)
c) iron + aluminium oxide → no reaction. (✓)
d) copper + iron oxide → no reaction. (✓)
e) zinc + silver nitrate solution
→ silver + zinc nitrate solution. (2✓)

7 a) Used metal objects (✓) are collected (✓) and the metal is used again (✓) to make new objects. (✓)
b) Aluminium never corrodes. (✓) **c)** By using a magnet to attract the iron. (✓) **d)** Your choice! (4✓)

8 See table at the bottom of the page. (16✓)

9 Y > X > W > Z (✓ for Z last, ✓ for Y first, ✓ for all correct). Z did not displace any of the other metals; put Z last. (✓) Both W and X displace Z; put both W and X before Z. *Either:* W > X >Z or X > W > Z. (✓) X displaces W; put X before W: X > W > Z. (✓) Y displaces X; put Y before X: Y > X > W > Z. (✓)

Total = 23 marks

Topic 10 Acids and bases

Test yourself

1 a) SA. **b)** WA. **c)** WB. **d)** WB. **e)** WA. **f)** N.
g) SB. (7✓)

2 Two of: Use an indicator (✓), e.g. litmus is red in acids (✓) and blue in alkalis. (✓) *Or* Add a piece of magnesium ribbon (✓) (or another reactive metal). It fizzes in acids (✓) but not in alkalis. (✓) *Or:* Add a carbonate (✓), which fizzes in acids (✓) but not in alkalis. (✓)

3 a) Hydrochloric acid. (✓) **b)** Example: magnesium hydroxide. (✓) **c)** Citric acid. (✓) **d)** Ammonia. (✓)

Total = 17 marks

Round-up

1 a) A. **b)** B. **c)** A. **d)** C. **e)** B. **f)** B. **g)** A. (6✓)

2 A bee sting is acidic; (✓) a wasp sting is alkaline. (✓)

3 Pour a little acid into a test tube. (✓) *Either:* Add a piece of magnesium ribbon. (✓) Hydrochloric acid reacts faster than citric acid, which is a weak acid. (✓) *Or:* add a chip of limestone (calcium carbonate). (✓) Again the stronger acid reacts faster. (✓)

4 a) zinc sulphate + hydrogen. (2✓) **b)** magnesium sulphate + water. (2✓) **c)** calcium chloride + carbon dioxide + water. (3✓) **d)** potassium chloride + water. (2✓)

5 a) sodium sulphate + water. (2✓) **b)** zinc chloride + hydrogen. (2✓) **c)** copper sulphate + water. (2✓)
d) calcium chloride + carbon dioxide + water. (3✓)

6 Calcium hydroxide is a base (✓) and neutralises some of the acid present. (✓)

7 The rock contains a carbonate. (✓) (With acid this gives carbon dioxide.)

Total = 32 marks

Metal	Metal salt solution			
	Copper chloride	**Iron chloride**	**Zinc chloride**	**Magnesium chloride**
copper	✗	✗	✗	✗
Iron	✓	✗	✗	✗
Zinc	✓	✓	✗	✗
Magnesium	✓	✓	✓	✗

Electricity & magnetism

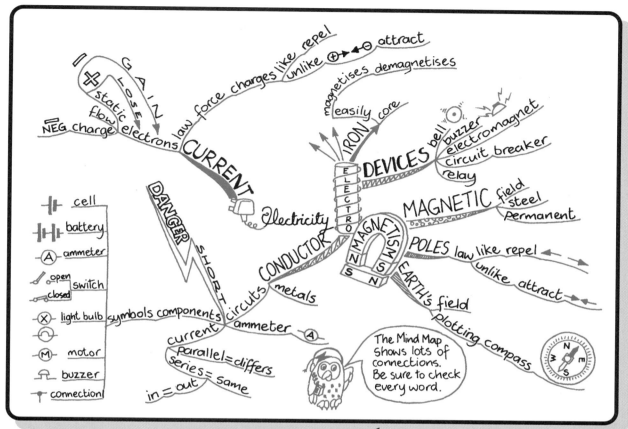

preview

At the end of this topic you will be able to:

- **explain charging of an insulator by friction**
- **relate the direction of force between two bodies to the type of charge on each body**
- **understand what current is**
- **describe what determines the current in a series circuit**
- **describe how to measure current in series and parallel circuits**
- **sketch the field pattern of a bar magnet and explain why permanent magnets are made of steel**
- **describe the construction of an electromagnet and explain why the core of an electromagnet is made of iron**
- ★**describe and explain some uses of electromagnets**

How much do you already know?

Test yourself

1 A charged balloon is hung on a thread. The diagram shows what happens when a second charged balloon is held near the balloon on the thread. Which two statements are correct?
(a) The two balloons repel each other. **(b)** The two balloons attract each other. **(c)** The two balloons carry opposite types of charge. **(d)** The two balloons carry the same type of charge   [2]

2 The circuit diagram below shows two ammeters in series with a torch bulb, a switch and a battery.

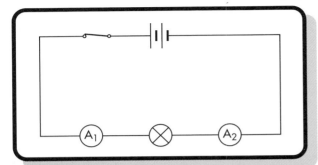

(a) Which one of the following statements is correct? **(i)** Ammeter A_1 reads more than ammeter A_2 **(ii)** Ammeter A_1 reads less than ammeter A_2 **(iii)** Ammeter A_1 reads the same as Ammeter A_2 [1]
(b) If the switch is left closed for a long time, the torch bulb gradually becomes dimmer and dimmer. What can you say about the reading of the two ammeters now? [2]

3 This circuit diagram shows three torch bulbs and a battery. **(a)** Which two torch bulbs are in parallel with each other? **(b)** What would be the effect on bulbs Y and Z if bulb X is disconnected? **(c)** What would be the effect on bulbs X and Y if Z was disconnected? [4]

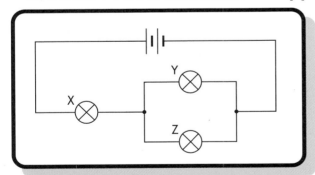

4 The diagram shows the lines of force between two magnets lined up end to end. Complete the paragraph below, using *each* of the following words *once only*:

north south repel attract

The two magnets shown _____ each other. Pole X is a _____ pole. If magnet A is turned round the two magnets would _____ each other. This is because a _____ pole is now facing a north pole. [4]

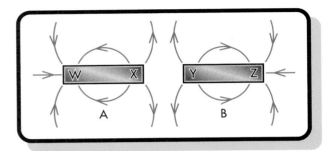

5 (a) Why is a permanent magnet made from steel rather than from iron? **(b)** Why is iron used rather than steel for the core of an electromagnet? [2]

Conductors and insulators

Metals conduct electricity. In the figure below the light bulb will light up if a metal object is connected in the gap XY. The light bulb will not light up if a plastic object is connected in the gap. Plastic is an insulator, not a conductor of electricity. Which substances in the list below are insulators and which are conductors? The answers are at the foot of the page.

wood, tap water, pure water, rubber, brass, glass, nylon, polythene, lead, cork

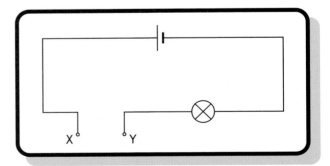

Answers

Conductors: tap water, brass, lead. The rest are insulators

1.1 Electric charge

Fact file

★ Certain insulating materials become charged when they are rubbed with a dry cloth. Examples include most plastic materials, glass and resin. This process of charging an insulator is called **charging by friction**.

★ There are two types of electric charge, **positive** and **negative**. A given insulating material always gains the same type of charge.

★ When an insulator is charged by rubbing it with a dry cloth, friction between the insulator and the cloth causes the insulator to gain one type of charge and the cloth to gain the other type of charge.

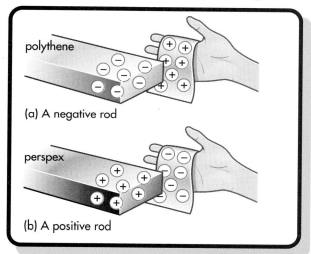

(a) A negative rod

(b) A positive rod

Charging by friction

The law of force between charged objects

Like charges repel: Unlike charges attract

The figure below shows a charged balloon hanging from a string. The balloon is attracted to the cloth used

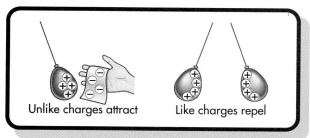

Unlike charges attract   Like charges repel

to charge it. This is because the balloon and the cloth carry unlike charges.

The figure also shows two charged balloons, each suspended by a string. The two balloons repel each other because they carry the same type of charge.

Electrons

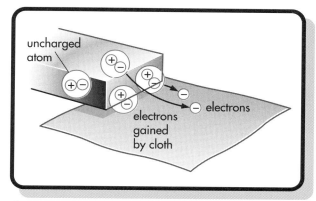

Electron transfer

Every atom contains a positively charged nucleus surrounded by much lighter negatively charged particles called **electrons**.

1 An insulator that loses electrons when rubbed with a dry cloth becomes positively charged.

2 An insulator that gains electrons when rubbed with a dry cloth becomes negatively charged.

Questions

1 A plastic ruler becomes charged positively when it is rubbed with a dry cloth. What type of charge does the cloth gain in this process?

2 A charged balloon is suspended from a cotton thread. A negatively charged rod held near the balloon attracts the balloon. **(a)** What type of charge does the balloon carry? **(b)** When the rod was charged, did it gain or lose electrons?

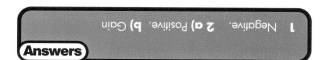
1 Negative. **2 a)** Positive. **b)** Gain

Answers

1.2 Electric circuits

Charge on the move

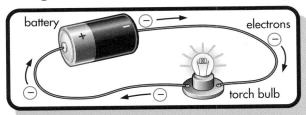

Charge flow

An electric current is a flow of charge. When a torch bulb is connected to a battery, electrons are forced from the negative terminal of the battery to its positive terminal through the bulb. Each electron carries a tiny negative charge so there is a flow of charge round the circuit.

The bigger the current through a wire or a component, the greater the number of electrons moving round the circuit each second.

The two essential conditions for an electric current in a circuit are:

1 The circuit must include a source of charge, such as a battery
2 The circuit must be complete, without a break, from one terminal of the battery to the other.

Components in circuits

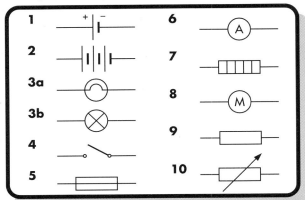

Circuit symbols

A circuit is made up of parts called **components**. The figure shows the symbols for some circuit components. Can you identify them? The key is at the bottom of the page.

A current problem

André Ampère in the eighteenth century discovered that an electric current is a one-way flow of charge round an electric circuit. He thought that an electric current is a flow of **positive** charge. This is why the direction of an electric current in a circuit is always marked from + to − We know now that an electric current in a wire is a flow of negative charge carried by electrons – but we still use Ampère's direction rule.

Measuring electric current

★ An **ammeter** is used to measure an electric current. The electric current through a component is measured by connecting the ammeter in **series** with the component so that all the electrons that pass through the ammeter also pass through the component. The current through the ammeter is the same as the current through the component.

★ Electric current is measured in **amperes** (symbol A). For example, a fuse marked 13 A will melt if the current through it exceeds 13 amperes.

★ The current leaving a component in an electric circuit is the same as the current entering the component. A component in an electric circuit does *not* 'use up' current.

★ The figure on the next page shows what is meant by connecting components in **parallel**. The current from the battery is divided between components that are connected in parallel with each other.

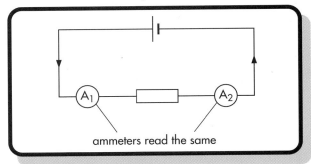

ammeters read the same

Current out = current in

Series and parallel circuits

Components in series have the same current

This is because all the electrons pass through every component if the components are in series. This can be demonstrated using two ammeters as in the figure below.

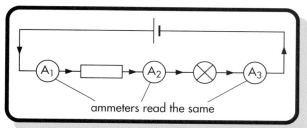

Components in series

Components in parallel have different currents

The figure below shows two torch bulbs in parallel with each other. Electrons from the battery pass through X or through Y. The battery current is therefore equal to the current through X plus the current through Y. The figure also shows how this can be demonstrated using three ammeters.

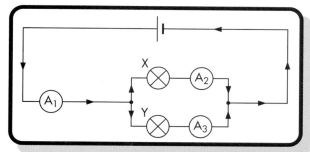

Components in parallel

Controlling the current in a circuit

★ A switch in series with a component is used to switch the component on or off. When the switch is closed, current passes through the switch and the component. When the switch is open, no current can pass.

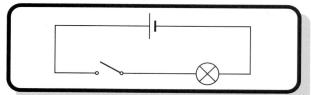

Using a switch

★ A **resistor** limits the amount of electric current in a circuit. This is because the resistor doesn't allow electrons to pass through very easily. The **resistance** of a resistor is a measure of how much the resistor limits the current.
★ The energy used by electrons to force their way through a resistor causes a **heating effect** in the resistor. This heating effect increases if the current increases. A **fuse** is a thin wire that melts if too much current passes through it, cutting the current off as a result.

A circuit short cut

A short-circuit is where there is a low-resistance path between two points in different parts of a circuit. The current through a short-circuit could be very large and cause overheating.

Question

3 The figure shows three circuits. **(a)** Which circuit allows each torch bulb to be switched on and off without affecting the other bulbs? **(b)** Which circuit only allows both torch bulbs to be either both on or both off? **(c)** In circuit 2, how could both torch bulbs be switched on?

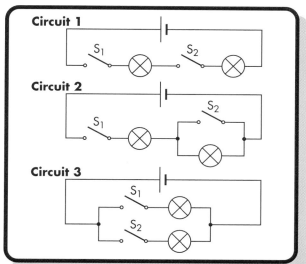

3 a) Circuit 3. **b)** Circuit 1. **c)** Close S1 and open S2.

Answers

49

1.3 Magnetism

Using a magnet as a compass

★ A bar magnet hung horizontally by a thread lines up so one end points north and the other end points south. The end that points north is its **north-seeking** pole (or north pole). The other end is its **south-seeking** pole.

★ A **plotting compass** is a tiny magnet on a pivot. Its north pole is an arrowhead that points north. The earth's magnetism makes a plotting compass point north. The line along which a plotting compass points is called a **line of force**.

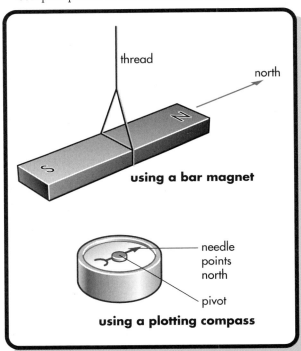

using a bar magnet

using a plotting compass

Direction finding

Magnetic materials

★ A **magnetic material** is any material that can be attracted by a magnet. Iron, steel and nickel are examples of magnetic materials. A magnet can be used to separate **ferrous** (iron-based) metals and other magnetic material from non-ferrous metals.

★ **Magnets are made of steel**. Magnets can be made of iron but iron loses its magnetism more easily than steel. However, steel is harder to magnetise than iron.

The law of force between magnets

Like poles repel: unlike poles attract

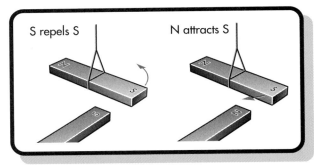

S repels S   N attracts S

The law of force between magnetic poles

If the north pole of a bar magnet is held near the north pole of a second bar magnet, the two magnets repel each other. The same happens if both poles are south poles. However, if the two poles are different the magnets attract each other.

Like = same
Unlike = different

Question

4 Figure a shows a plotting compass on its own pointing north. When an iron nail is held near the plotting compass, the plotting compass turns as shown in figure b. **(a)** What two deductions can you make from this observation? **(b)** What would you expect to observe if the nail is moved nearer the plotting compass?

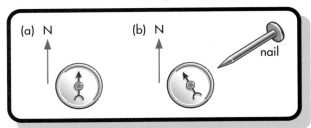

(a) N   (b) N
                         nail

4 a) The nail is magnetised; the pointed end of the nail is a north pole. **b)** The compass needle turns further.

Answers

Magnetic fields

A bar magnet affects a plotting compass without touching it. The magnet creates a **magnetic field** in the surrounding space. The pattern of the magnetic field caused by the bar magnet can be seen by sprinkling iron filings onto a sheet of paper placed on top of the magnet. The filings form lines along the **lines of force** (or field lines) that loop round from the north pole to the south pole.

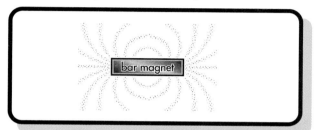

Using iron filings

A plotting compass can be used to plot the lines of force of a magnetic field. The figure below shows what some different field patterns look like. The direction of a line of force is the direction along which a plotting compass needle points.

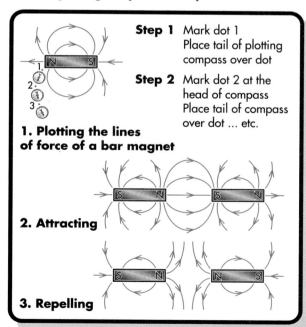

Step 1 Mark dot 1 Place tail of plotting compass over dot

Step 2 Mark dot 2 at the head of compass Place tail of compass over dot ... etc.

1. Plotting the lines of force of a bar magnet

2. Attracting

3. Repelling

Using a plotting compass

1 The lines of force of a bar magnet are concentrated most at the poles, where the

magnetic field is strongest. The lines loop round from the north pole to the south pole.

2 For two bar magnets lined up to attract each other, the lines of force pass from the north pole of one magnet to the south pole of the other.

3 For two bar magnets lined up to repel each other, the lines from each magnet curve away from the lines of the other magnet.

4 The lines of force of the Earth's magnetic field point north. Over a small region, they are effectively parallel.

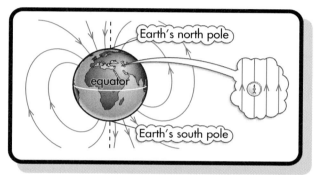

The Earth's magnetic field

Question

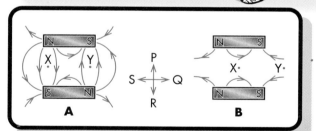

5 Above are two arrangements of two magnets side by side. Some lines of force are shown in each arrangement. **(a)** In one of the two arrangements, the magnets attract each other and in the other they repel each other. Which is which? **(b)** Which direction P, Q, R or S will a plotting compass point if placed at **(i)** X, **(ii)** Y in each arrangement?

5 a) They attract in A and repel in B. **b)** A (i) R, (ii) P; B (i) Q, (ii) S.

Answers

1.4 Electromagnetism

The magnetic effects of an electric current

★ A current along a straight wire produces a magnetic field round the wire. The direction of the lines of force depends on the direction of the current.

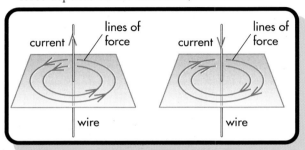

The magnetic field round a current-carrying wire

★ A current through a long coil of wires produces a magnetic field like the field of a bar magnet. The direction of the lines of force depends on the direction of the current.

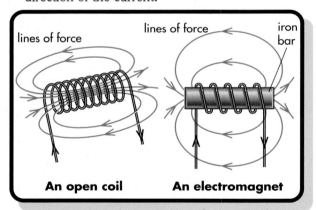

An open coil   **An electromagnet**

The magnetic field of a long coil

★ The magnetic field produced by a coil carrying a current is much stronger if there is an iron bar inside the coil. The current through the coil magnetises the bar. The magnetic field of the bar is much stronger than the magnetic field of the empty coil. The bar loses its magnetism when the current is switched off. The bar and the coil form an **electromagnet**. The bar is called the core of the electromagnet.

★ Iron is much easier to magnetise and demagnetise than steel. This is why the core of an electromagnet is iron.

Question

6 (a) Why is iron, rather than steel, used in an electromagnet? **(b)** Why do the wires of an electromagnet need to be insulated?

Uses of electromagnets

Lifting and moving scrap iron and steel

A large electromagnet on the end of a crane jib is used to move iron and steel objects about. When the electromagnet is switched off, the objects drop off the electromagnet.

The electric bell

A metal hammer repeatedly hits a gong due to the action of an electromagnet. The operation of the bell takes place in three stages, as follows.

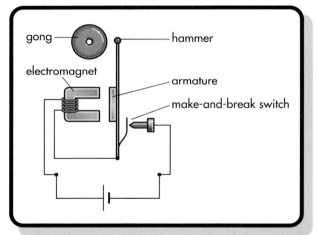

The electric bell

1 **Attraction:** when current passes through the electromagnet coil, an iron plate called the armature is attracted onto the electromagnet. The hammer attached to the armature hits the gong.
2 **Breaking the circuit:** The armature moves onto the electromagnet. It opens a 'make and break' switch which switches the electromagnet current off.
3 **Recoil:** The electromagnet loses its magnetism. The armature (and hammer) recoil back to close the 'make and break switch'. This switches the electromagnet on again and the sequence begins once more.

The relay

A relay will open or close a switch in a separate circuit. It depends on passing a current through the electromagnet coil to pull an iron armature onto the electromagnet core.

★ In a normally open (NO) relay, the movement of the armature closes a springy switch.

★ In a normally closed (NC) relay, the movement of the armature opens a springy switch.

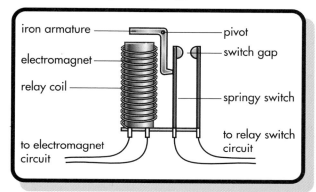

The relay

Question

7 (a) In an electric bell and a relay, why is the armature made from iron rather than steel?

(b) The figure shows a relay used to switch a light bulb on and off. Put the following statements in correct order to explain what happens when the switch S is closed.

  1 The movement of the armature closes the relay switch.

  2 Current passes through the light bulb.

  3 Current passes through the relay coil.

  4 The electromagnet attracts the iron armature.

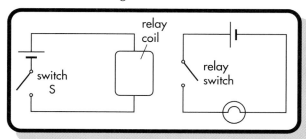

round-up

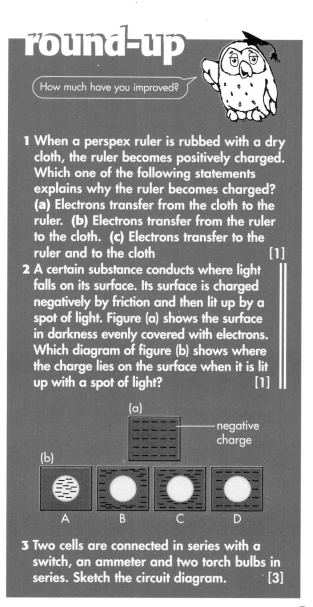

How much have you improved?

1 When a perspex ruler is rubbed with a dry cloth, the ruler becomes positively charged. Which one of the following statements explains why the ruler becomes charged? **(a)** Electrons transfer from the cloth to the ruler. **(b)** Electrons transfer from the ruler to the cloth. **(c)** Electrons transfer to the ruler and to the cloth [1]

2 A certain substance conducts where light falls on its surface. Its surface is charged negatively by friction and then lit up by a spot of light. Figure (a) shows the surface in darkness evenly covered with electrons. Which diagram of figure (b) shows where the charge lies on the surface when it is lit up with a spot of light? [1]

3 Two cells are connected in series with a switch, an ammeter and two torch bulbs in series. Sketch the circuit diagram. [3]

round-up

4 The ammeter in the circuit in question 3 read 0.5 A when the switch was closed. Which one of the following statements is correct?
(a) The current through each torch bulb was less than 0.5 A. **(b)** The current from the cells was more than 0.5 A. **(c)** The current through each torch bulb was 0.5 A. **(d)** The current returning to the cells was less than 0.5 A. [1]

5 and 6 The figure shows a cell in series with a switch, an ammeter and two identical torch bulbs X and Y in parallel. When the switch was closed, the ammeter reading was 0.6 A.

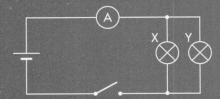

5 Which of the following statements is correct?
(a) The current through torch bulb X is 0.6 A.
(b) The current through torch bulb X is less than 0.6 A. **(c)** The current through torch bulb X is more than the current through bulb Y. **(d)** The current through Y is 0.6 A. [1]

6 Torch bulb Y is disconnected from the circuit with the switch still closed. Describe what happens to **(a)** the ammeter reading, and **(b)** the brightness of torch bulb X. [2]

7 and 8 Two bar magnets are lined up end-to-end so they repel each other. A plotting compass near the other end of one of the magnets points away from the magnet, as shown in the figure.

7 On the diagram, mark each end of each bar magnet with the correct polarity. [4]

8 (a) Explain your choice of polarity for the left-hand end of bar magnet A. **(b)** Explain your choice of polarity for the two facing poles. [4]

9 and 10 Alan designs and makes a buzzer, which is shown below.

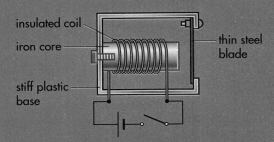

9 Alan tests the buzzer by connecting it in series with a switch S and a battery. Unfortunately, it does not buzz when Alan closes the switch. Complete the paragraph below to explain what happens when the switch is closed.

When the switch is closed, the core becomes _____ because current passes through the _____. The thin steel blade is _____ onto the core. The blade sticks to the core because _____. [4]

10 A make-and-break switch is needed to make the buzzer work. The figure shows how the blade may be used as part of a make-and-break switch. Explain why the blade vibrates when switch S is closed. [4]

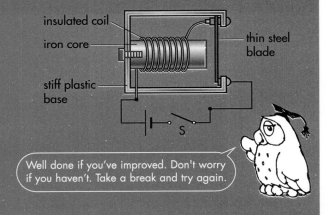

Well done if you've improved. Don't worry if you haven't. Take a break and try again.

Forces

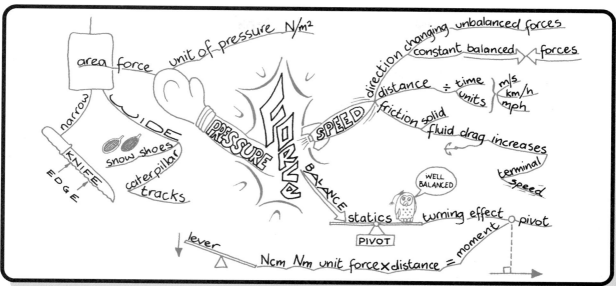

How much do you already know?

preview

At the end of this topic you should be able to:

- **understand how speed, distance and time are related for an object moving at constant speed**
- ★**carry out calculations using the equation speed = distance/time**
- **describe the effect of balanced or unbalanced forces on the motion of an object**
- **explain the effect of frictional forces on the motion of an object**
- **describe and use the principle of moments**
- ★**carry out calculations using the equation pressure = force/area**
- **describe and explain applications of the relationship between pressure, force and area.**

Test yourself

1 A cyclist sets off from home at 8.00 a.m. and arrives at school 6 km away at 8.30 a.m. Calculate the cyclist's average speed in
(a) km/h, **(b)** m/s. [2]
2 The figure shows a manual punch used to punch a hole in sheets of paper.

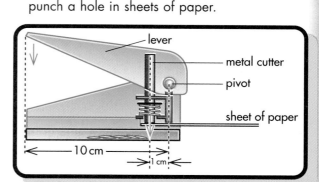

(a) Explain why a small force exerted on the end of the lever causes the cutter to exert a much larger force on the paper. [3]
(b) A force of 30 N is exerted on the end of the lever, as shown in the figure. Calculate the force exerted by the cutter on the paper. [3]
3 Explain why a toboggan will slide on ice but not on snow. [3]
4 Explain why a sharp knife cuts more easily than a blunt knife. [2]

2.1 **Making objects move**

Fact file

★ Different types of force include weight (the force of gravity), tension (forces that stretch or pull), compression (forces that squeeze or push), twisting forces, electrical and magnetic forces.

★ The unit of force is the **newton** (N). Note that 10 N is the weight of 1 kg of mass at the Earth's surface.

★ If the forces on an object balance each other out, the object stays at rest or moves at constant speed without change of direction.

★ An object changes its speed or its direction of motion if the forces acting on it are unbalanced.

Balanced and unbalanced forces

Constant speed

An object moving at constant speed travels the same distance every second. Its speed is calculated from the equation

$$\text{Speed} = \frac{\text{distance}}{\text{time}}$$

★ Rearranging this equation gives

$$\text{Distance} = \text{speed} \times \text{time}$$

and

$$\text{Time} = \frac{\text{distance}}{\text{speed}}$$

★ Speed is measured in metres per second (m/s) (the scientific unit of speed) or kilometres per hour (km/h) or miles per hour (mph).

★ You need to be able to be able to convert from m/s to km/h or km/min and from km/h to mph. Note that 1 mile = 1.6 kilometres, 1 kilometre = 1000 metres and 1 hour = 60 minutes = 3600 seconds.

★ For an object moving at constant speed, a graph of distance (on the vertical axis) against time (on the horizontal axis) is a straight line. The gradient is equal to the speed.

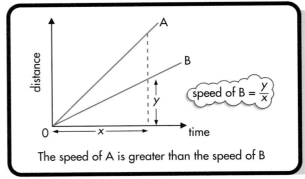

The speed of A is greater than the speed of B

A distance versus time graph for constant speed

Question

1 A walker set off from a car park at 10.00 a.m. and walked at constant speed a distance of 10 km in 2 hours 30 minutes. She then stopped for a break of 30 minutes, then returned at an average speed of 3 km/h by a different route, arriving back at the car park at 4.00 p.m.
(a) Calculate the average speed of the walker on her outward journey. **(b)** Calculate the distance she walked on the return journey.
(c) Calculate her average speed on the return journey in metres per second.

Answers

1 a) 4 km/h. b) 9 km. c) 0.83 m/s (= 3000 m/3600 s).

Changing speed

When an object accelerates (speeds up) or decelerates (slows down), the forces on it are unbalanced. Its average speed over a given time is calculated by

$$\text{Average speed} = \frac{\text{distance moved}}{\text{time taken}}$$

Friction

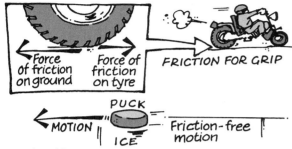

Examples of friction

★ Solid surfaces that rub against each other create **friction**. The force of friction on each surface acts in the opposite direction to the direction in which the surface moves or tries to move. Friction is essential to achieve grip for moving.

★ Fluid flow past an object causes a drag force on the object. This is due to friction between the fluid and the object. Examples include air resistance on a vehicle or drag on a ship moving through water. The drag force increases with speed.

Terminal speed

When an object moves through a fluid, the drag force acts against its motion. If the object is 'driven' by a constant force (e.g. the engine force for a vehicle or weight for a falling object), its speed increases until it reaches a constant speed known as the **terminal speed**. The speed reaches this limit because the drag force increases with speed. At the terminal speed, the drag force is equal and opposite to the driving force. The figure shows how the speed of an object released in water changes with time.

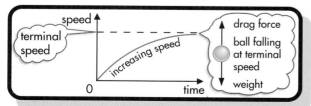

Terminal speed

Dropping in

A parachutist falls at constant speed because the force of air resistance on the parachute is equal and opposite to the force of gravity (i.e. the weight) on the parachutist.

Balanced forces again

Questions

2 The Highway Code advises motorway drivers to follow the 'two second' rule. This means that there should be at least 2 seconds between the car in front passing a roadside marker and their car passing the same marker. **(a)** The speed limit on any motorway is 31 m/s. Calculate the shortest distance to the car in front for a motorist following the 'two second' rule. **(b)** How long would it take for a motorist travelling at 31 m/s to travel a distance of 80 km? **(c)** Show that 31 m/s is equal to 110 km/h.

3 (a) A ship at sea moves at constant speed with its engines on full power. Explain why the ship moves at constant speed, even though its engines are on full power. **(b)** Explain why a cyclist can reach a higher top speed as a result of crouching over the handle bars instead of sitting upright.

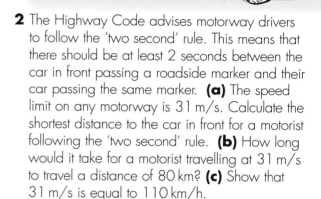

Answers

2 a) 62 m. **b)** $\text{Time} = \frac{\text{distance}}{\text{speed}} = \frac{80\,000\,\text{m}}{31\,\text{m/s}} = 2580\,\text{s}$
= 43 minutes.
c) 31 m/s = 31 × 3600 metres per hour
= 31 × 3.6 km/h = 110 km/h.
3 a) The drag force due to friction between the ship and the water balances the force of the engines. **b)** The air resistance increases with speed. At any given speed, there is less air resistance in the crouched position than upright. At top speed, the air resistance is equal and opposite to the 'driving force', which is constant. The cyclist achieves this amount of air resistance at a higher top speed when crouched than when upright.

2.2 Making objects turn

Whenever you open or close a door, you are applying a force that makes the door turn about its hinges. The door is pivoted on its hinges. Someone pushing on the other side of the door with the same force will not be able to push past if you apply your force as far from the hinge as possible.

The **moment** of the force about a pivot = force × perpendicular distance from the pivot to the line of action of the force. The unit of moment is the newton metre (N m).

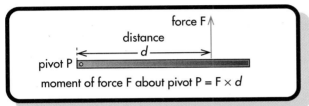

The moment of a force

Levers as force multipliers

The handle of a spanner is a lever used to turn a nut on a screw thread. The further from the nut the force is applied to the spanner, the greater the moment of the force about the nut.

Worked example

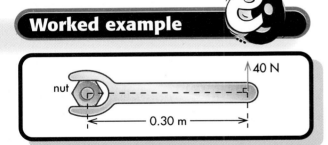

A spanner at work

A force of 40 N is applied perpendicular to a spanner at a distance of 0.30 m from the nut. Calculate:
(a) the moment of this force about the nut
(b) the distance that a force of 50 N would need to be applied from the nut to give an equal moment.

Solution

a) Moment = force × distance = 40 N × 0.30 m
    = 12 N m
b) Let the distance = d. Therefore 50 d = 12,
    so d = 12/50 = 0.24 m

More force multipliers

In each of the following applications, the moment of the applied force about a pivot must overcome the moment of an opposing force acting about the same pivot.

★ A large force can be applied to the cap of a bottle by applying a small force to the bottle opener. The opposite side of the bottle top acts as the pivot.

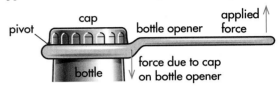

★ A pair of scissors cuts through material because the force applied exerts a large enough moment to overcome the force of the material on the blades.

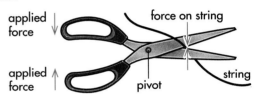

★ A wheelbarrow is used to lift and shift a heavy load with a much smaller force. The wheel acts as a pivot. Provided the moment of the force on the handles is greater than the moment of the load about the pivot, the load can be raised. It works because the force applied to the handles is much further from the pivot that the load.

★ A door handle turns a lock as a result of a small force applied to the end of the handle. The moment of the applied force must be enough to overcome the friction between the moving parts in the lock.

A seesaw problem

A seesaw problem

The figure shows a boy and a girl on a seesaw, which is horizontal. Who is heavier?

The boy's weight tries to turn the seesaw anticlockwise. The girl's weight tries to turn it clockwise. The moment of the boy is equal to the moment of the girl about the pivot. Since the boy is nearer the pivot than the girl is, he must be heavier than the girl to cause an equal moment.

The principle of moments

A pivoted object will not turn if the sum of the clockwise moments about the pivot is equal to the sum of the anticlockwise moments about the pivot.

Applying the principle of moments to the seesaw problem above gives

clockwise moment = anticlockwise moment

weight of boy ×
distance of boy to pivot = weight of girl ×
distance of girl to pivot

Question

4 The boy's weight was 400 N and he was seated 1.5 m from the pivot. The girl was seated 2.0 m from the pivot on the other side. Calculate the girl's weight.

A simple balance

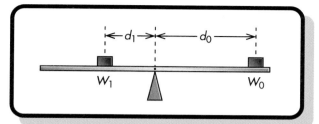

A simple balance

The figure shows how to find the weight W_1 of an object, given a pivoted metre rule and a known weight W_0. The weights are adjusted as far as possible from the pivot so the rule is horizontal. The distance d_1 from the unknown weight to the pivot and the distance d_0 from the known weight to the pivot is measured.

At balance, the moment of W_1 about the pivot = the moment of W_0 about the pivot.

so $\quad W_1 d_1 = W_0 d_0$

hence $\quad W_1 = \dfrac{W_0 d_0}{d_1}$

Question

5 Calculate the unknown weight W or distance d for each arrangement in the figure.

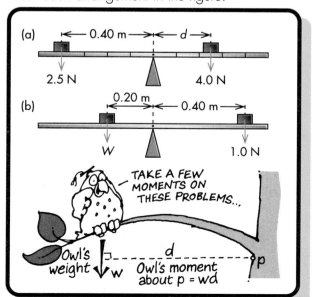

2

2.3 Force and pressure

Fact file

★ The pressure of a force acting on an object depends on the surface area the force acts on. The smaller the area, the greater the pressure of the force.
★ The pressure of a force on a surface is defined as the **force per unit area** acting at right angles to the surface. This may be written as an equation:

$$\text{Pressure} = \frac{\text{Force}}{\text{Area}}$$

★ The unit of pressure is the newton per square metre (N/m²), which is also known as the pascal (Pa). The newton per square centimetre (N/cm²) is also sometimes used for pressure measurements.

In the snow

Walking across deep snow is difficult unless you are wearing snowshoes. Without snowshoes, your boots press on a small area of the snow's surface and sink into it. With snowshoes, you don't sink in to the snow because the shoes have a larger area than ordinary boots – so your weight exerts a smaller pressure.

Reducing the pressure

Vehicles crossing snow and ice (and sand!) are fitted with caterpillar tracks instead of tyres. With caterpillar tracks fitted, the weight of the vehicle is spread out over the area of the tracks in contact with the ground. This area is much greater than the area of the tyres in contact with the ground so the caterpillar tracks exert less pressure on the ground than tyres would.

At the sharp end

★ When you push a drawing pin into a board, the force from your thumb on the drawing pin is concentrated at its sharp end. The area of the sharp end is much smaller than the area your thumb presses on. Some more examples of concentrating a force over a small area are given below. In each case, the pressure of the force is increased if the force acts over a smaller area.

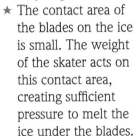 

★ The area of contact between the sharp edge of the knife and the cheese is small. The pressure on the cheese is therefore very large.
★ The contact area of the blades on the ice is small. The weight of the skater acts on this contact area, creating sufficient pressure to melt the ice under the blades. The water layer enables the blade to move over the ice with little friction. The water freezes again after the blade has moved on.
★ An air bag fitted to the steering column of a vehicle inflates rapidly in a collision. The force of impact on the driver is spread over a large area by the air bag. This could save the driver's life by reducing the pressure of the impact on the driver.

Using the pressure equation

Rearranging the equation

$$\text{pressure (p)} = \frac{\text{force (F)}}{\text{area (A)}}$$

gives

$$F = pA$$
or
$$A = \frac{F}{p}$$

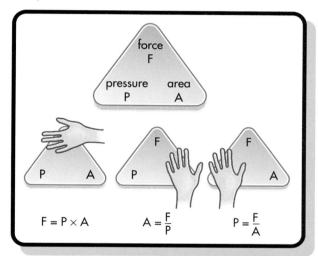

$$F = P \times A \qquad A = \frac{F}{P} \qquad P = \frac{F}{A}$$

The triangle rule

Worked example

(a) The contact area of each tyre of a car of weight 7200 N on the ground is 120 cm². Show that the pressure of the car's weight on the ground is 15 N/cm².

(b) Calculate the area of contact of each tyre of a four-wheel vehicle of weight 9000 N for the same pressure.

Solution

(a) Total contact area
$$= 4 \times 120\,\text{cm}^2 = 480\,\text{cm}^2$$
$$\text{Pressure} = \frac{\text{force}}{\text{area}} = \frac{7200\,\text{N}}{480\,\text{cm}^2} = 15\,\text{N/cm}^2$$

(b) Total area $= \dfrac{\text{force}}{\text{pressure}} = \dfrac{9000\,\text{N}}{60\,\text{N/cm}^2} = 150\,\text{cm}^2$

So contact area of each tyre $= \dfrac{150}{4} = 37.5\,\text{cm}^2$

Questions

6 The picture shows a fire-fighter crawling along a ladder laid on an icy pond in an attempt to rescue a dog that has fallen through the ice. Why is a ladder vital in this situation?

Rescuers at work

7 Explain why **(a)** beach vehicles are fitted with caterpillar tracks, **(b)** a blunt sewing needle is difficult to use.

8 A rectangular brick of weight 40 N has dimensions of 8.0 cm × 10.0 cm × 20 cm. Calculate the pressure of the brick on the ground when it rests **(a)** with its largest face on the ground, **(b)** with its smallest face on the ground (i.e. end-on).

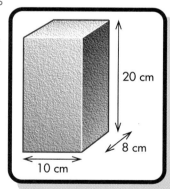

9 Complete the table below by using the pressure equation.

	Force (N)	Area (m²)	Pressure (N/m²)
(a)	20	2.5	
(b)	1200		6000
(c)		0.0050	120 000

round-up

How much can you remember? Check out your score on page 95.

1 A car was towed along a straight level road by a tow rope attached to another car. The force opposing the motion of the car was 800 N. Which of the following statements about the tension in the tow rope is correct? **(a)** The tension is greater than 800 N. **(b)** The tension is equal to 800 N. **(c)** The tension is less than 800 N. **(d)** There is no tension in the tow rope. [1]

2 A train leaves London at 14.25 and arrives at its destination 320 km away at 16.33. Calculate **(a)** the journey time, **(b)** the average speed in **(i)** km/min, **(ii)** m/s. [3]

3 The diagram shows a parachutist descending safely to the ground. Explain why the parachutist falls at a constant speed. [3]

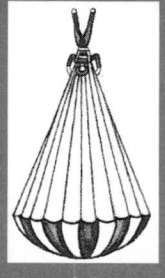

4 Would a wide parachute give a faster or a slower descent than a narrower parachute? Explain your answer. [3]

5 The diagram shows a spanner of length 0.20 m used to tighten a wheel nut. The moment of the force applied to the wheel nut must not be greater than 40 N. m. Calculate the maximum force that can be applied to the spanner. [2]

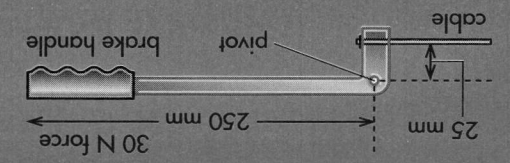

force

wheel nut

0.20 m

6 The design of a handbrake is shown in the figure. When a force is applied to the handbrake lever, the cable pulls the brakes on. Explain why the force of the cable is much greater than the force applied to the handbrake lever. [3]

7 A force of 30 N is applied to the handbrake lever as shown in the figure. Calculate the resulting force on the cable. [3]

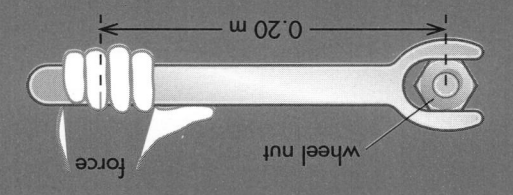

30 N force

250 mm

25 mm

brake handle

pivot

cable

8 Explain why tractor wheels are fitted with much wider tyres than car wheels. [3]

9 A 5 cm cube weighing 10 N rests on a table. Calculate the pressure exerted by the cube on the table. [3]

10 A small elephant of weight 5000 N has feet each of area 500 cm². A cat of weight 50 N has feet each of area 5 cm². Which animal exerts the greater pressure when standing upright on all fours? Explain your answer. [3]

How did you do? Don't worry if you couldn't answer everything. Take a break and try again.

Answers

6 The ladder spreads the weight of the fire-fighter over a much larger area. The pressure on the ice is therefore much smaller.

7 a) The vehicle weight is spread out over the area of the track. The pressure on the beach is reduced. The vehicle doesn't sink into the sand. **b)** The area of contact is larger than for a sharp needle so the force needs to be larger to exert the same pressure.

8 a) A = 20 × 10 = 200 cm²: therefore $p = \dfrac{F}{A} = \dfrac{40\,N}{200\,cm^2}$ = 0.2 N/cm²

b) A = 8 × 10 = 80 cm²: therefore $p = \dfrac{F}{A} = \dfrac{40\,N}{80\,cm^2}$ = 0.5 N/cm²

9 a) 8.0 N/m² **b)** 0.20 m² **c)** 600 N.

Energy

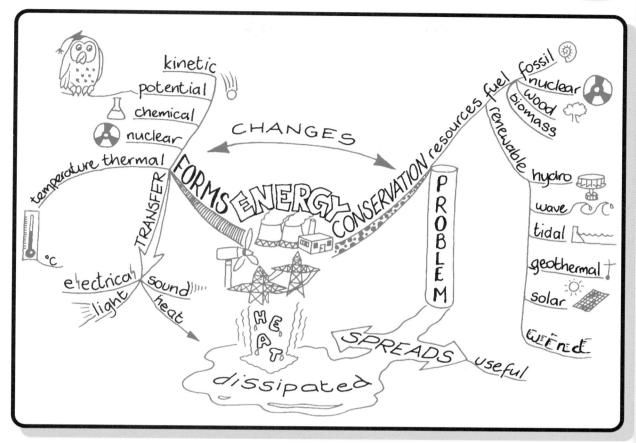

preview

At the end of this topic you will be able to:

- describe situations where energy is transferred or stored
- explain the difference between the temperature of an object and the energy it contains
- ★ understand that energy is conserved in any change, although it becomes less useful
- list a variety of energy resources and know which ones depend on the Sun
- explain whether an energy resource is renewable or non-renewable
- describe energy resources used to generate electricity.

How much do you already know? Check the Mind Map to energise your memory!

Test yourself

1 Complete the passage below using words from the list.

kinetic   potential   thermal   elastic

A catapult can store _____ energy. When an object is 'fired' from a catapult, energy from the catapult is converted into _____ energy. If the object is directed upwards, its _____ energy decreases and its _____ energy increases as it gains height. If air resistance is large enough, some of the object's _____ energy is converted into _____ energy of the air.   [6]

2 A weightlifter gives a weight 200 J of potential energy by lifting it by a height of 1.0 m from the floor. He then releases the weight so it falls to the floor. **(a)** Just before the weight hits the floor, **(i)** how much potential energy did it have? **(ii)** How much kinetic energy did it have? **(b)** When the weight was 0.5 m above the floor as it fell, **(i)** how much potential energy did it have? **(ii)** how much kinetic energy did it have? [4]

3 (a) Which of the following fuels are fossil fuels:
coal, gas, wood, uranium?
(b) (i) Which one of these fuels has not stored energy from the Sun? **(ii)** Name another energy resource that does not store or use energy from the Sun. [4]

4 Which three of the following energy resources are renewable and dependent on energy from the Sun?
geothermal energy, hydroelectricity, oil, solar cells, tidal energy, wind energy.
[3]

3.1 Using energy

Fact file

Energy transfer

★ Energy is needed when an object is forced to move. For example, you need energy to push a loaded luggage trolley across the floor. More energy is needed if the force needed is increased (for example if the trolley is loaded more) or if the distance moved is increased.

★ Energy is possessed by an object if the object is able to make something move. For example, a runaway trolley contains energy due to its motion because it will force a stationary trolley to move if they collide.

★ Energy is transferred when one object forces another object to move. For example, a runaway trolley that collides with a stationary trolley passes some of its energy to the other trolley when they collide.

★ Energy can also be transferred due to a temperature difference.

Forms of energy

Forms of energy

Objects possess energy in different forms, including

★ **kinetic** energy, which is the energy of a moving object
★ **potential** energy, which is the energy of an object due to its position
★ **chemical** energy, which is energy released by chemical reactions
★ **elastic** energy, which is energy stored in an object by changing its shape
★ **thermal** energy, which is the energy of an object due to its temperature
★ **nuclear** energy, which is energy released in nuclear reactions.

In addition, transfer of energy can take place in the form of

★ **light** energy, which is energy carried by light
★ **sound** energy, which is energy carried by vibrations travelling through a substance
★ **electrical** energy, which is energy carried by an electric current
★ **heat**, which is energy transfer due to temperature difference.

Temperature and thermal energy

The thermal energy of an object is the energy the object has due to its temperature. For example, a kettle full of boiling water has much more thermal energy than a kettle full of cold water. A sealed container of food placed in boiling water would explode if enough energy was transferred to its contents. This would demonstrate that boiling water has more energy than cold water!

The temperature of an object is a measure of how concentrated its thermal energy is. If a cup of hot water is poured into a bath of cold water, the temperature of the bath water scarcely rises because the thermal energy of the small volume of hot water spreads out when the hot water is poured into the bath. Temperature is measured on the Celsius scale (°C) by defining the temperature of
1 pure melting ice as 0 °C, and
2 steam at atmospheric pressure as 100 °C.

Storage of energy

★ Potential energy is stored by raising a weight. Energy stored by raising a weight is sometimes called 'gravitational potential energy' to distinguish it from other forms of stored energy such as elastic energy.
★ Elastic energy is stored by stretching a spring or an elastic band or by winding up a clockwork spring.
★ Kinetic energy can be stored in a flywheel.
★ Chemical energy is stored in a rechargeable battery or in fuel.

Questions

1 Name two objects that can easily be stored at home as energy sources for use in a power cut. For each object, state the form in which the energy is stored and the form of energy it releases.

2 In the figure, energy is stored and transferred in different forms. Identify the form of energy indicated by each letter in each picture.

Answers

1 A torch battery – chemical energy, light; a candle – chemical energy, light; a gas cylinder – chemical energy, heat and light; a clockwork electricity generator – elastic energy, electrical energy. **2 a)** A and C = gravitational potential energy, B = kinetic energy. **b)** D = chemical energy, E = electrical energy, F = light energy. **c)** G = Chemical energy, H = heat, I = light energy, J = thermal energy. **d)** K = elastic energy, L = kinetic energy, M = thermal energy, N = sound energy.

3.2 Conservation of energy

Measuring energy

Energy is measured in joules (J). One joule of energy is the amount of energy needed to raise a weight of one newton by a height of one metre.

OWLS NEED TO CONSERVE THEIR ENERGY IN WINTER

CRISP
CHOCC
BIS

The **principle of conservation of energy** states that:

In any change, the total energy before the change is equal to the total energy after the change.

Using the principle of conservation of energy

The two examples below show you how the principle of conservation of energy works. The total number of joules at the end is always equal to the total number of joules at the start.

A falling object loses potential energy as it falls.

★ Provided air resistance is very small, the object speeds up as it falls and therefore gains kinetic energy. The loss of potential energy is equal to its gain of kinetic energy. For example, if an object in free-fall with no air resistance loses 1000 J of potential energy over a certain distance, its gain of kinetic energy over that distance must be 1000 J.

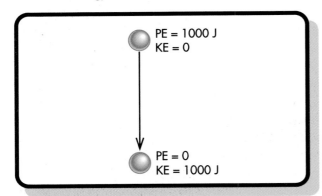

PE = 1000 J
KE = 0

PE = 0
KE = 1000 J

Losing potential energy

★ If air resistance is not very small, some or all of the potential energy of a falling object is converted into thermal energy of the air.
★ If it falls at constant speed, all its potential energy is converted into thermal energy of the air.

A torch battery loses chemical energy when it is used. The energy changes that take place in a torch can be seen in the figure. Chemical energy is changed to electrical energy in the battery. When a current flows, electrons transfer electrical energy from the battery to the light bulb. In the filament of the light bulb, electrical energy is converted to heat and light. The wires that carry the electrons gain some thermal energy because the electrons have to use some energy to move round the circuit. For every 100 J of chemical energy released by the battery, suppose 30 J is delivered to the filament. The remaining 70 J is wasted as thermal energy of the wires.

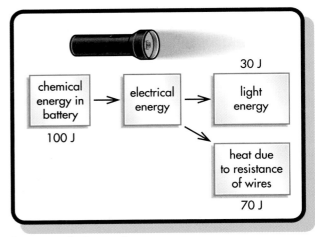

chemical energy in battery
100 J

electrical energy

light energy
30 J

heat due to resistance of wires
70 J

Energy transfer in a torch

Energy problems

The energy used in doing jobs like lifting weights or making machines move is called **useful** energy. Energy is wasted in the process of supplying useful energy to where it is needed. For example, in Fig 5.2C, 70 J of energy is wasted in supplying 30 J of energy to the filament. Energy that is wasted cannot be stored or used to do a job because it spreads out to heat the surroundings. It is **dissipated** and can no longer be used for work. 'Dissipate' means 'squander' and is perhaps a better word than 'waste' to describe energy that spreads out and can't be used again.

Friction and air resistance in machines causes energy to be dissipated as heat. No machine can convert all the energy supplied to it into useful energy because friction is always present between its moving parts.

Energy dissipated due to friction

Electrical resistance of the wires of an electric circuit causes energy to be dissipated as heat in the wires. Using thick cables reduces the resistance of a circuit but doesn't eliminate it.

Energy dissipated due to resistance heating

Questions

3 Describe the energy changes that occur when a battery-operated cassette player is used to listen to music.

4 (a) A weightlifter raises a heavy weight through a height of 2.0 m above the floor, increasing the potential energy of the weight by 400 J. Why is the chemical energy used by the weightlifter to do this task more than 400 J?
(b) The weightlifter lowers the weights by 0.5 m then holds the weights at a height of 1.5 m above the floor. **(i)** How much potential energy has been lost by the weight through lowering it by 0.5 m? **(ii)** What form(s) of energy is produced as a result of this loss of potential energy?

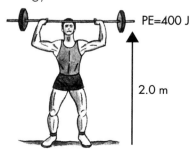

PE=400 J

2.0 m

3.3 Energy resources

Demand and supply

The total energy demand for the United Kingdom in one year is about 10 million million million joules. This works out at about 5000 joules per second for every person in the country. The pie charts show

★ how the total energy is obtained (i.e. our energy resources)
★ what it is used for.

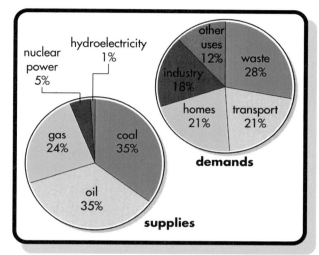

UK energy supplies and demand

Fuels

Fuels are substances which release energy as a result of reacting with oxygen and releasing energy. This is known as **combustion** and it changes the fuel into other substances. Fuels cannot be reused.

Fossil fuels

Fossil fuels include coal, oil, gas, wood and peat. The energy stored in fuel is chemical energy which was converted from the Sun's energy by living plants millions of years ago.

★ Coal is formed from the decayed remains of plants that lived millions of years ago. Layers of sand and clay formed over the decayed plants, creating pressure which eventually changed the dead plants into coal.
★ Oil and gas formed from the decayed remains of sea animals and other marine life that lived millions of years ago. On the bed of the oceans, these remains became covered with layers of silt and mud, creating pressure which eventually changed the dead animals into oil.

Nuclear fuel

Nuclear fuel is extracted from natural uranium which has existed on the Earth since the time the Earth was formed.

Fuel from biomass

Biomass fuel is material from living organisms such as wood from trees or methane gas from rotting plants or animal waste – or even rotting rubbish!

Energy at home

Mains electricity is produced in a power station by an electricity generator. The generator is forced to rotate by a turbine which is usually driven by steam at high pressure. The steam is raised by heating water, using either chemical energy from fossil fuels or nuclear energy from a nuclear reactor. In a hydroelectric power station, the turbines are driven by water running downhill off high ground.

Gas is a convenient fuel for heating and cooking. Our gas supplies are from pockets of natural gas trapped underground or under the sea bed. Oil and coal are also used for heating but they need to be stored unlike gas which is supplied through the gas main.

Petrol and diesel fuel are obtained from oil at oil refineries.

Batteries also supply electrical energy. They can provide emergency lighting and can be carried round. However, a battery needs recharging and cannot store enough energy to operate household appliances like washing machines.

In remote areas with no mains electricity or gas, bottled gas and wood are used for cooking, heating and lighting. Renewable energy resources listed below will become more and more important in remote areas as well as helping to meet the growing world-wide demand for energy.

Food for thought!

Muscle energy

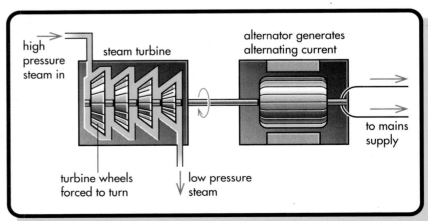

high pressure steam in

steam turbine

alternator generates alternating current

turbine wheels forced to turn

low pressure steam

to mains supply

Producing electricity

Food provides the energy needed by our muscles. Chemical energy from food is used to make a muscle contract and to keep it contracted. Holding a heavy book at arm's length is tiring because energy is needed to keep the arm muscles contracted. For every 100 J of chemical energy supplied to a muscle through food, only about 25 J is used for work and the rest is dissipated as heat in the muscle.

Renewable energy resources

These are energy resources which do not change the substances involved, allowing them to be reused.

The Sun as a source

The Sun is the ultimate source of energy for most of our energy resources. This means that most of our energy resources can be traced back to the Sun. The Sun radiates more than 400 million million million million joules of energy each second. The tiny fraction of this energy that falls on the Earth each day would provide enough energy for the entire population of the world for 20 years – if only it could all be used!

1 Plants converted solar energy into chemical energy of fossil fuels millions of years ago.
2 Wood and biomass converted solar energy into chemical energy
3 The Sun provides the energy for the following renewable energy resources – either directly, or by heating the Earth's atmosphere causing rain, wind and waves.

★ **Solar panels** for water heating
★ **Solar cells** to convert sunlight directly into electricity
★ **Hydroelectricity** is generated by channelling rainwater running off mountains through turbines. The potential energy of the rainwater is converted into electrical energy.
★ **Wind energy** generates electricity in windmills and aerogenerators, their modern equivalents. The kinetic energy of the wind is converted to electrical energy in an aerogenerator.
★ **Wave energy** can turn electrical generators on floating platforms. The waves rock the platform up and down, forcing the generators to turn. The kinetic and potential energy of the waves is converted into electricity.

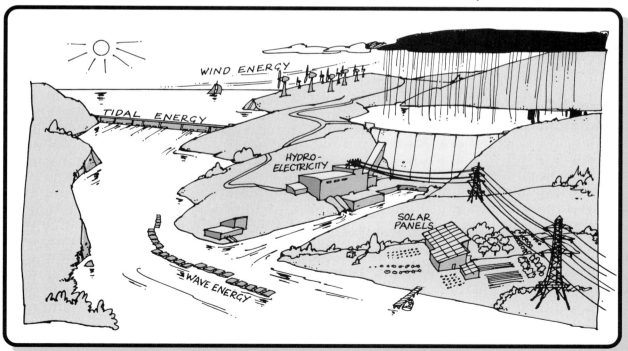

Renewable energy resources

Other sources of renewable energy

Renewable energy resources not driven by the Sun include

★ **Tidal energy**, which is harnessed by trapping each incoming tide behind a tidal barrage and later releasing it gradually through turbines to generate electricity. The tides are created as result of the gravitational pull of the Moon on the Earth. The potential energy of the high tide is converted to electrical energy.

★ **Geothermal energy**, which is the thermal energy of hot rocks deep underground. In certain parts of the Earth. the hot rocks are nearer the surface. Water can be pumped down to these rocks to return as steam which is used to drive turbines to generate electricity.

Clean energy

We all need energy but not at the expense of the environment. Fossil fuels create pollution when burned. Spent nuclear fuel must be stored for many years because it is harmful. Hydroelectricity and other renewable resources do not pollute the atmosphere and produce no harmful products. However, they cannot at present provide enough energy to meet all our needs. Greater use of renewable resources, like tidal energy, wind energy or solar panels, would help to meet our energy demands.

Questions

5 Which of the following **(a)** are renewable energy resources? **(b)** do not use the Sun's energy? **(c)** do not pollute the atmosphere or create harmful products?

coal, geothermal energy, hydroelectricity, tidal energy, oil, wind energy

5 (a) geothermal energy, hydroelectricity, tidal energy, wind energy. **(b)** Geothermal energy, tidal energy. **(c)** Geothermal energy, hydroelectricity, tidal energy, wind energy.

Answers

round-up

How much do you remember?

1 What form of energy is possessed by
   (a) a stretched rubber band,
   (b) a runaway train?   [2]
2 Describe the energy changes that take place when **(a)** a skier slides down a hillside, **(b)** a battery-operated hand drill is used to drill a hole in a brick wall.   [6]
3 The figure shows a girl standing on a box about to lower a plate from a high shelf onto a table. **(a)** What form of energy did she use to climb onto the box? **(b)** What form of energy does the plate possess? **(c)** Describe the energy changes of the plate as it is lowered safely from the shelf onto the table. **(d)** Why does the girl need to use energy to lower the plate onto the table?   [5]

4 Complete the passage below using the words in the following list.
   chemical   electrical   light   thermal   kinetic   potential
In a fuel-burning power station, _____ energy from the fuel changes into _____ energy, which is used to raise steam. The steam is then used to drive a turbine, which drives a generator that produces _____ energy from the _____ energy of the steam.   [4]

round-up

5 A ball gained 2.0 J of potential energy when it was raised 2.0 m from a flat surface and held above the surface. It was then released and rebounded to a maximum height of 1.5 m.
   (a) Assuming there is no air resistance on the ball, how much kinetic energy did it have just before it hit the ground?
   (b) How much potential energy did it have at a height of 1.5 m after rebounding?
   (c) (i) How much of its original potential energy did it lose as a result of hitting the floor? (ii) What form of energy was produced as a result of the impact? [4]

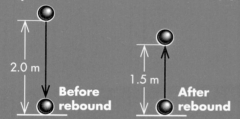

Before rebound | **After rebound**
2.0 m | 1.5 m

6 Biomass and wood are not fossil fuels.
   (a) Why are they not called fossil fuels?
   (b) Why are they called fuels, not renewable resources? [2]

7 The figure shows a variety of energy resources. Identify each energy resource and state whether or not it is a renewable resource. [10]

8 (a) Which energy resources in the figure can be traced back to the Sun as the ultimate source of energy? (b) For each energy resource not derived from the Sun, state where the energy comes from. [2]

9 (a) Describe the energy changes that occur when an electric torch is switched on.
   (b) Why is mains electricity used instead of batteries for lighting at home? [5]

10 Copy and complete the following passage, using the words from the list (each word may be used once, more than once or not at all).

   burned   conserved   dissipated   recovered   released   stored   used

   Energy is always _____ when it changes from one form into other forms. However, whenever energy is_____ to force an object to move, some energy is always _____ and can never be _____. Except for uranium, fuel contains energy _____ as chemical energy. This energy is _____ when the fuel is _____. Burnt fuel can not be _____ again. [8]

> How did you get on? Don't worry if you couldn't answer everything. Take a break and try again

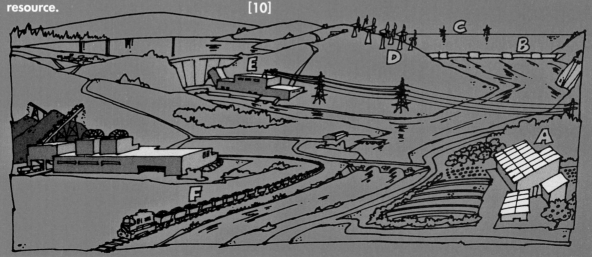

The Earth and beyond

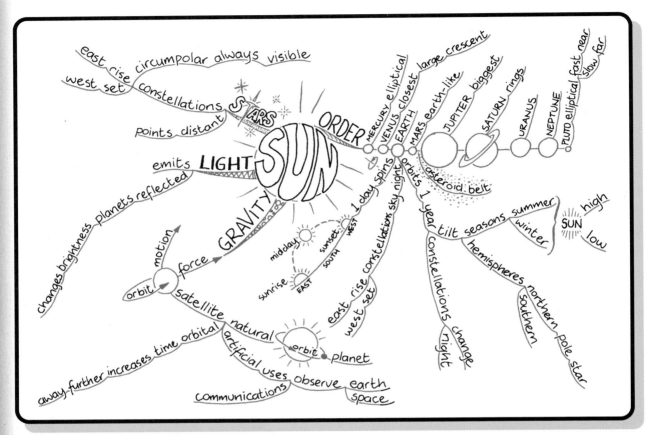

What do you already know? Look at the Mind Map to help you out.

preview

At the end of this topic you will be able to:

- **explain how and why the Sun moves across the sky during the day and why the stars move across the sky at night**
- **explain why the Sun at midday is higher in summer than in winter and why the stars in the night sky change during the year**
- **explain the difference between stars and planets and state the relative positions of the planets in the solar system**
- ★**understand that the force of gravity between the Sun and each planet makes the planet orbit the Sun**
- **describe some uses of artificial satellites**

Test yourself

1 **(a)** In which direction (north, south, east or west) is the Sun at **(i)** midday? **(ii)** sunrise in March? **(b)** In which month is the Sun at midday in the northern hemisphere lowest in the sky?   [3]
2 Complete the passage below by using words from the list.

**summer winter southern northern
rise set some all**

The Earth spins on its axis once every 24 hours. Its axis is tilted in a fixed direction in space. In December, the _____ hemisphere is tilted towards the Sun so it is _____ in Britain. Circumpolar constellations are groups of stars near the Pole Star that never _____.

An observer at the North Pole can see
_____ of the constellations in the
_____ hemisphere on any clear night. [5]

3 (a) In the figure below, the Earth is at position E. **(i)** Mark the position where Venus is furthest from Earth. **(ii)** Explain why Venus cannot be seen at this position from the Earth.
(b) (i) Mark the position where Mars is nearest to Earth. **(ii)** Why is Mars easy to see when it is at this position? [4]

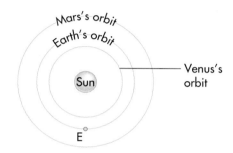

4 (a) Which of the three planets in the figure orbits the Sun in **(i)** the shortest time **(ii)** the greatest time? **(b) (i)** Mark on the figure the approximate orbit of Mercury. **(ii)** Why is Mercury much more difficult to see than Mars or Venus? [4]

5 A minor planet orbits the Sun mid-way between Mars and Jupiter. It experiences forces of attraction due to Mars, Jupiter and the Sun. **(a)** Which of these three forces of attraction is strongest? Give a reason for your answer. **(b)** Which of these three forces is weakest? Give a reason for your answer. [4]

Did you know?

The Earth is one of nine planets in orbit round a star we call the Sun. It takes about 8 minutes for light to reach Earth from the Sun. It takes over 4 years for light to reach Earth from the next nearest star, Proxima Centauri.

Answers

1 a) The Sun is then due south and is at its highest position in the sky. b) The height of the Sun increased from sunrise to midday then decreased after midday. The higher the Sun, the shorter the shadow.

4.1 The Sun in the sky

From sunrise to sunset

★ The Sun always rises in the east and sets in the west. At midday, the Sun is always due south.
★ The Sun moves across the sky because the Earth is spinning about an axis through its poles.
★ The Sun at midday in summer is higher than in winter. There are more daylight hours in summer than in winter because the Sun rises earlier and sets later in summer than in winter.
★ The Sun is in the sky for longer in summer than in winter because in summer in the northern hemisphere the north pole is tilted towards the Sun. In the northern winter, the north pole is tilted away from the Sun.

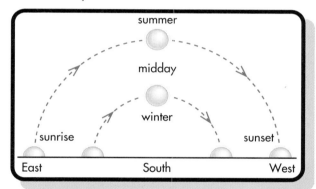

Sunrise and sunset

Question

1 The figure shows a shadow stick on a sunny day. **(a)** Why is the shadow shortest when it points due north? **(b)** Why did the shadow become shorter then longer between sunrise and sunset?

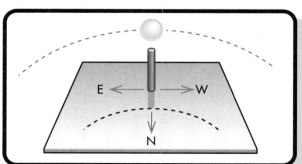

4

One day in your life

★ One full day is the time it takes for the Earth to spin one full turn.
★ At night, our part of the Earth faces away from the Sun.

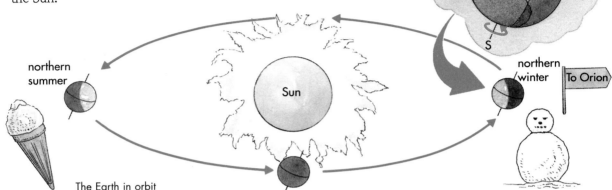

The Earth in orbit

★ Sunrise happens when our part of the Earth moves into daylight.
★ Sunset happens when our part of the Earth moves out of the daylight.
★ From sunrise to sunset, the place we live in moves through the daylight half of the Earth. This causes the movement of the Sun across the sky.

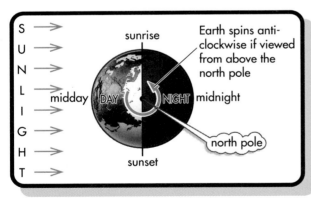

Night and day

One year in your life

★ The Earth moves round the Sun on an orbit which is almost circular.
★ The Earth takes $365\frac{1}{4}$ days to orbit the Sun once.
★ The Earth's axis is tilted and always points towards the Pole star in the northern sky.
★ The north pole is tilted away from the Sun in the northern winter and towards the Sun in the northern summer.

The midnight Sun

People who live in the Arctic Circle can see the Sun at midnight in midsummer, because the north pole is tilted towards the Sun at midsummer. The Arctic Circle is on the daylight side of the Earth then. In midwinter the Sun never rises in the Arctic Circle.

Question

2 The figure shows the path of the Sun across the sky as seen from Britain during a clear day in March. **(a)** Mark the position of the Sun at sunrise, midday and sunset. **(b)** Mark the path the Sun would take on a clear day in January.

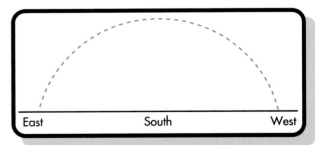

East   South   West

4.2 The sky at night

Constellations

* The Sun is a star. It is so close to us that when we see it we can't see any other stars because sunlight fills the sky. At night, we are on the dark side of the Earth – hidden from the Sun – and we can see many stars on a clear night.
* All the stars and the Sun emit light. The stars in the night sky are so far away from us that they all appear as pinpoints of light.
* The stars do not change their positions relative to each other. They are so far away that they appear stationary relative to each other.
* The stars were mapped out in groups, called **constellations**, thousands of years ago. The constellations are exactly the same today.

Watching the stars

The stars move across the sky during the night because the Earth is spinning.

Because the Earth turns through 360° in 24 hours, the stars move across the sky at a rate of 15° every hour. Therefore each constellation turns through 15° per hour as it moves across the sky.

Some stars rise and set. Stars that rise always rise in the east. They reach their maximum height when due south then set in the west later.

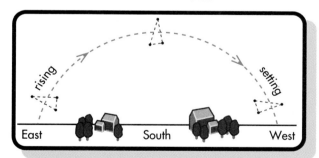

Rising and setting of stars

Some stars never set. The Pole Star (or Polaris) is *always* directly above the Earth's north pole because the Earth's axis always points in the same direction in space. Stars near the Pole Star can be seen from Britain on any clear night because they never set. These stars are called **circumpolar** because they go round the Pole Star without setting.

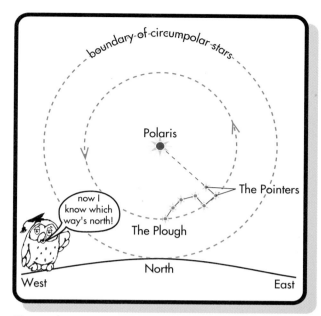

Circumpolar stars

* How to find due north on a clear night
  The Plough is a prominent pattern of stars in the circumpolar constellation Ursa Major, the Great Bear. The two stars at the front of the Plough are called the 'pointers' because they lie along a line that passes through the Pole Star. The Plough is known as the Big Dipper in North America.

A year with the stars

The constellations that rise and set in the night sky change during the year. This is because the night sky is in the opposite direction to the Sun and the Earth moves round the Sun each year.

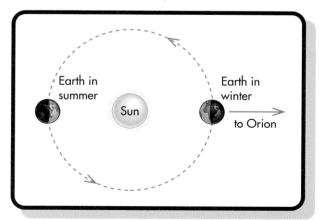

The changing night sky

The planets

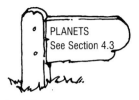

PLANETS
See Section 4.3

There are nine planets, including the Earth, in orbit round the Sun. We can see them because they reflect sunlight. They appear to the unaided eye as pinpoints like stars. Seen from Earth, each of the other planets changes its position against the constellations as it moves round the Sun. The planets orbit the Sun in the same direction at different distances. Planets are sometimes called 'wandering stars' because they move through the constellations – in fact 'planet' means wanderer!

You and your star sign

As the Earth orbits the Sun, the constellation in the direction of the Sun changes. If we could see the stars in daylight, we would see that the Sun moves round a band of constellations each year. We cannot see where the Sun appears against the stars because the Sun is so bright. However, just before sunrise, we can see part of the constellation the Sun is in because the sky is still dark. Your star sign is the constellation the Sun was in on the day you were born. Although astrologers attach great importance to star signs, there is no scientific evidence that the distant stars affect people physically.

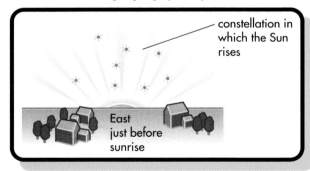

constellation in which the Sun rises

East just before sunrise

Star signs

Questions

3 (a) Why does the Pole Star always lie due north? **(b)** Look at the figure on page 75 and sketch the position of the Plough **(i)** 6 hours later, **(ii)** 12 hours later. **(c)** Would the Pole Star seen from the Earth's equator appear higher or lower in the sky?

4 Betelgeuse is a bright star in the constellation of Orion. The figure shows the constellation as seen from Britain in mid-December. **(a)** Mark the approximate position on the horizon where the constellation rose. **(b)** On the diagram, show where the constellation will appear 2 hours later. **(c)** Why is it not possible to see Orion from Britain in summer?

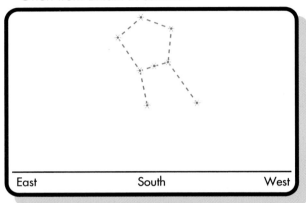

East   South   West

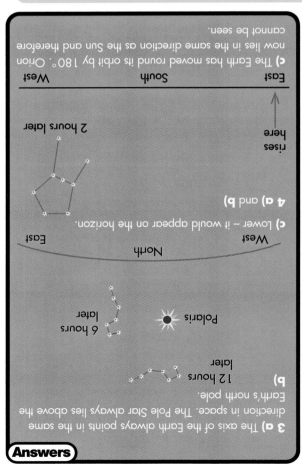

Answers

3 a) The axis of the Earth always points in the same direction in space. The Pole Star always lies above the Earth's north pole.

b)
6 hours later
12 hours later

Polaris

North

West   East

c) Lower – it would appear on the horizon.

4 a) and b)

rises here

2 hours later

East   South   West

c) The Earth has moved round its orbit by 180°. Orion now lies in the same direction as the Sun and therefore cannot be seen.

4.3 The Solar System

Fact file

★ There are nine planets in orbit round the Sun. They are, in order of distance from the Sun, Mercury, Venus, Earth, Mars, Jupiter, Saturn, Uranus, Neptune and Pluto.

★ The planets all move round the Sun in the same direction. The path of a planet round the Sun is called its **orbit**.

★ Their orbits are almost circular, except for Pluto, and are in the same plane as the Earth's orbit.

★ The planets reflect sunlight, which is why we see them.

★ The further a planet is from the Sun, the longer it takes to go round its orbit.

★ When we observe the planets from the Earth, they move through the constellations as they go round the Sun.

★ The asteroid belt consists of rocks and some minor planets in orbit round the Sun between Mars and Jupiter.

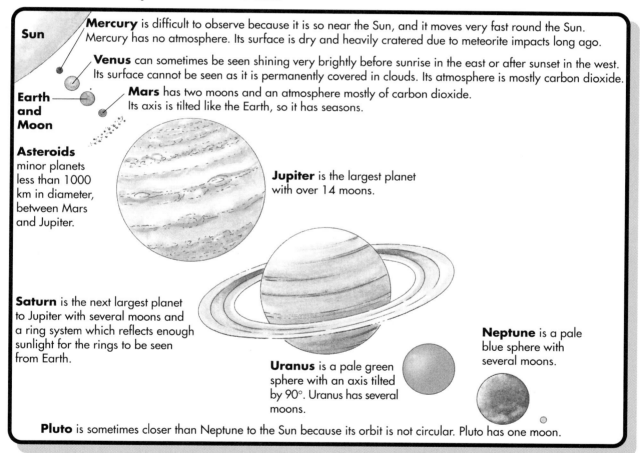

Sun

Mercury is difficult to observe because it is so near the Sun, and it moves very fast round the Sun. Mercury has no atmosphere. Its surface is dry and heavily cratered due to meteorite impacts long ago.

Venus can sometimes be seen shining very brightly before sunrise in the east or after sunset in the west. Its surface cannot be seen as it is permanently covered in clouds. Its atmosphere is mostly carbon dioxide.

Earth and Moon

Mars has two moons and an atmosphere mostly of carbon dioxide. Its axis is tilted like the Earth, so it has seasons.

Asteroids minor planets less than 1000 km in diameter, between Mars and Jupiter.

Jupiter is the largest planet with over 14 moons.

Saturn is the next largest planet to Jupiter with several moons and a ring system which reflects enough sunlight for the rings to be seen from Earth.

Neptune is a pale blue sphere with several moons.

Uranus is a pale green sphere with an axis tilted by 90°. Uranus has several moons.

Pluto is sometimes closer than Neptune to the Sun because its orbit is not circular. Pluto has one moon.

The planets

	Mercury	Venus	Earth	Mars	Jupiter	Saturn	Uranus	Neptune	Pluto
Distance from the Sun in astronomical units	0.40	0.70	1.00	1.50	5.20	9.60	19.20	30.10	39.50
Time to orbit the Sun in years	0.24	0.62	1.00	1.90	11.90	29.50	84.00	165.00	249.00

Distances from the Sun
1 astronomical unit (AU) is the mean distance from the Earth to the Sun.

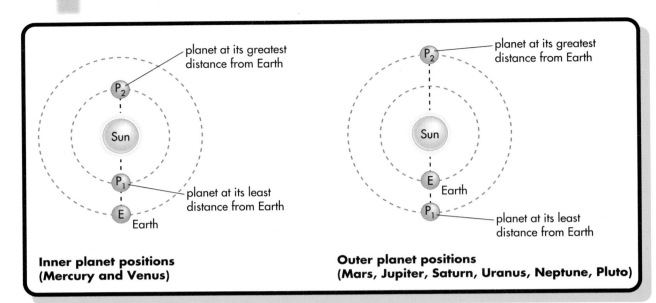

planet at its greatest distance from Earth

P₂

Sun

planet at its least distance from Earth

P₁

E Earth

Inner planet positions (Mercury and Venus)

planet at its greatest distance from Earth

P₂

Sun

E Earth

P₁

planet at its least distance from Earth

Outer planet positions (Mars, Jupiter, Saturn, Uranus, Neptune, Pluto)

Distances to the planets

Distances to the other planets from Earth

The distances of the planets from the Sun are shown in the table on page 77.

1 The shortest distance from Earth to another planet is when it is on the same side of the Sun as the Earth.

2 The longest distance to a planet is when it is on the opposite side of the Sun to the Earth.

3 A planet appears largest when it is closest to the Earth and smallest when it is furthest from the Earth. This apparent change of size is most noticeable for Venus.

Handy hint

Here's how to remember the order of the planets from the Sun:

Hints & Tips

Make **V**ery **E**asy **M**ash; **J**ust **S**tart **U**sing **N**ew **P**otatoes!

Brightness comparisons

The brightness of a planet depends on various factors including its distance from the Sun, its distance from the Earth, its diameter and how good its surface is as a reflector. In addition, Saturn's rings reflect sunlight with varying effect according to their direction relative to Earth.

★ The two inner planets, Mercury and Venus, show phases like the Moon. This is most noticeable for Venus. Mercury is difficult to see because it is near the Sun. Venus is covered in cloud and therefore reflects sunlight very effectively. At its brightest, Venus is brighter than the brightest star.

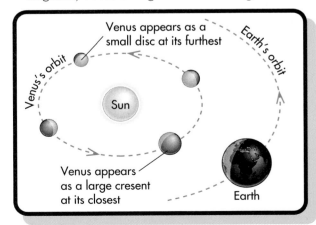

Venus appears as a small disc at its furthest

Earth's orbit

Venus's orbit

Sun

Venus appears as a large crescent at its closest

Earth

The changing appearance of Venus

★ Mars and Jupiter are brightest when they are in the opposite direction to the Sun. We can then see all the sunlit face of Mars or Jupiter from Earth and it is at its closest to us. The four innermost moons of Jupiter can be seen with a small telescope or binoculars.

★ Saturn is at its brightest when its rings are as shown in the figure and it lies in the opposite direction to the Sun. Since it takes about 29 years to orbit the Sun, Saturn is at its maximum brightness every $14\frac{1}{2}$ years.

★ Uranus, Neptune and Pluto can only be seen using a large telescope. Pluto's orbit is elliptical (egg-shaped) and is closer to the Sun at times than Neptune.

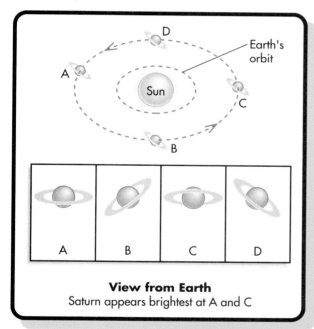

View from Earth
Saturn appears brightest at A and C

Saturn's rings

Questions

5 (a) Using the data in the table, calculate the least distance in astronomical units from Earth to **(i)** Mars, **(ii)** Venus, **(iii)** Jupiter. **(b)** In the time it takes Jupiter to go once round the Sun, how many times does **(i)** Earth, **(ii)** Mars go round the Sun?

6 The figure shows the orbits of Venus, Earth and Jupiter. **(a)** Mark on this diagram **(i)** position X, where Jupiter is at its brightest as seen from the Earth at E, **(ii)** position Y, where Venus is at its brightest, **(iii)** position Z, where Venus is seen from Earth as a large crescent and **(iv)** the orbit of Mars. **(b)** Explain why the brightness of Saturn as seen from Earth changes as it moves round the Sun.

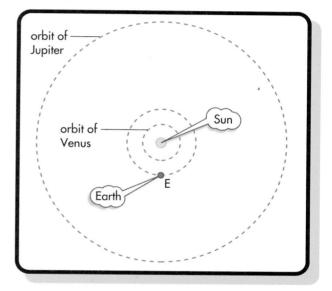

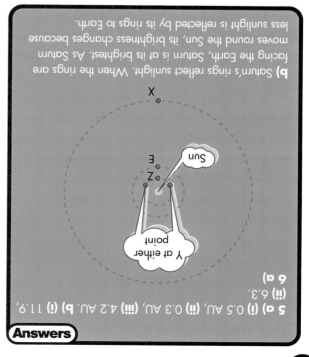

Answers

6 (b) Saturn's rings reflect sunlight. When the rings are facing the Earth, Saturn is at its brightest. As Saturn moves round the Sun, its brightness changes because less sunlight is reflected by its rings to Earth.

6 (a)

(ii) 6.3.

5 a) (i) 0.5 AU, **(ii)** 0.3 AU, **(iii)** 4.2 AU, **b) (i)** 11.9,

4.4 In orbit

Round in circles

What will happen to an object that is being whirled round on the end of a string if the string breaks? The object will fly off at a tangent because there is no longer any force to keep it moving round in a circle. Any object going round in a circle needs a force to keep it on a circular path. A planet moving round the Sun stays on a circular path because of the force of gravity between the planet and the Sun.

The force of gravity

Throw an object directly up into the air and it will return to you. The force of gravity between the object and the Earth stops the object from rising and pulls it back again. This force exists between any two objects due to their mass.

The force of gravity between any two objects:
1 is always attractive
2 increases with increased mass of either object
3 decreases with increased distance apart

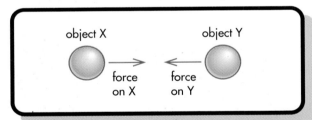

The force of gravity

Planets and their orbits

Apart from Mercury and Pluto, the other planets go round the Sun on orbits which are almost circular.

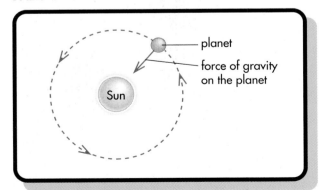

A planet in a circular orbit

The force of gravity between each planet and the Sun keeps the planet moving round the Sun. It is much greater than the force of gravity between any two planets because the Sun is much more massive than any other planet.

The greater the radius of orbit of a planet, the longer it takes to go round the Sun. The further a planet is from the Sun, the weaker the force of gravity is between the planet and the Sun. It takes longer to orbit the Sun than a planet nearer the Sun. This is because
1 it moves more slowly on its orbit, and
2 it has a greater distance to cover.

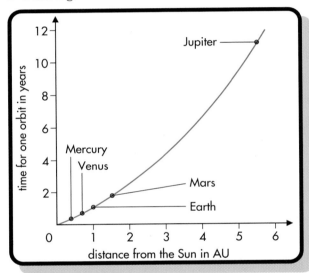

Orbital time versus distance

Mercury and Pluto go round the Sun on elliptical (egg-shaped) orbits. The speed of a planet on an elliptical orbit increases the nearer it is to the Sun.

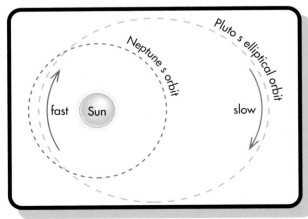

An elliptical orbit

Question

7 A minor planet orbits the Sun at a distance of 2.2 AU. **(a)** Use the figure on circular orbits to estimate how long a minor planet at this distance takes to orbit the Sun. **(b)** Calculate the least distance between this minor planet and Mars.

Satellites

★ The planets are **satellites** of the Sun because they go round the Sun.

★ The Moon is a satellite of the Earth because it goes round the Earth. It is kept on its orbit by the force of gravity between it and the Earth.

★ Artificial satellites orbit the Earth above the atmosphere. The higher a satellite is above the Earth, the longer its orbit takes.

★ Communication satellites are in orbits directly over the equator. A communications satellite takes exactly 24 hours to orbit the Earth so it always appears to be above the same point on the equator.

★ Satellites are used to observe the Earth. For example, weather satellites are in circular orbits that pass over each pole every 2 hours, sending back images of weather systems. Military satellites are vital sources of information about the movements of hostile troops and weapons.

★ The Hubble Space Telescope is a satellite used to observe objects in space. Being above the atmosphere, it is unaffected by the atmosphere and can view deep-space objects far better than telescopes on the ground.

★ Space vehicles have been put into orbit round the Moon and round Mercury, Venus and Mars.

Question

8 Why is it essential for a military satellite to be in an orbit that is not too high and not too low?

Answers

7 a) 3.3 years. **b)** 0.7 AU.
8 If it is too high, the cameras will be too far away to take detailed pictures. If it is too low, it will be slowed down by the atmosphere and dragged to the ground.

round-up

How much can you remember? Check out your score on page 00.

1 In which direction are **(a)** the Sun at sunset? **(b)** the Pole Star? [2]

2 (a) Which months of the year have 12 daylight hours per day? **(b)** At midday in June on the Equator, is the Sun **(i)** directly overhead, **(ii)** towards the north **(iii)** towards the south or **(iv)** directly overhead in Britain? [3]

3 Orion is visible from Britain at night in winter but not in summer. **(a)** Which direction should you look to find Orion at night in winter? **(b)** Why is it not possible to see Orion in summer? [3]

4 The figure shows a constellation due south at midnight in the night sky. **(a)** State whether the same constellation two hours later will be **(i)** east or west of due south, **(ii)** higher or lower than when it was due south. **(b)** Explain why the constellations move across the sky. [4]

East   South   West

5 (a) Why does the Pole Star always lie due north? **(b)** Circumpolar stars never set. The figure shows the path over 24 hours of a circumpolar star that just touches the horizon when observed from Britain. Its position at 10.00 p.m. one evening is marked as X. **(i)** Mark its position 6 hours later with the letter Y. **(ii)** Would this star be visible further south? Explain your answer. [4]

Polaris   X

West   North   East

round-up

6 The figure shows the orbits of Jupiter, Mars and the Earth. **(a)** When Mars is at position M on its path, **(i)** mark with the letter J the position of Jupiter where it would appear brightest as seen from Mars and **(ii)** with the letter E the position of the Earth where it would appear at its brightest as seen from Mars. **(b)** Calculate the least distance between Mars and **(i)** Jupiter, **(ii)** the Earth.[4]

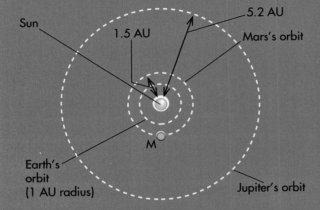

7 (a) Which of the three planets in the figure takes longest to go round the Sun? **(b)** Mark the orbit of Venus on the figure. **(c)** Mark the position of Venus on its orbit with the letter V when it would appear as seen from Mars at M as a crescent. [3]

8 and 9

Two photographs of the night sky, looking south from the same location one month apart

8 (a) Identify the planet on photograph 1 with the letter P. **(b)** Explain why the planet could not be Mercury or Venus. [3]

9 (a) Photograph 1 was taken at midnight. The star marked X was exactly due south when the photograph was taken. The figure shows the positions of the Earth and the Sun when photograph 1 was taken. Mark with an arrow labelled 'to X' the direction to star X. **(b)** Photograph 2 was taken 1 month later, when star X was exactly due south again. Mark on the diagram below the approximate position of the Earth when photograph 2 was taken. [2]

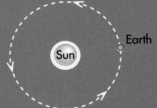

10 Pluto's orbit is elliptical, as shown in the figure. **(a)** When Pluto is at position P on its orbit, mark the direction of **(i)** the force of gravity on Pluto due to the Sun, **(ii)** the direction of motion of Pluto. **(b) (i)** Mark the point X on the orbit where Pluto is moving fastest and the point Y where it is moving slowest. **(ii)** Explain why it slows down when it moves from X to Y. [5]

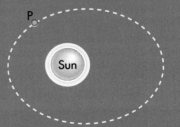

How did you get on? Don't worry if you found some of these questions too difficult. Take a short break and try again.

Light and sound

How much do you already know?
The Mind Map will be able to help you.

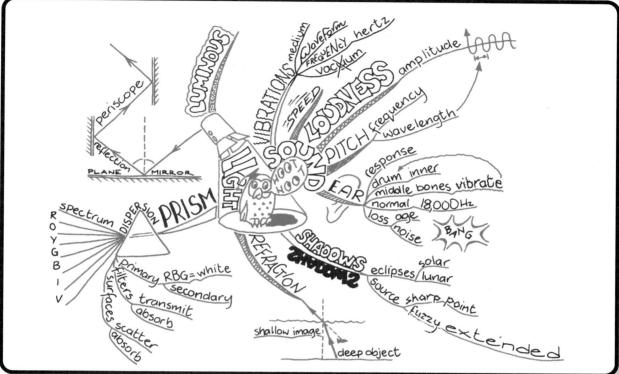

preview

At the end of this topic, you should:

- **know how non-luminous objects are seen and how shadows are formed**
- **know how light is reflected and refracted**
- **know how white light is split into colours and know the effect of colour filters on white light**
- ★ **be able to explain the appearance of coloured objects in white light and in other colours of light**
- **know that light is much faster than sound and that sound can't travel through a vacuum**
- ★ **know how the loudness and pitch of a sound depend on the amplitude and frequency of the vibrations causing it**
- **be able to explain the effect of sound on the ear, including the effect of loudness and pitch.**

Test yourself

1 The figure shows three sound waveforms.
(a) Which sound is quietest? **(b)** Which sound has the highest pitch? [2]

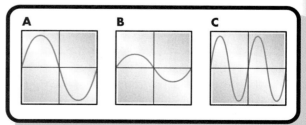

2 (a) Which frequency is the upper frequency limit of the human ear? **(i)** 50 Hz **(ii)** 3000 Hz **(iii)** 18 000 Hz **(iv)** 50 000 Hz [1]
(b) What happens to the bones of the middle ear to cause hearing loss in an old person? [3]

3 (a) In the figure below, which points on the screen are in the shadow of the plate? [2]

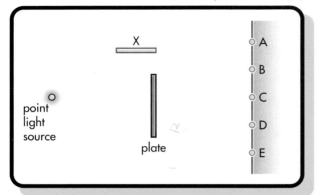

(b) In the figure, a plane mirror is placed at X. Which points on the screen are still in darkness? [2]

4 A beam of white light directed into a prism is split into the colours of the spectrum by the prism. **(a)** What is the name for this process? **(b)** Which colour changes direction most? [2]

5.1 Sound

Fact file

★ When a solid surface in contact with another substance vibrates, sound waves spread out from the surface throughout the substance.

★ Sound travels through solids, liquids and gases but not through a vacuum.

★ Sound waves make the particles of a substance vibrate to and fro, parallel to the direction in which the sound travels.

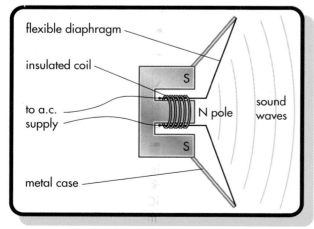

The loudspeaker

★ A loudspeaker (usually just called a 'speaker') creates sound when alternating current passes through it. The alternating current makes a coil move to and fro repeatedly in the magnetic field. The movement of the coil makes the diaphragm vibrate, sending vibrations through the surrounding air.

Sound cannot pass through a vacuum

This can be shown by listening to a ringing bell in a bell jar as the air is evacuated from the bell jar. The ringing sound is no longer heard after a while even though you can clearly see that the bell is operating. The sound of the bell cannot pass through the vacuum in the bell jar.

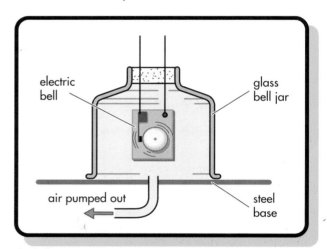

The bell jar experiment

Modelling sound waves

Figure (a) shows waves travelling along a slinky spring as a result of pushing and pulling one end of the slinky. The waves on the slinky are like sound waves in air. Each coil of the slinky vibrates about a certain position.

Figure (b) shows how the position of a coil changes with time. This type of graph is called a **waveform**. A particle of air moves in this way when sound passes through the air. Each particle moves from one side to the other side and back again in one complete cycle of vibration.

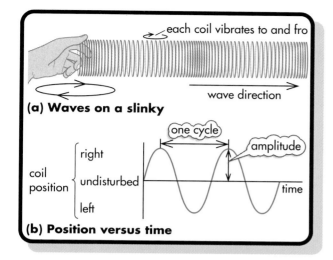

(a) Waves on a slinky

each coil vibrates to and fro

wave direction

one cycle
amplitude
coil position { right / undisturbed / left }
time

(b) Position versus time

★ The **amplitude** of a wave is the maximum distance of a particle from the centre of vibration.

★ The **frequency** of vibration is the number of complete cycles of vibration a particle makes each second. The unit of frequency is the hertz (Hz), equal to 1 cycle per second.

Displaying sound waves

A microphone connected to an **oscilloscope** can be used to display sound waveforms. The microphone generates an alternating current when sound waves fall on it. The alternating current traces out the sound waveform on the oscilloscope screen.

Controlled sounds can be created from a loudspeaker connected to a signal generator (a source of alternating current). The amplitude and frequency of the sound can be changed by adjusting the signal generator.

Increasing the amplitude of the waveform makes the sound louder. The peaks of the trace becomes higher when the sound is made louder.

Increasing the frequency makes the pitch of the sound higher. The peaks of the trace become closer together when the pitch is raised. This is because there are more cycles each second.

Making music

Musical instruments

Musical notes are easy to listen to because they are rhythmic. This means the waveform of a musical note shows smooth changes. Each type of instrument produces a waveform with its own identity. Noise is unpleasant to listen to because the waveform shows jagged changes.

★ In a string instrument the string is made to vibrate, either using a bow as in a violin or plucking it as in a guitar. The vibrations make the surface of the instrument vibrate which makes the surrounding air vibrate.

★ In a percussion instrument such as a drum, a surface vibrates when it is struck. The vibrating surface makes the surrounding air vibrate.

★ In a wind instrument, the mouthpiece is used to make the air in the tubes of the instrument vibrate.

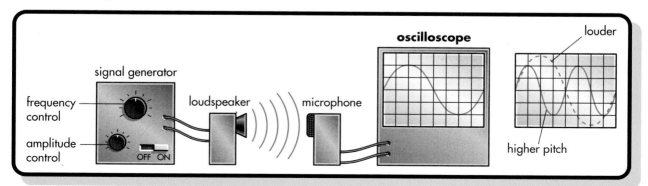

Using an oscilloscope to display sound waves

Questions

1 (a) Explain how sound waves are produced when a guitar string is plucked. **(b)** Complete the paragraph below, using each of the words in bold after the paragraph.

When sound passes through a medium, the particles of the medium _____. The louder the sound, the larger the _____ of vibration of the particles. The higher the _____ of a sound, the greater the frequency of vibration of the particles. The unit of frequency is the

_____.

amplitude   hertz   pitch   vibrate

2 The figure shows waveforms of sound produced by two different tuning forks, X and Y.
(a) Which tuning fork produces the higher pitched note? **(b)** Use the figure to sketch the waveform X would have produced if it had produced a quieter note. **(c)** If Y was replaced by a different tuning fork Z, what two tests could you carry out to find out if Z produces a higher pitch or a lower pitch than Y?

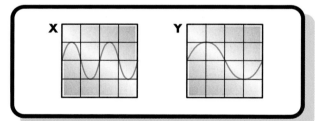

5.2 Hearing

The ear

Your ears are incredibly sensitive and robust detectors of sound. The loudest sound that the ear can cope with is a million million times more powerful than the faintest sound it can detect.

The frequency response of the human ear

★ The normal human ear can detect sound frequencies from about 20 Hz to about 18 000 Hz.
★ The human ear is most sensitive at about 3000 Hz
★ Sound above about 18 000 Hz is called **ultrasound** and cannot be heard by the human ear.
★ Other animals hear in different frequency ranges. For example, bats communicate through ultrasound and dolphins are thought to communicate at very low frequencies.

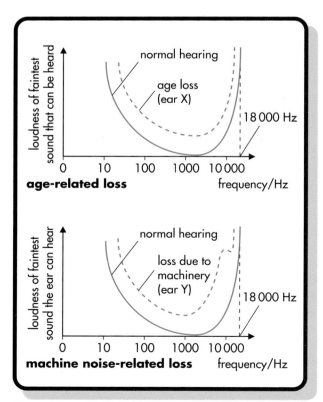

The ear's frequency response

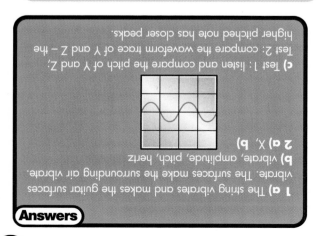

Answers

1 a) The string vibrates and makes the guitar surfaces vibrate. The surfaces make the surrounding air vibrate.
b) vibrate, amplitude, pitch, hertz
2 a) X, **b)**

c) Test 1: listen and compare the pitch of Y and Z;
Test 2: compare the waveform trace of Y and Z – the higher pitched note has closer peaks.

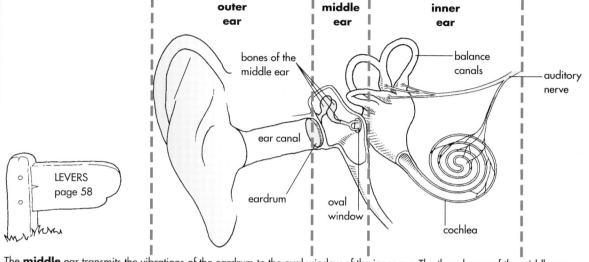

The **outer ear**, the **pinna**, funnels sound waves down the ear canal. The sound waves make the ear drum vibrate.

The **inner ear** channels the vibrations down the cochlea where they stimulate the auditory nerves. The signals from the auditory nerves are interpreted by the brain.

outer ear | middle ear | inner ear

bones of the middle ear

balance canals

auditory nerve

ear canal

LEVERS page 58

eardrum

oval window

cochlea

The **middle** ear transmits the vibrations of the eardrum to the oval window of the inner ear. The three bones of the middle ear, the ossicles, are known as the hammer, the anvil and the stirrup because of their shapes. These three bones act as a lever system to increase the force of the vibrations. Because the oval window is smaller than the eardrum, the increased force acts on a smaller area. The pressure (= force/area) of the vibrations on the oval window is therefore much greater than on the eardrum.

The human ear

Look after your hearing

Hearing loss or partial deafness is due to two main causes.

1 Age causes hearing loss at all frequencies but is most noticeable at higher frequencies. The upper frequency limit becomes lower due to age. Age-related loss of hearing is due to the bones of the middle ear gradually becoming worn away where they rub against each other.

2 Excessive noise causes hearing loss at all frequencies, if the noise covers all frequencies. If the ear is repeatedly subjected to loud noises at a certain frequency, hearing loss occurs at this frequency. For example, a machine operator not wearing ear protectors would eventually suffer hearing loss at the machine's frequency. Think how your hearing can be affected by the loud music in a disco!

Questions

3 Listen to your recorded voice. You will find it sounds different to your normal voice.
(a) Does your recorded voice sound deeper or higher than normal? **(b)** A recording of a certain voice sounds deeper than normal. Which part of the frequency range of the voice has been lost in the recording?

4 **(a)** Explain why hearing loss is caused if the ear drum is punctured. **(b)** Look at the graphs on page 86, and estimate **(i)** the frequency at which ear X is most sensitive, **(ii)** the frequency range over which ear Y is suffering hearing loss.

Answers

3 a) Higher. b) The lower part. 4 a) The eardrum is unable to vibrate properly when sound falls on it. b) (i) about 3000 Hz. (ii) about 5000–8000 Hz

5

5.3 Shadows

Light sources

★ The Sun, the stars, light bulbs, fluorescent tubes, flames and lasers are all light sources. They are **luminous**, which means they are sources of light.
★ A **point source** is a luminous object that emits its light from a point. A source will appear as a point source if it is observed from far enough away.

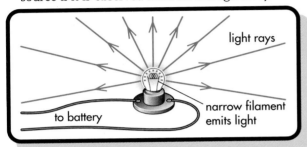

Light rays from a point source

★ An **extended source** is a luminous object which is not a point source. For example, the Sun is an extended source as it appears as a bright disc not a point. However, the stars are point sources because they are much further away than the Sun.
★ Light travels in straight lines from a light source. This is usually shown by means of light rays, as in the figure. An **opaque** object (one that you can't see through) in the path of a light ray stops the light ray, either reflecting it or absorbing it.

The speed of light

Light travels through space at a speed of 300 000 000 m/s. Sound in air travels about a million times slower, at a speed of about 340 m/s. You can notice the difference when a distant thunderstorm occurs. A stroke of lightning creates a flash of light that you see almost instantly. This is followed by a clap of thunder after a few seconds.

Making shadows

Interesting shadows can be made by placing your hand between a white screen and a light bulb in a dark room. Your hand stops the light reaching the screen. The shadow on the screen is the area that light from the source cannot reach. It has the same shape as your hand because light travels in straight lines. Light rays that miss your hand form a bright patch.

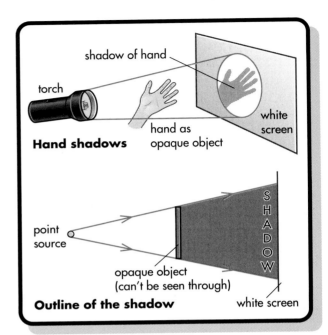

Making a sharp shadow

★ Strong sunlight also casts shadows behind opaque objects because strong sunlight is much brighter than normal daylight. This effect is used in the shadow stick and the sundial (see page 73).
★ A point source of light and a white screen in a dark room give the best shadows. The edge of such a shadow is very sharp and the shadow itself is much darker than the bright areas of the screen.
★ An extended source gives a fuzzy shadow. For example, a fluorescent tube casts a poor shadow of an object because each point on the tube casts an outline of the object in a different position. The shadow boundary is not clear.

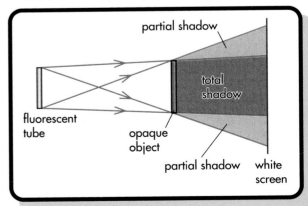

Poor shadows

Eclipses

A **lunar eclipse** takes place when the shadow of the Earth moves across the face of the Moon. On a clear night, the eclipse can be seen by anyone on the night side of the Earth.

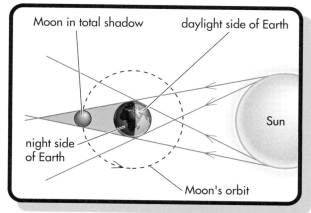

A lunar eclipse

A **solar eclipse** takes place when the Moon passes in front of the Sun. The Moon's shadow sweeps across the Earth. The region of total shadow is called the **umbra**. Note that a total eclipse is seen only by people in the umbra.

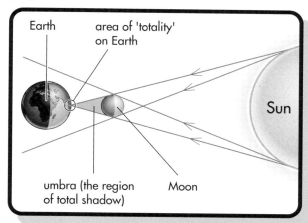

A solar eclipse

Questions

5 A stone is thrown into the middle of a pond. An observer on the bank sees and hears the stone hit the water and watches the waves spread out on the water surface. **(a)** Which travels fastest, light or sound or water waves? **(b)** Which travels slowest?

6 A cardboard figure can be used to cast a shadow on a white screen in a darkened room, as shown below.

(a) Draw some light rays to show where the shadow of the object is formed on the screen. **(b)** Why is it necessary to use a light source that is bright and as small as possible?

7 The shadow of a stick was marked at intervals throughout a sunny day. **(a)** Why did the direction of the shadow change during the day? **(b)** Why did the shadow shorten then become longer?

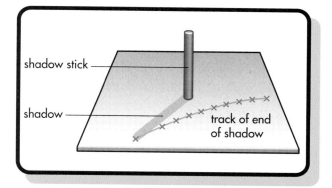

shadow stick

shadow

track of end of shadow

5.4 **Reflection and refraction**

Look and learn

★ We see a luminous object because the light from such an object enters our eyes. We see a non-luminous object because the object scatters the light that falls on it. Some of the scattered light enters our eyes. The fact that a non-luminous object can be seen from any direction proves that it must scatter light in all directions.

★ The light that enters the eye forms a pattern on the retina, a layer of light-sensitive nerve cells at the back of the eye. The brain receives signals from these nerve cells and turns the signals into patterns.

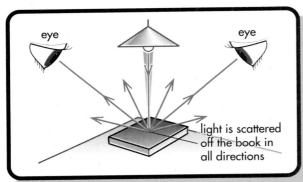

Using scattered light

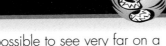

Question

8 Why is it not possible to see very far on a foggy day?

Reflection by plane mirrors

★ A plane mirror is a smooth flat silvered surface that reflects all the light directed at it.

★ A light ray directed onto a plane mirror (the **incident** ray) is reflected off the mirror in one direction only. The light is *not* scattered in all directions.

★ As you can see from the figure, the angle of reflection is always equal to the angle of incidence.

8 Light that is on its way from an object to the eye is scattered by the fog.

Answers

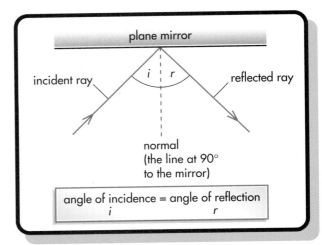

The law of reflection

angle of incidence = angle of reflection
i = r

The periscope

This is a useful device to see over the heads of people in a crowd. The user can see over the crowd because the periscope mirrors reflect light from an object into the eye. Periscopes are used in submarines to see above the water and by soldiers in trenches to see the enemy.

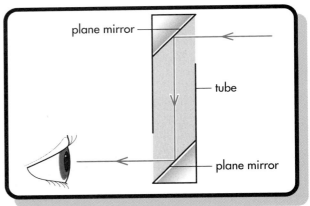

The periscope

Mirror images

The image of an object in a plane mirror lies behind the mirror. The figures on page 91 shows how the image is formed.

★ The image and the object are at the same distance from the mirror.

★ The image is the same size as the object and is laterally inverted. This means that the left hand side of an object appears on the right hand side of the image.

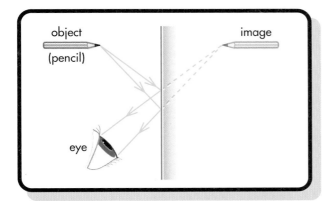

Mirror images

Refraction of light

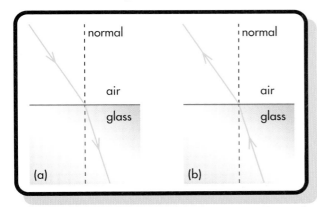

Refraction of light – a light ray passing from air into glass and from glass into air

Light travels at different speeds in different substances. When a light ray travels across the boundary between two transparent substances, its speed changes. This change of speed causes the light ray to change direction, unless it is travelling along the normal. The change of direction at the boundary is called **refraction**.

In general, a light ray is refracted

★ towards the normal when it travels from air into a denser substance

★ away from the normal when it travels from a denser substance into air.

Prisms and lenses

A prism changes the direction of a light ray twice. A convex lens changes the directions of light rays from a point object to make them meet again.

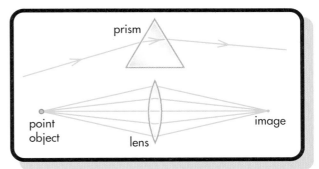

A prism and a convex lens

Questions

9 Look at the plan of an art gallery, below. The partition wall increases the number of pictures that can be displayed. A mirror on one wall allows the supervisor S at the entrance desk to see behind the partition.
(a) Why is a viewer standing at X unlikely to obtain a good view of picture A? **(b)** Which pictures cannot be seen from the desk?
(c) Where would you position a second identical mirror to increase the number of pictures the supervisor can see behind the partition? **(d)** The supervisor reckons that a large fish tank at T would enable him to see more pictures. Do you agree? Explain your answer.

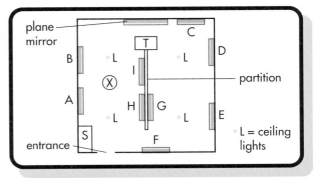

5.5 Colour

The white light spectrum

A beam of sunlight or a torch light beam projected on a white screen appears white. However, if the beam is passed through a prism, it is split into a spectrum of colours. This effect is known as **dispersion**.

The figure shows how dispersion is achieved by directing a narrow beam at a prism. The colours are the same as the colours of the rainbow and the pattern is called the white light spectrum.

Remember

★ Roy G. Biv! The colours of the spectrum are red, orange, yellow, green, blue, indigo and violet.
★ Blue Bends BetteR than Red. The glass prism refracts blue light more than red light because blue light travels more slowly than red light in glass.
★ White light contains all the colours of the spectrum. A torch beam projected on a white screen appears white because all the colours of the spectrum are present.

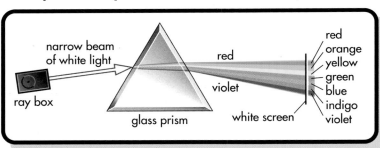

Splitting white light into colours

Why are coloured objects coloured?

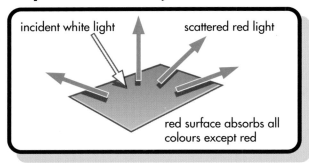

A coloured object

When white light falls on a coloured object, the surface molecules scatter light of one colour only. All the other colours are absorbed by the surface molecules. The colour of the surface is the colour of the light it scatters.

Primary and secondary colours

Primary colours

The primary colours of light are red, green and blue. This is because any other colour of light, including white light, can be produced by overlapping combinations of the three primary colours on a white screen. Note that overlapping red, green and blue spots give white light.

R + G + B = W

Secondary colours

Each secondary colour is produced where two primary colours overlap.

Yellow = red + green
Cyan = blue + green
Magenta = red + blue

White light is seen where a secondary colour formed from two primary colours overlaps the third primary colour. A secondary colour and the primary colour that overlap to give white are **complementary colours**. Yellow and blue are complementary colours because they overlap to give white light.

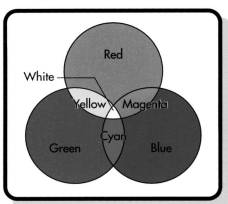

Overlapping colours

Colour filters

A filter lets light of one colour only through. The filter molecules absorb all other colours of light.

A **primary colour filter** lets light of one primary colour through. For example, if a beam of white light is passed through a blue filter, only blue light emerges. All the other colours in the white light beam are absorbed by the filter.

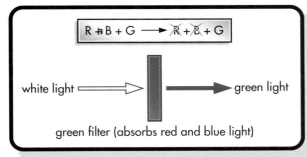

A primary colour filter

A **secondary colour filter** absorbs light of its complementary primary colour only and lets all other colours through. For example, a yellow filter absorbs blue light and allows all the other colours of white light through.

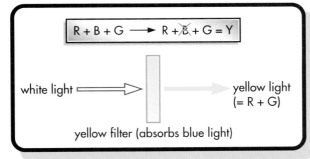

A secondary colour filter

Question

10 What colour light beam emerges when **(a)** a white light beam is directed at **(i)** a blue filter, **(ii)** a yellow filter, **(b)** a blue light beam is directed at **(i)** a red filter, **(ii)** a magenta filter?

Changing colour

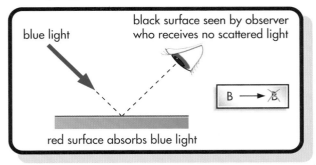

Using coloured light

The colour of an object can appear different in coloured light. For example, a red book observed in blue light appears black. This is because the book surface scatters red light only and absorbs all other colours of light except red. It therefore appears black in blue light because it absorbs the blue light and scatters none.

To work out the observed colour:
1 Write down the primary colours in the beam of light.
2 Write down the primary colours the surface can scatter.
3 Write down the colour or colours that are in both lists. If there are two primary colours in *both* lists, work out the observed secondary colour.

Questions

11 Look at the prism on page 92. What colours would you see on the screen if **(a)** a red filter is placed in the path of the beam before it passes through the prism, **(b)** a yellow filter replaces the red filter in (a)?

12 Look at the overlapping colours diagram. What colours would be seen if **(a)** a blue screen, **(b)** a cyan screen, was used?

round-up

How much can you remember?

1 The figure shows a sound waveform on an oscilloscope screen. Complete the passage below, using words from the following list to fill in the gaps.

higher louder lower closer quieter

Increasing the loudness of the sound makes the waveform _____. If the pitch of the sound is increased, the frequency is made _____ and the waveform peaks become _____. [3]

2 (a) Which frequency is closest to the frequency at which the human ear is most sensitive? 50 Hz, 3000 Hz, 18 000 Hz, 50 000 Hz. **(b)** Telephone channels do not carry frequencies above 4000 Hz. What difference does this make to someone's voice over the phone? [3]

3 'Glue ear' is a hearing disorder which makes sound muffled and quieter. It is usually caused as a result of fluid in the middle ear, usually caused by infection. Why would fluid in the middle ear cause this difficulty in hearing? [3]

4 (a) Which travels slower, light or sound? **(b)** What is the difference between scattering of light and reflection of light? [3]

5 The figure shows a board between an extended light source and a screen. **(a)** Complete the diagram below to show why a shadow of the board B cannot be formed on the screen. **(b)** Describe one change that could be made to obtain a shadow on the screen. [4]

extended light source

board B

white screen

6 Why are you more likely to see an eclipse of the Moon than an eclipse of the Sun? [3]

7 The figure shows a plane mirror used in a restaurant to observe the entrance door from the kitchens.

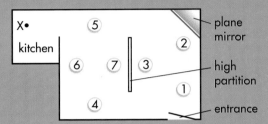

(a) Which two tables can be seen in the mirror from point X in the kitchen? **(b)** Which tables can be seen by someone at table 1? [4]

8 (a) When a light ray travels from air into glass, does it refract towards or away from the normal? **(b)** Complete the diagram below, showing the path of the light ray into then out of the semicircular glass block. [3]

9 (a) Name the colours of the spectrum. **(b)** Name the secondary colour that is complementary to red. [3]

10 (a) A blue spot of light partly overlaps a green spot of light on a white screen. What colours are seen on the screen? **(b)** If the white screen was replaced by a yellow screen, what colour would now be seen on the screen? [3]

How did you do? Don't be too worried if you didn't do too well. Have a break then try again.

Answers

Topic 1 Electricity and magnetism

Test yourself

1 a) and d). (2✔)
2 **a)** (iii). (✔) **b)** The readings are less than before. The two ammeters read the same as each other. (2✔)
3 **a)** Y and Z. (✔) **b)** Both Y and Z go off. (✔) **c)** X and Y become equally bright. (2✔)
4 Repel, north, attract, south. (4✔)
5 **a)** Steel keeps its magnetism better than iron. (✔) **b)** Iron becomes magnetised and loses its magnetism easier than steel. (✔)

Total = 15 marks

Round-up

1 (b). (✔)
2 (c). (✔)
3 Look at the figure to see cells in series and correctly connected (✔), torch bulbs in series (✔), ammeter and switch in series with cells and torch bulbs (✔).

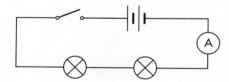

4 (c). (✔)
5 (b). (✔)
6 a) Lower reading. (✔) **b)** Unchanged brightness. (✔)
7 Left-hand end of A is north. (✔) Right-hand end of A and left-hand end of B are south. (2✔) Right-hand end of B is north. (✔)
8 a) Left-hand end of A repels north pole of plotting compass. (✔) Like poles repel, therefore left-hand end of A is north (✔). **b)** Right-hand end of A is south because the other end is north. (✔) The left-hand end of B repels the right-hand end of A, so the left-hand end of B must be south – and so the right-hand end of B must be north. (✔)
9 Magnetised (or magnetic), coil, attracted (or pulled), the core stays magnetised (or magnetic). (4✔)
10 Current passes through the coil. The iron core becomes magnetised and attracts the steel blade. (✔) The make-and-break switch is opened and the current is switched off. (✔) The iron core demagnetises and releases the blade. (✔) The make-and-break switch closes so current passes through the coil again and the sequence is repeated. (✔)

Total = 25 marks

Topic 2 Forces

Test yourself

1 a) 12 km/h. (✔) **b)** 3.3 m/s. (✔)
2 a) The cutter is nearer the pivot. (✔) The moment of the force on the lever is equal to the moment of the force on the cutter. (✔) The force of the cutter is therefore greater than the force on the lever. (✔) **b)** $F \times 1$ (✔) $= 30 \times 10$ (✔) $F = 300\,N$. (✔)
3 The contact area of the blades is small (✔) so the pressure of the blades (= force/area) will be large enough to sink into snow but not into ice. (✔) The pressure of the blades on ice melts the ice under the blades, allowing the blades to slide freely over the ice. (✔)
4 The contact area of a sharp edge is much less than the contact area of a blunt edge. (✔) Pressure = force/area, therefore the pressure is greater for the same force if a sharp knife is used instead of a blunt knife. (✔)

Total = 13 marks

Round-up

1 (b). (✔)
2 a) 2 hours, 8 minutes. (✔) **b) (i)** 2.5 km/min, (✔) **(ii)** 42 m/s. (✔)
3 Air resistance on the parachute opposes the motion. (✔) The air resistance increases with speed until the air resistance is equal and opposite to the weight. (✔) The parachutist falls at constant speed when the air resistance becomes equal and opposite to the weight. (✔)
4 A wider parachute would descend more slowly. (✔) There would be more air resistance with a wide parachute, (✔) so the parachutist would not reach as high a speed. (✔)
5 $F \times 0.20 = 40$, (✔) therefore $F = 40/0.20 = 200\,N$. (✔)
6 The force on the lever acts further from the pivot than the force on the cable. (✔) The moment of the force on the lever is equal to the moment of the force on the cable. (✔) Since moment = force × distance, the nearer to the pivot the force acts, the greater the force needed to give the same moment. (✔)
7 $T \times 25$ (✔) $= 30 \times 250$ (✔). Therefore $T = 300\,N$. (✔)
8 Tractors need to go on soft ground without sinking into the ground. (✔) The pressure of a vehicle on the ground is less the greater the contact area of the tyres with the ground. (✔) The wider the tyre, the greater the contact area. (✔)
9 $A = 5 \times 5 = 25\,cm^2$. (✔) $p = F/A = 10/25$ (✔) $= 0.4\,N/cm^2$. (✔)
10 Same. (✔) Elephant's weight of 5000 N is spread over 2000 cm², giving a pressure of 2.5 N/cm². (✔) The cat's weight of 50 N is spread over 20 cm², giving a pressure of 2.5 N/cm². (✔)

Total = 27 marks

Topic 3 Energy

Test yourself

1 Elastic, kinetic, kinetic, potential, kinetic, thermal. (6✓)
2 **a) (i)** 0, (✓) **(ii)** 200 J. (✓) **b) (i)** 100 J, (✓) **(ii)** 100 J. (✓)
3 **a)** Coal and gas. (2✓) **b) (i)** Uranium. (✓) **(ii)** Tidal energy or geothermal energy. (✓)
4 Hydroelectricity, wind energy, electricity from solar cells. (3✓)

Total = 17 marks

Round-up

1 **a)** Elastic. (✓) **b)** Kinetic. (✓)
2 **a)** Potential energy → kinetic energy + heat dissipated (due to friction and air resistance). (3✓)
  b) Chemical energy → electrical energy (+ heat dissipated in the wires) → kinetic energy → sound + heat dissipated due to friction. (3✓)
3 **a)** Chemical energy. (✓) **b)** Potential energy. (✓)
  c) It loses potential energy. (✓) It does not gain kinetic energy. (✓) **d)** Energy is needed to keep her muscles contracted so she can lower the plate safely. (✓)
4 Chemical, thermal, electrical, kinetic. (4✓)
5 **a)** 2.0 J. (✓) **b)** 1.5 J. (✓) **c) (i)** 0.5 J. (✓) **(ii)** Thermal energy or sound energy. (✓)
6 **a)** They are not produced from organisms that lived millions of years ago. (✓) **b)** They cannot be reused once they have released their energy. (✓)
7 A is solar energy (✓) and is renewable (✓). B is tidal energy (✓) and is renewable. (✓) C is gas. (✓) It is not renewable. (✓) D is wind energy (✓) and is renewable (✓). E is hydroelectricity. (✓) It is renewable. (✓) F is coal (✓) and is not renewable. (✓)
8 **a)** All except B. (✓) **b)** Kinetic energy of the Moon round the Earth. (✓)
9 **a)** Chemical energy → electrical energy → light and heat. (2✓) **b)** Batteries cannot store enough energy. (✓) They would need to be recharged. (✓) Batteries could not supply energy at a fast enough rate. (✓)
10 Conserved, used, dissipated, recovered, stored, released, burned, used. (8✓)

Total = 50 marks

Topic 4 The Earth and beyond

Test yourself

1 **a) (i)** South, **(ii)** east. (2✓) **b)** December. (✓)
2 Southern, winter, set, all, northern. (5✓)
3 **a) (i)** See figure. (✓) **(ii)** It is hidden by sunlight (or by the Sun). (✓) **b) (i)** See figure. (✓) **(ii)** It is in the opposite direction to the Sun and is therefore easily seen at night. (✓)

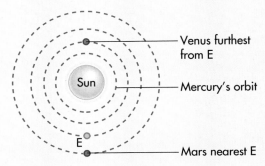

4 **a) (i)** Venus. (✓) **(ii)** Mars. (✓) **b) (i)** See figure (✓) **(ii)** It is never far from the Sun. (✓)
5 **a)** The Sun, (✓) because the Sun is much bigger (or more massive) than Mars or Jupiter. (✓) **b)** Mars, (✓) because Mars is much less massive than Jupiter and the distance to each is the same. (✓)

Total = 20 marks

Round-up

1 **a)** West. (✓) **b)** North. (✓)
2 **a)** March and September. (2✓) **b)** (ii). (✓)
3 **a)** South. (✓) **b)** The Earth moves halfway round its orbit in six months. (✓) From the Earth, Orion lies in the same direction as the Sun six months later. (✓)
4 **a) (i)** West, (✓) **(ii)** lower. (✓) **b)** The Earth spins about an axis through its poles towards the East. (✓) We see the constellations rise in the east and set in the west due to the Earth's spinning motion. (✓)
5 **a)** The Earth's north pole always points towards the Pole Star. (✓) **b) (i)** See figure. (✓) **(ii)** Yes, (✓) but it would not be circumpolar as it would sometimes be below the horizon. (✓)

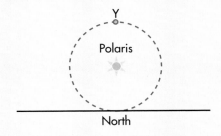

6 **a) (i)** and **(ii)** see figure. (2✓) **b) (i)** 3.7 AU, (✓) **(ii)** 0.5 AU. (✓)
7 **a)** Jupiter. (✓) **b)** and **c)** See figure. (2✓)

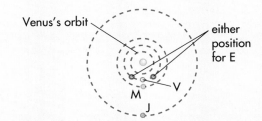

8 a) Look at the figure. (✓) **b)** Neither planet could be so far away from the Sun. (✓) Both planets can only be seen in the west after sunset or in the east before sunrise. (✓)

9 a) The arrow should point in the opposite direction to the Sun. (✓) **b)** See figure. (✓)

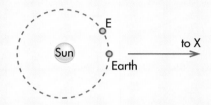

10 a) (i) and **(ii)** See figure. (2✓) **b) (i)** See figure. (2✓) **(ii)** The force of gravity due to the Sun slows it down as it moved away from the Sun. (✓)

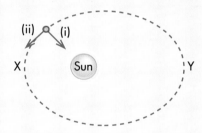

Total = 33 marks

Topic 5 Light and sound

Test yourself

1 **a)** B. (✓) **b)** C. (✓)
2 **a)** (iii). (✓) **b)** They become worn (✓) where they rub against each other, (✓) they transmit vibrations less effectively. (✓)
3 **a)** B, C, D and E. (2✓) for all four correct, (✓) for three correct. **b)** B and C. (2✓)
4 **a)** Dispersion. (✓) **b)** Violet. (✓)

Total = 12 marks

Round-up

1 Higher, higher, closer. (3✓)
2 **a)** 3000 Hz. (✓) **b)** The phone voice is deeper than normal (✓) (unless their normal voice is very deep). (✓)
3 The bones of the middle ear would not be able to vibrate easily. (✓) The fluid absorbs some of the sound. (✓) Sound vibrations reach the oval window after a delay. (✓)
4 **a)** Sound. (✓) **b)** Scattering is where light leaves a non-luminous surface in all directions. (✓) Reflection is where light leaves a surface in one direction only. (✓)
5 **a)** See figure. (3✓) **b)** Replace the extended source with a point source or move the board nearer to the screen. (✓)

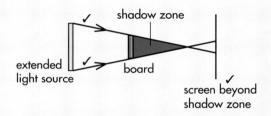

6 Everyone on the night side of the Earth can see a lunar eclipse. (✓) A solar eclipse can only be seen from a small part of the Earth. (✓) The Earth's shadow is much wider than the Moon's shadow. (✓)
7 **a)** 1, 2. (2✓) for both correct; (✓) for one correct. **b)** 2, 3, 4 and 5. (2✓) for all four correct, (✓) for two correct.
8 **a)** Towards. (✓) **b)** See figure. (2✓)

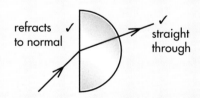

9 **a)** Red, orange, yellow, green, blue, indigo, violet. (✓) for all correct, (✓) in correct order. **b)** Cyan. (✓)
10 **a)** Blue, green (✓) and cyan. (✓) **b)** Green only. (✓)

Total = 32 marks

Life processes & living things

STRUCTURE

PLANT CELLS and ANIMAL CELLS

NUCLEUS – controls the cell at work

MITOCHONDRIA – where oxygen breaks down sugar releasing energy

CYTOPLASM – fills the cell giving it shape

MEMBRANE – separates cell from other cells and from the outside environment

PLANT CELLS only

PLUS

CHLOROPLASTS – where photosynthesis takes place

WALL – gives cell its shape

VACUOLE – contains a solution of sugar and salts

EXAMPLES

CILIATED cells – hair-like cilia move mucus and other substances from place to place in the body.

SPERM cells swim towards an egg. One of them fertilises it.

EGG cells are fertilised by sperm.

ROOT HAIR cells absorb water from the soil.

PALISADE cells in the leaf contain chloroplasts where photosynthesis occurs, making sugar.

CELLS

CELLS suited (adapted) jobs / functions

Different structures enable cells to do their job

Different functions of cells enable TISSUES→ORGANS→ORGAN SYSTEMS to do their job

DIVISION

HALF-SET OF CHROMOSOMES

meiosis produces sex cells

sperm cells

eggs

mitosis produces identical daughter cells

BUILDING

make of bodies BLOCKS

TISSUES Groups of similar cells

ORGAN Group of different tissues

ORGAN SYSTEMS Group of different organs

Enable LIFE'S PROCESSES to take place

Movement
Respiration
Sensitivity
Growth
Reproduction
Excretion
Nutrition

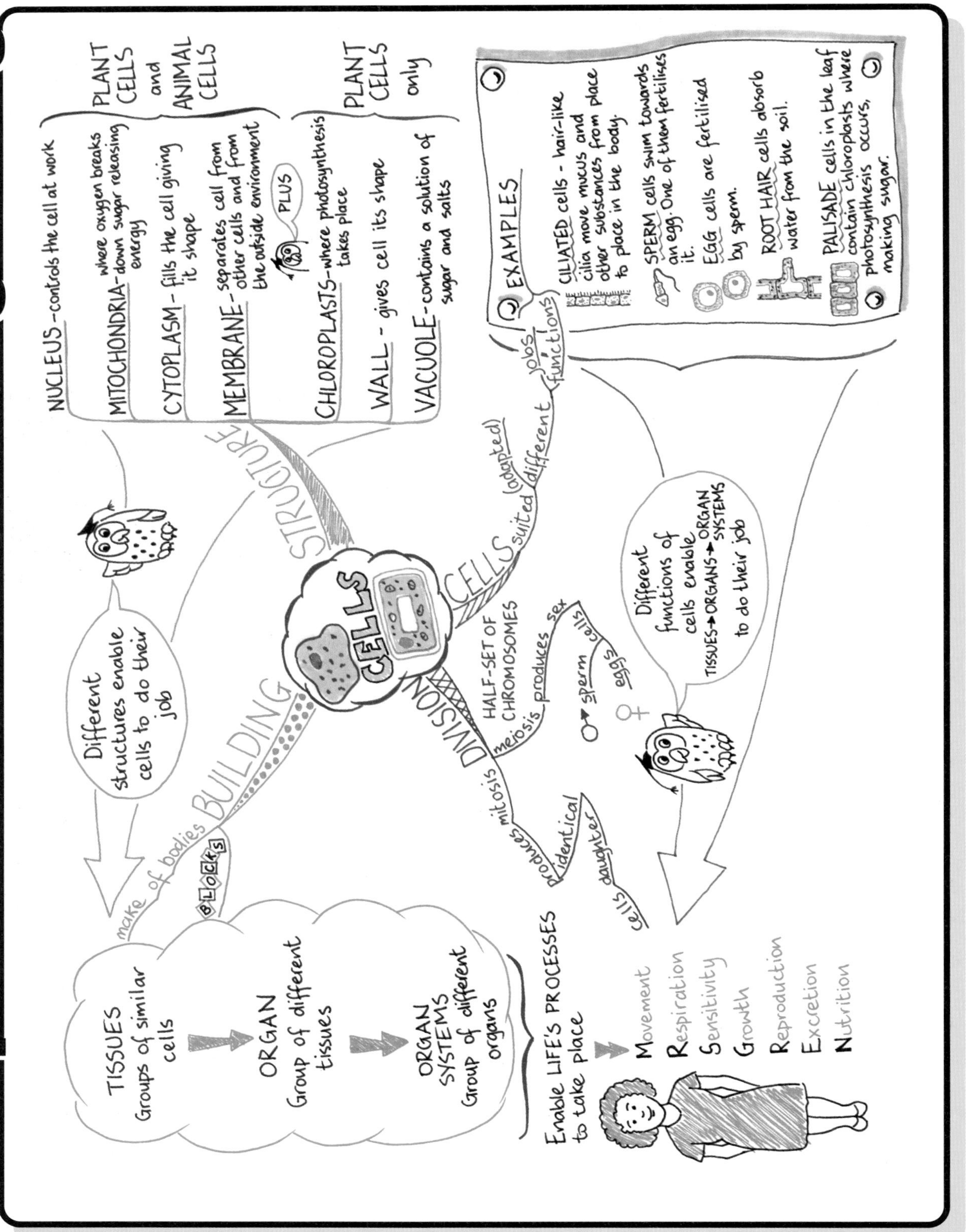

Test yourself

How much do you know already? The Mind Map will help you to organise your thoughts and answer the questions below.

1 The table below lists different cell structures. Put a tick in each space if the structure is present. [7]

Cell structure	Plant cell	Animal cell
Cell membrane		
Cell wall		
Cytoplasm		
Nucleus		
Chloroplast		
Mitochondrion		
Large vacuole		

2 The diagram shows different cells. Briefly describe how the appearance of each one helps you understand what it does. [6]

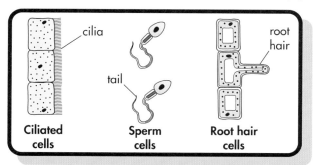

Ciliated cells   **Sperm cells**   **Root hair cells**

3 Complete the following paragraph using the words provided below. Each word may be used once, more than once or not at all.

chloroplasts   nucleus   membrane   cilia   vacuole   mitochondria   cytoplasm

A cell is surrounded by a _____, which forms its surface. Inside is the jelly-like _____, in which are different structures. For example, the _____ contains the chromosomes and _____ are structures where energy is released from the breakdown of glucose. Only plant cells have a cell wall and _____, which trap light energy. Inside plant cells there is a large space called the _____, which contains a solution of sugar and salts. [6]

4 'Cells are the building blocks from which living things are made.' Briefly comment on this statement. [3]

1.1 Cell structure

preview

At the end of this section you will:
- **be able to identify different parts (structures) of animal cells and plant cells**
- **know the similarities and differences between plant and animal cells**
- **understand that cells are adapted to do different jobs (their function)**

Some structures are a part of all **cells**. Other structures are found in some cells but not in others. The figure shows you the structure of animal cells and plant cells. Notice the similarities and differences. Also notice that the structures of different types of cells are suited (adapted) for their particular functions in the body.

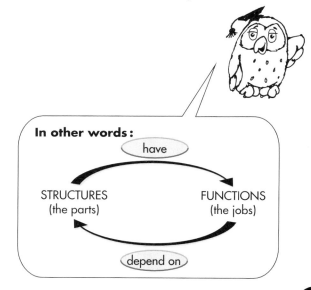

In other words:

STRUCTURES (the parts)   have   FUNCTIONS (the jobs)

depend on

CELL STRUCTURE

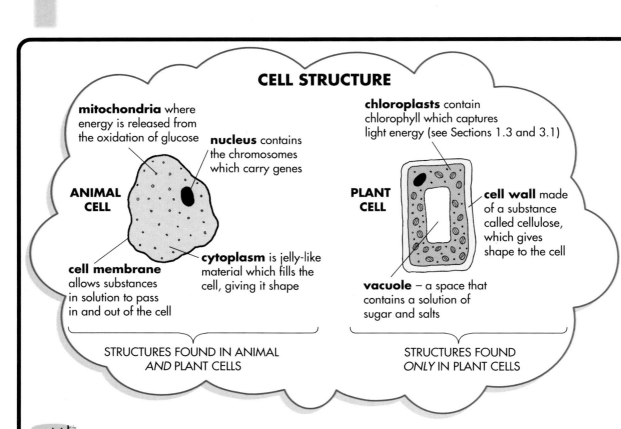

mitochondria where energy is released from the oxidation of glucose

nucleus contains the chromosomes which carry genes

ANIMAL CELL

cell membrane allows substances in solution to pass in and out of the cell

cytoplasm is jelly-like material which fills the cell, giving it shape

chloroplasts contain chlorophyll which captures light energy (see Sections 1.3 and 3.1)

PLANT CELL

cell wall made of a substance called cellulose, which gives shape to the cell

vacuole – a space that contains a solution of sugar and salts

STRUCTURES FOUND IN ANIMAL *AND* PLANT CELLS

STRUCTURES FOUND *ONLY* IN PLANT CELLS

Ciliated cells – cilia are rows of fine hairs which sway to and fro. Ciliated cells line the windpipe. They sweep a covering layer of mucus, which traps bacteria, viruses and other particles, into the pharynx. The mucus is either swallowed, sneezed out or coughed up.

cilia

sperm – the male sex cell which swims to the egg (see Section 4.4)

tail-like flagellum lashes from side to side

ovum (egg) – the female sex cell which is fertilised when a sperm fuses with it (see section 4.4)

Different types of animal cell

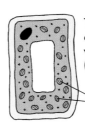

The **leaf palisade cell** contains numerous chloroplasts, where photosynthesis takes place (see Sections 1.3 and 3.1)

chloroplasts

Root hair cell absorbs water from the soil. The hair-like extension of the cell increases the surface area available for the absorption of water from the soil.

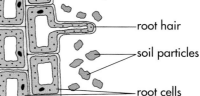

root hair

soil particles

root cells

Different types of plant cell

Cells: what they look like and what they do

Remember:

★ Most cells are too small to be seen with the naked eye.

★ The light microscope helps you to see the structure of cells by magnifying their details (see the figure below).

★ The human body is made of more than 200 different types of cell.

1.2 Cells, the building blocks

At the end of this section you will:

● **know that animals and plants are made up of cells**

● **understand that cells are organised into tissues, tissues into organs and organs into organ systems**

● **know that tissues, organs and organ systems enable life processes to take place.**

Cells are to bodies as bricks are to houses. Cells build bodies. Each of us is made of thousands of millions of cells. Different types of cell are adapted to do different jobs.

Plants and animals are said to be **multicellular** because they are made of many cells.

Remember the sequence:

A group of similar cells makes a tissue → Different tissues together make up an **organ** → Different organs make up an **organ system**

The figure on the next page shows you how cells, tissues, organs and organ systems come together to build bodies. Notice that the tissues, organs and organ systems enable life processes to take place.

Life processes happen because of the link between structures and their function (see page 99).

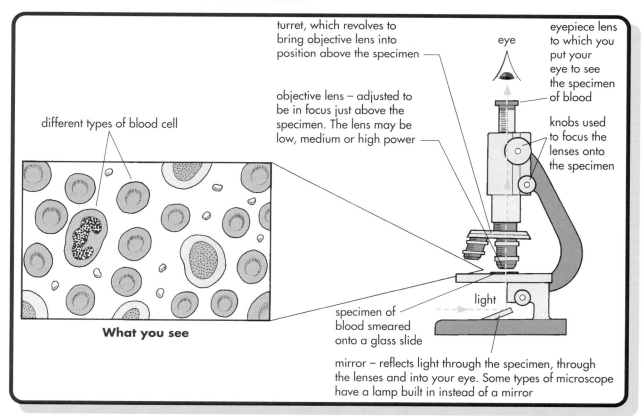

turret, which revolves to bring objective lens into position above the specimen

objective lens – adjusted to be in focus just above the specimen. The lens may be low, medium or high power

eye

eyepiece lens to which you put your eye to see the specimen of blood

knobs used to focus the lenses onto the specimen

different types of blood cell

What you see

specimen of blood smeared onto a glass slide

light

mirror – reflects light through the specimen, through the lenses and into your eye. Some types of microscope have a lamp built in instead of a mirror

Looking at blood cells through the light microscope

In other words, each part of the body – tissue, organ, organ system – is suited (**adapted**) to do a particular job (their **function**). For example the blood system transports blood to all parts of the body, and a leaf makes food by photosynthesis.

BLOOD
Page 131.

GREEN PLANTS
Page 118.

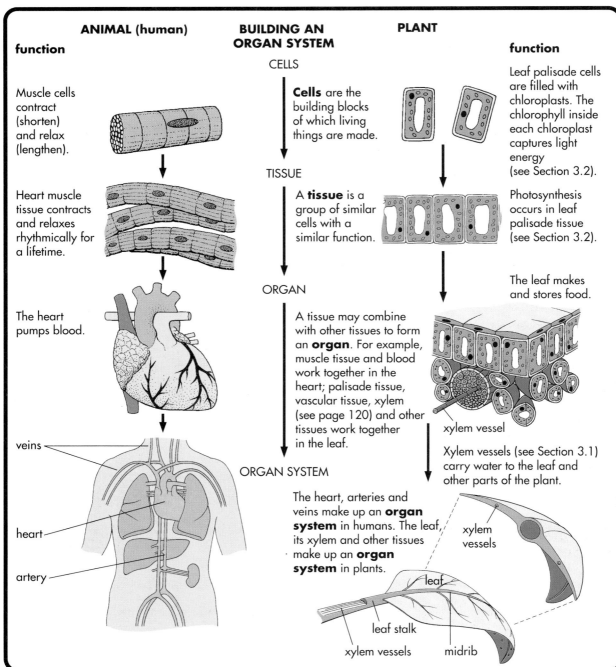

ANIMAL (human)

function

Muscle cells contract (shorten) and relax (lengthen).

Heart muscle tissue contracts and relaxes rhythmically for a lifetime.

The heart pumps blood.

veins

heart

artery

BUILDING AN ORGAN SYSTEM

CELLS

Cells are the building blocks of which living things are made.

TISSUE

A **tissue** is a group of similar cells with a similar function.

ORGAN

A tissue may combine with other tissues to form an **organ**. For example, muscle tissue and blood work together in the heart; palisade tissue, vascular tissue, xylem (see page 120) and other tissues work together in the leaf.

ORGAN SYSTEM

The heart, arteries and veins make up an **organ system** in humans. The leaf, its xylem and other tissues make up an **organ system** in plants.

PLANT

function

Leaf palisade cells are filled with chloroplasts. The chlorophyll inside each chloroplast captures light energy (see Section 3.2).

Photosynthesis occurs in leaf palisade tissue (see Section 3.2).

The leaf makes and stores food.

xylem vessel

Xylem vessels (see Section 3.1) carry water to the leaf and other parts of the plant.

xylem vessels

leaf

leaf stalk

xylem vessels

midrib

Cells to tissues, to organs, to organ systems

Other organ systems enable different life processes to take place, as you can see in the table.

	Organ system	Life processes	Reference
Animals (humans)	Digestive system	Breaks down large food molecules, which the body cannot absorb, into small molecules that can be absorbed	page 128
	Muscles and skeleton	The bones of the skeleton protect delicate organs and give shape to the body. Muscles pull on bones, moving the skeleton	page 133
	Reproductive systems	The male system produces sperm; the female system produces eggs and protects the developing fetus (baby)	page 134
	Lungs	Consist of sac-like surfaces where oxygen can diffuse into the blood and carbon dioxide can diffuse from the blood	page 136
Plants	Stem	Supports the leaves and flowers, connecting them to the roots	page 119
	Roots	Anchor the plant and absorb water from the soil	page 119

The life processes carried out by different organ systems

1.3 Cells at work

preview

At the end of this section you will:
- **understand that cells convert energy from one form to another**
- **know that plant cells convert light energy into the chemical energy of food**
- **understand that plant and animal cells release energy by breaking down sugars (glucose)**
- **know that the energy released by cells powers life's processes**
- **understand the importance of cell division.**

Cells are able to convert energy from one form to another. The energy used in cells enables life's processes to take place (see Section 1.2).

Important!!

Energy can be converted from any one form to any other form.

This is a **really, really, important** scientific idea. Looking at pages 29 and 66 will help you to understand it.

Even reading this announcement transfers energy. The chemical energy released by cells from the breakdown of foods is converted into the electrical energy of nerve impulses. The information carried in nerve impulses is understood by your brain.

Energy conversion: plant cells

Plant cells convert light energy into the chemical energy of food. The process, called photosynthesis, is described on pages 120–122.

Plant cells, animal cells and the cells of most other living things use the oxygen produced by photosynthesis to **oxidise** sugar (see page 120 for more on photosynthesis). The process releases energy and is called aerobic respiration.

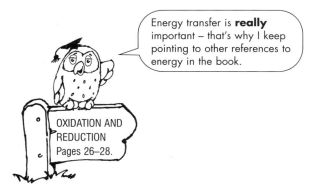

Energy transfer is **really** important – that's why I keep pointing to other references to energy in the book.

OXIDATION AND REDUCTION Pages 26–28.

The oxidation (**respiration**) of sugar by cells occurs in the **cytoplasm** and in very tiny structures called **mitochondria** (see page 100). It is the **aerobic** part of respiration which takes place in the mitochondria. Here, respiration is completed, releasing lots of energy. The chemical reactions of aerobic respiration can be summarised as follows:

$$\text{Sugars} + \text{Oxygen} \rightarrow \text{Carbon dioxide} + \text{Water}$$

Energy released

The energy released by aerobic respiration powers life's processes, which are summarised by MRS GREN (see page 98).

Handy hint

Hints & Tips

The mnemonic Mrs Gren will help you remember life's processes.

Now you know why I've 'gone on' about energy transfer. It powers life: it's why we are alive!

New cells from old

When cells divide, new cells are formed:

★ **parent** cells are the old cells which divide
★ **daughter** cells are the new cells formed when parent cells divide. 'Daughter' doesn't mean that the cells are female – it means that they are the new cells formed in cell division.

When a parent cell divides, the chromosomes in its nucleus and the **genes** which are a part of the chromosomes are passed on to the daughter cells. Genes are parts of the threads of a substance called **deoxyribonucleic acid** (**DNA**). They carry the **genetic code**, which contains all the information cells need to do their jobs. Daughter cells therefore inherit the information for their 'job description' from their parent cell. How much information they inherit depends on the way the parent cell divides.

Ways of dividing

Mitosis

Mitosis produces daughter cells with the *same number* of chromosomes as the parent cell. The chromosomes that the daughter cells inherit are replicas of the parent cell's chromosomes. The daughter cells are therefore genetically identical to the parent cell.

Mitosis is the way living things:

★ **repair damage** – for example, mitosis replaces damaged skin cells with identical new skin cells
★ **grow** – for example, the root of a plant grows because root cells divide by mitosis to produce new root tissue
★ **reproduce asexually** – for example, cells of parts of a stem dividing by mitosis produce roots. Stem and roots grow into a new plant.

ASEXUAL REPRODUCTION Page 126.

Meiosis produces daughter cells with *half the number* of chromosomes of the parent cell. Only cells in the sex organs divide by meiosis. The daughter cells are the sex cells:

★ **sperm** in males
★ **eggs** in females.

Sexual reproduction depends on a sperm joining with an egg. The process of 'joining' is called **fertilisation**.

SEXUAL REPRODUCTION
Pages 122 & 134.

How do half numbers of chromosomes come together again to make a full set of chromosomes?

Each human body cell has 46 chromosomes: the FULL SET

An example of a man's body cell which divides by **meiosis** to produce sperm
 (46) (46) **Parent cells**
An example of a woman's body cell which divides by **meiosis** to produce an egg

Each human sex cell has 23 chromosomes – a HALF SET

 (23) **Sperm**
(23) **Egg**

 – Why? –

Because the sex cells are produced from parent cells that divide by meiosis

FERTILISATION

FERTILED EGG
has 46 chromosomes: the FULL SET. 23 chromosomes are inherited from the male parent and 23 are inherited from the female parent

Fertilisation restores the full set of chromosomes

During fertilisation the chromosomes from each cell combine in the offspring. You can see how this works in the figure.

 Is there more?

Yes – because the offspring formed by sexual reproduction inherit genes from each parent they are genetically different from each other (unless they are identical twins) and their parents. In other words, they show variation.

VARIATION Page 146.

Words to remember

You have read some important words in this chapter. Here's a list to remind you what the words in red mean.

Adapted	suited for a particular job or to a particular way of life in a particular environment
Aerobic respiration	uses oxygen to release energy from food
Inheritance	passing on characteristics from parent to offspring
Offspring	new individuals produced by parents
Photosynthesis	the chemical reactions that use the light energy trapped by chlorophyll to convert carbon dioxide and water into sugars and oxygen
Replica	an exact copy
Tissue	a group of similar cells that are adapted to perform a particular biological task
Variation	the word used to describe the differences between individuals

round-up

How well have you revised? These round up questions will help you to know how well you are doing.

1 Match each of the structures in column A with their function in column B   [5]

A	B
Mitochondrion	Allows substances to pass into and out of the cell
Cell membrane	Where energy is released from the oxidation of glucose
Chloroplast	Made of a substance called cellulose
Cell wall	Controls the cell at work
Nucleus	Where light energy is captured

2 Which of the structures listed below are found in **(a)** animal cells and plant cells **(b)** plant cells only?   [7]

nucleus, cell membrane, cell wall, large vacuole, mitochondria, chloroplasts, cytoplasm

3 Here is a series of words that describe the different parts that come together to build bodies:

organ systems, cells, living thing, tissue, organs

Arrange the words in a sequence that shows how simpler parts combine to make more complicated parts which form a living thing.   [5]

4 (a) What process in plant cells converts light energy into the chemical energy of food (sugars)? Where does the process take place in plant cells?   [2]

(b) What process in animal cells and plant cells releases energy from the oxidation of sugars? Where does the process take place in animal cells and plant cells?   [2]

(c) Briefly describe the link between the chemistry of the processes mentioned in parts (a) and (b)   [3]

You might want to answer the Test yourself questions again so that you can measure how well you've improved compared with your first try. Well done if you've improved.

Living things in their environment

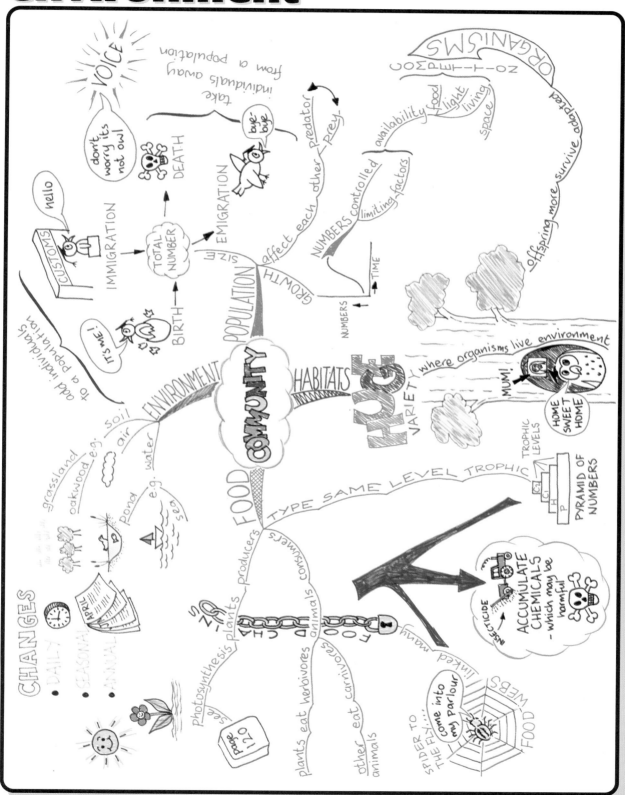

Test yourself

How much do you know already? The Mind Map will help you to organise your thoughts and answer the questions below.

1 Match the list of terms in column A with the correct description in column B [3]

A	B
Community	The place where a group of organisms live in the community
Habitat	A group of individuals of the same species
Population	All of the organisms that live in a particular environment

2 'Who eats whom' between predators, prey and scavengers? [3]

3 Why is a food web a more accurate description of feeding in a community than a food chain? [2]

4 Why do food chains and food webs always begin with plants? [4]

5 Why doesn't a pyramid of numbers accurately describe the feeding relationships within a woodland community? [2]

6 The diagram at the bottom of the page shows a soil profile of grassland in East Africa (savanna) showing the wet and dry season water tables.
(a) Which type of plant grows in the wet season but dies down in the dry season? Explain your answer. [3]
(b) Suggest possible features of plants that die down in the dry season which allow them to survive until the next growing season. [4]
(c) Which type of plant grows all year round? Explain why it is able to grow all year round. [3]

7 Look at this model population growth curve and then explain as accurately as you can what is happening to the rate of population growth at stages A, B, C and D. [7]

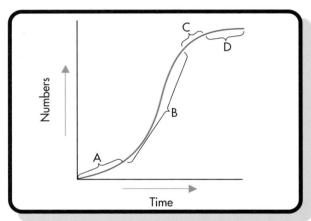

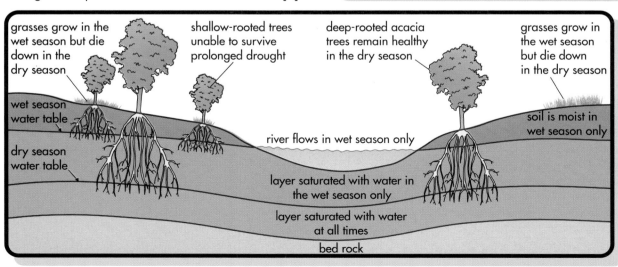

2.1 Places to live

preview

At the end of this section you will:
- **know that different environments are homes for life on Earth**
- **understand what is a community**
- **be able to explain the relationship between an environment, its community and the habitats where organisms live.**

Planet Earth is our home and the home of all life as we know it. Elsewhere in the universe there may be other planets with organisms on them but we don't know anything about them. The figure shows different **environments**, which are homes for life on Earth.

Wherever there is light, plants can make food by photosynthesis.

Notice that in the dark ocean depths life depends on the dead remains of organisms falling from above or on the heat and chemical energy given out by underwater volcanoes.

PHOTOSYNTHESIS
Page 120.

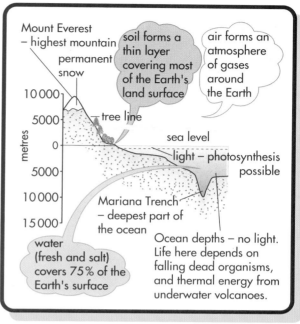

Each environment consists of air, soil or water and the plants, animals and microorganisms which live in it

Living things are not found just anywhere. For example, trees are rooted in the soil, fish swim in the sea, and so on. In other words, each living thing is adapted to the environment where it lives.

Communities and habitats

A wood or a pond are homes for a community of organisms. Members of the community live in different habitats. The figure on the next page shows you the idea.

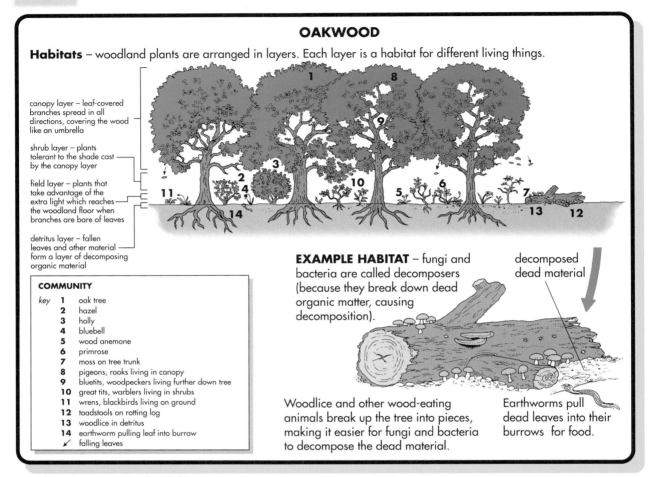

OAKWOOD

Habitats – woodland plants are arranged in layers. Each layer is a habitat for different living things.

canopy layer – leaf-covered branches spread in all directions, covering the wood like an umbrella

shrub layer – plants tolerant to the shade cast by the canopy layer

field layer – plants that take advantage of the extra light which reaches the woodland floor when branches are bare of leaves

detritus layer – fallen leaves and other material form a layer of decomposing organic material

COMMUNITY

key		
	1	oak tree
	2	hazel
	3	holly
	4	bluebell
	5	wood anemone
	6	primrose
	7	moss on tree trunk
	8	pigeons, rooks living in canopy
	9	bluetits, woodpeckers living further down tree
	10	great tits, warblers living in shrubs
	11	wrens, blackbirds living on ground
	12	toadstools on rotting log
	13	woodlice in detritus
	14	earthworm pulling leaf into burrow
	↙	falling leaves

EXAMPLE HABITAT – fungi and bacteria are called decomposers (because they break down dead organic matter, causing decomposition).

decomposed dead material

Woodlice and other wood-eating animals break up the tree into pieces, making it easier for fungi and bacteria to decompose the dead material.

Earthworms pull dead leaves into their burrows for food.

An oakwood community and its habitats

2.2 Changing environments

preview

At the end of this section you will:

- **know why temperature and the amount of light and water influence where organisms live**
- **understand how the balance of photosynthesis and respiration affects the physical and chemical conditions of a pond**
- **know about daily, seasonal and annual changes in different environments.**

Temperature and the amount of **light** and **water** are the most important physical (non-living) influences on where organisms live. Because of changes in temperature and the amount of light and water, environments alter during the day and change from season to season.

Here are some examples of different environments. These examples will help you to revise the influence that changes in temperature, light intensity and availability of water have on different communities of living things.

A pond's surface

The temperature, amount of light and concentration of particular substances at the surface of a pond change over 24 hours. The figure and table on the next page give you the idea.

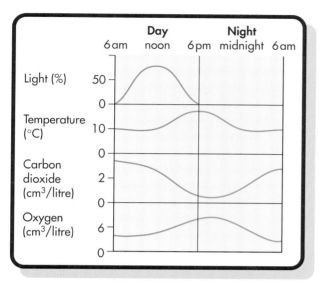

Changes in the physical and chemical conditions at the surface of a pond over 24 hours

Physical/chemical condition	During the day	At night
Light intensity	Increases	Decreases
Temperature	Rises	Falls
Carbon dioxide concentration	Decreases	Increases
Oxygen concentration	Increases	Decreases

Changes occurring over 24 hours at a pond's surface

Questions

Look at the table.

1 Why does the intensity of light change?

2 Why does the temperature rise and fall?

3 Why do the concentrations of oxygen and carbon dioxide change?

Answers

3 The concentration of the two gases depends on the balance between photosynthesis and respiration.

2 The sun warms up the water's surface, which cools when the sun sets.

1 Light changes occur because day begins as the sun rises and night begins as the sun sets.

Photosynthesis – plants produce more oxygen through photosynthesis than is used by the respiration of all of the pond's organisms (including plants). Photosynthesis stops at night.

Respiration – day and night, all of the pond's organisms (including plants) produce carbon dioxide through respiration. Photosynthesis, which uses carbon dioxide, stops at night.

Daily changes to the community

The pond's community responds to the daily changes in the physical and chemical conditions. For example:

★ Water lily flowers float on the water's surface during the day. Insects are attracted to the flowers' yellow pollen. The plants are rooted in the mud at the bottom of the pond. The flowers close at night and sink below the water's surface.

★ Microscopic plants and animals form a layer near the water's surface during the day. At night the tiny organisms sink to deeper parts of the pond.

2

Inside an oakwood

The amount of light affects life inside an oak wood. The more light there is, the greater is the rate of photosynthesis and the more plants grow. In turn, the growth of plants affects the animals that depend on them for food and shelter.

Seasonal changes to the community

The oakwood community responds to the seasonal changes in the amount of light entering the wood.

★ In **winter** sunlight streams through the branches bare of leaves, and reaches the woodland floor. However, it is too cold for plants to grow.

IT'S TOO COLD FOR ME, TOO!

★ In **spring**, sunlight streams through the branches, which are still bare of leaves, and reaches the woodland floor. It is warmer, therefore plants of the field layer (e.g. bluebells and primroses, see page 110) can grow as the rate of photosynthesis increases. The plants flower and produce seeds, which will develop into the next generation of plants the following spring.

★ In **summer**, the leaves of the trees unfold and the canopy (see page 110) develops, reducing the amount of light reaching the woodland floor. Here photosynthetic activity decreases but the plants of the field layer have already produced seeds for next year. Now it is the trees' turn to benefit from the long hours of sunlight for photosynthesis.

In the desert

Without rain, communities die. The desert community is adapted to cope with life in difficult conditions.

Annual changes to the community

The year-to-year (annual) pattern of rainfall in deserts affects the plant community:

★ the seeds of some plants survive years of drought
★ other plants dry out and survive in a state of 'suspended animation'
★ cacti store water in thick, fleshy stems.

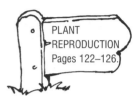

PLANT REPRODUCTION Pages 122–126.

What happens when it rains?

Flowers bloom, reproduce and scatter seeds. The burst of activity dies down when drought returns. However, the next generation of plants will grow when it rains again.

A desert before it rains

A desert after the rain

2.3 Who eats what and whom?

At the end of this section you will:

- **know that a food web consists of food chains linked together**

- **be able to explain how pyramids of numbers identify the amount of food in a community**

- **understand that poisonous substances accumulate in food chains.**

Finding out 'who eats what and whom' is one way of describing how a community works. For example, animals eat different types of food:

★ **herbivores** eat plants

★ **carnivores** eat meat

★ **omnivores** eat both plants and meat (most human beings are omnivorous).

Because they eat food, animals are called **consumers**.

Most carnivores are **predators** – they catch and eat other animals. The animals caught are called their **prey** and are often herbivores. **Scavengers** are animals that feed on the remains of prey left by predators, on the bodies of animals that have died for other reasons such as disease and old age, or on the dead remains of plants.

Food chains and food webs

A **food chain** shows the links between plants, prey, predators and scavengers. In the figure you can see examples of food chains. Notice in each example that:

★ the arrows represent the transfer of food between different organisms

★ the arrows point from the eaten to the eater

★ there are usually four or less links in a food chain.

EATING transfers food between different organisms

MMM... VOLE, FROG + MOZARELLA

PREDATOR PIZZA CO. FREE DELIVERY

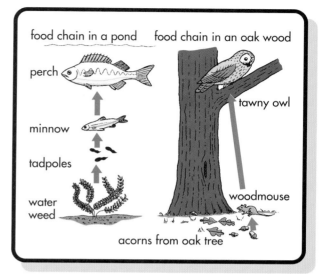

food chain in a pond   food chain in an oak wood

perch

minnow

tadpoles

water weed

acorns from oak tree

tawny owl

woodmouse

Food chains

A **food web** is usually a more accurate description of feeding relationships in a community because most animals eat more than one type of plant or other animal. The figure on the next page shows examples of food webs. Notice in each example that:

★ several food chains link up to form a food web

★ plants produce food by photosynthesis

★ different types of animal eat the same type of food.

Producers

Plants, algae and some bacteria are called **producers**, because they can use sunlight to produce food by photosynthesis. This is why food chains and food webs begin with plants (or algae or photosynthetic bacteria). Animals use this food when they eat plants. Even when they eat other animals, predators depend on plant food indirectly because somewhere along the line their prey has been a plant eater.

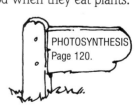

PHOTOSYNTHESIS Page 120.

Can you think when a food chain would *not* begin with photosynthetic organisms? Look back at Section 2.1 to find out.

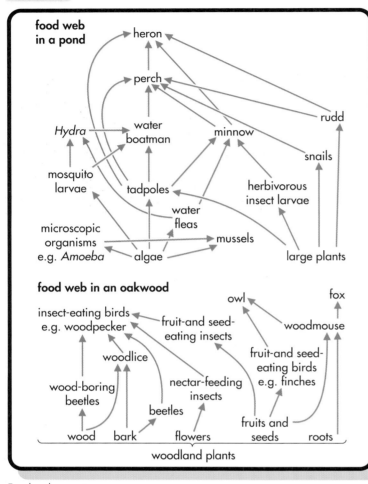

food web in a pond

food web in an oakwood

Food webs

★ Other trophic levels are made up of carnivores (see page 113). There are different categories of carnivore: **first carnivore**s (C_1) feed on herbivores, **second carnivores** (C_2) feed on first carnivores.

★ The group of organisms in each trophic level is smaller than the one below it. This gives the pyramid its shape.

A pyramid of numbers for a woodland points down as well as up (as you can see in the bottom figure). This is because relatively few producers (trees) support a large number of herbivores and carnivores. You might think that woodland consumers are in danger of starvation. However, the numbers pyramid does not allow for differences in the size of producers and consumers in a woodland. It takes tens of thousands of grass plants to equal an oak. No wonder a single tree can support so many consumers!

Pyramid of numbers

Food chains and food webs describe the feeding relationships within a community. However, they don't tell us about the number of individuals involved. **Pyramids of numbers** do. Many plants support a limited number of herbivores, which in turn support fewer carnivores.

The figure opposite shows a pyramid of numbers for a grassland community. Notice that:

★ Producers (**P**) occupy the base of the pyramid.

★ The pyramid has different feeding levels called **trophic levels**. Each trophic level groups together organisms that eat similar types of food. For example, a snail and a sheep are both herbivores (see page 113). Both belong to the second trophic level (**H**).

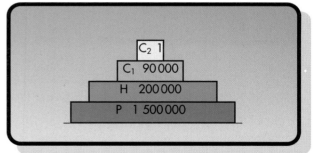

A pyramid of numbers for grassland in 0.1 hectare

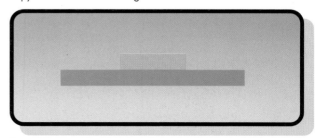

Pyramid of numbers for an oakwood

Insecticides accumulate in food chains

Eating sometimes transfers substances other than food through food chains. For example, until recently insecticides (substances that kill insects) like DDT were used to control the numbers of insects that eat our crops or cause disease. Unfortunately DDT does not break down easily, and it is soluble in fat. The body finds it difficult to remove DDT.

The figure below shows you what happened when Clear Lake in California, USA, was sprayed with DDT to get rid of mosquitoes. The insecticide accumulated in the food chain. At the beginning of the food chain the microorganisms of the plankton were unharmed by the low concentrations, but fish-eating grebes at the top of the food chain died because DDT built up in their bodies to lethal levels.

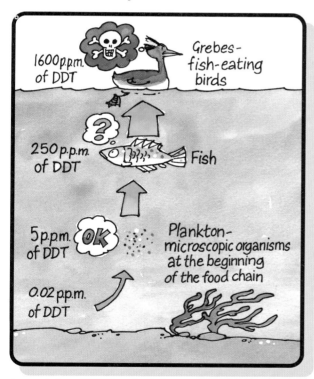

Accumulation of DDT in a food chain in Clear Lake, California

We are at the end of food chains and accumulate DDT in our bodies, even though the use of DDT has been banned and different substances are used to control insects. Because DDT doesn't break down easily, it will remain in the soil and water for many years to come.

2.4 Populations

preview

At the end of this section you will:
- **understand the factors affecting the size of a population**
- **know that limiting factors stop populations from growing indefinitely**
- **know how competition causes organisms to adapt to their environment.**

A **population** is a group of individuals of the same species living in a particular place at the same time.

Births and immigration increase the size of a population. **Deaths** and emigration decrease the size of a population.

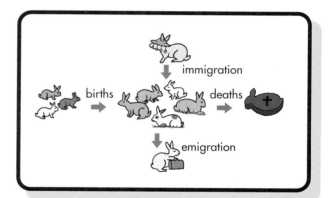

Factors affecting the size of a population

Populations grow in a particular way, as the figure on page 116 shows.

Populations need resources such as water, food and living space to grow. Resources are in short supply. As a result, resources are **limiting factors**, which stop populations from growing indefinitely. The individuals of a population are rivals for the limited resources. They compete. **Competition** means that the individuals that are best suited (adapted) to compete for resources are more likely to survive. Successful competitors reproduce more offspring than their rivals and therefore contribute more offspring to the next generation.

2

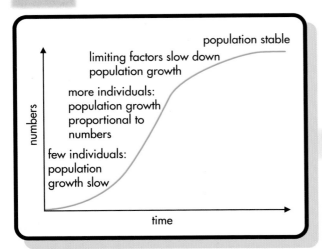

Population growth curve

Predator and prey populations

Predation affects the number of the prey population. The number of prey affects the predator population: if prey is scarce, then some of the predators will starve. The figure shows the relationships between the numbers of predators and prey.

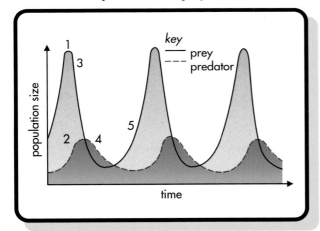

Predator–prey relationships

Follow the numbers in the diagram:

1 Prey breed and increase in numbers in favourable conditions (e.g. when there is a lot of food).
2 Predators breed and increase in numbers when there are large numbers of prey.
3 More predators means that the numbers of prey will decline.
4 Predator numbers drop when food is scarce.
5 Fewer predators means that numbers increase … and so on.

Notice that:

★ changes in predator numbers are smaller than changes in prey numbers
★ changes in predator numbers lag behind changes in prey numbers.

Question

Why is this?

The human population

The human population has grown dramatically since the beginning of the nineteenth century.

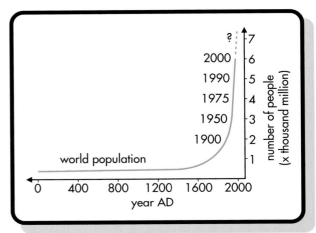

World population growth over the past 2000, years showing predicted future increase based on present trends

The populations of developed countries, for example European countries, are levelling off. The populations of developing countries, for example many of the countries in Asia and Africa, are still growing rapidly. This is a result of:

★ improvements in food production
★ more drugs being available for the treatment of disease
★ improved medical care
★ improved public health.

There are fewer predators than prey, and predators tend to reproduce more slowly than prey.

Answer

The rate of population growth is affected by the number of young people in the population. In particular, the more women of child-bearing age there are, the more children are born.

Words to remember

You have read some important words in this chapter. Here's a list to remind you what the words in red mean.

Adapted	suited for a particular job or to a particular way of life in a particular environment
Community	all the organisms living in a particular environment
Drought	the absence of rain for a long time
Emigration	movement of individuals out of a population
Habitat	the place in the environment where a group of organisms lives
Immigration	movement of individuals into a population
Organism	any living thing
Photosynthesis	the chemical reactions that use the light energy trapped by chlorophyll to convert carbon dioxide and water into sugars and oxygen
Predation	the action of predators in catching food (prey)
Species	a group of individuals able to mate to reproduce offspring, which themselves are able to mate and reproduce

round-up

How well have you revised?

1 (a) Explain the meaning of the phrase 'physical influences' on where organisms live in the environment. [1]
(b) Why is the amount of light an important physical influence on life inside a wood? [4]
2 Look at the figure of a food chain in a pond on page 113.
(a) How many links are there in the food chain? [1]
(b) Name the producers. Briefly explain why they are called producers. [2]
(c) Name the herbivores. Briefly explain why they are herbivores. [2]
(d) Name the carnivores. Briefly explain why they are carnivores. [3]
3 Look back at the food webs on page 114. Construct two different food chains, one with three links, the other with four links. [2]
4 Name the ultimate source of energy for all organisms in a woodland. [1]
5 When is the pyramid of numbers an accurate description of the feeding relationships in a community? [1]

6 The table below shows the change in numbers of sheep for 105 years since their introduction into South Australia.

Year	Number of sheep (millions)
1830	0.1
1840	0.2
1850	1.0
1860	3.0
1870	5.0
1880	6.5
1890	6.9
1900	5.2
1910	6.1
1920	7.4
1930	6.0
1935	8.0

(a) Plot the data on graph paper. [8]
(b) Between which years was population growth proportional to the numbers of sheep? [2]
(c) In which years did limiting factors stop the growth in numbers of sheep? [2]
(d) What was the overall effect of limiting factors on the numbers of sheep between 1890 and 1935? [1]

Green plants

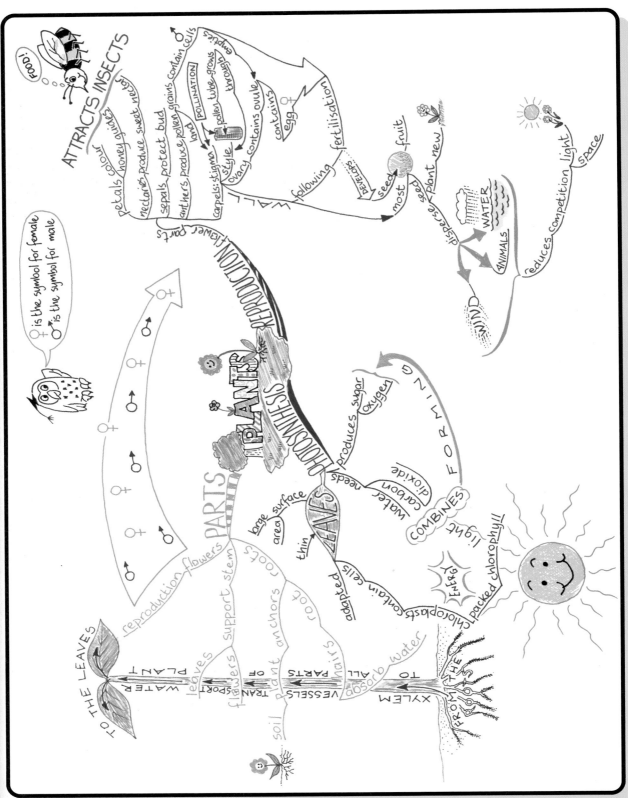

How much do you know already? The Mind Map will help you to organise your thoughts and answer the questions below.

Hey! I do the introductions!

Test yourself

1 Summarise the chemical changes that take place during photosynthesis [5]

2 Briefly describe two ways in which the leaf is adapted for photosynthesis [2]

3 Briefly describe what happens when water evaporates from the leaves of a plant [3]

4 Match the structure in column A with its correct description in column B [5]

A	B
Nectary	Develops from the ovary after fertilisation
Stigma	A fertilised ovule
Fruit	Contains the egg nucleus
Ovule	Produces a sugar solution
Seed	Structure to which pollen grains attach

5 (a) Briefly explain two different ways in which pollination occurs in plants [4]
(b) What is the difference between pollination and fertilisation? [4]

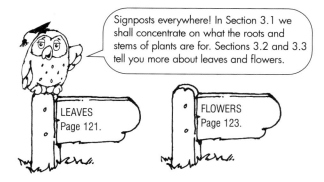

Signposts everywhere! In Section 3.1 we shall concentrate on what the roots and stems of plants are for. Sections 3.2 and 3.3 tell you more about leaves and flowers.

LEAVES Page 121.

FLOWERS Page 123.

3.1 Plants at work

preview

At the end of this section you will:
- be able to identify the different parts of a flowering plant
- understand that roots are adapted for the absorption of water and minerals in solution
- know that xylem vessels transport water and minerals in solution from the roots to all parts of the plant.

Parts of a plant

Buttercups grow in meadows. The figure shows the different parts of a buttercup and explains what each part is for. Although plants come in all shapes and sizes, they are all made up of similar parts.

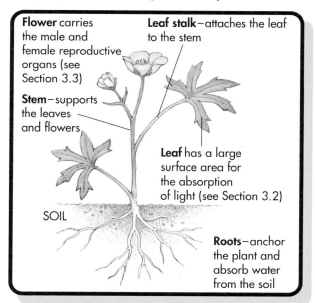

Flower carries the male and female reproductive organs (see Section 3.3)

Leaf stalk – attaches the leaf to the stem

Stem – supports the leaves and flowers

Leaf has a large surface area for the absorption of light (see Section 3.2)

SOIL

Roots – anchor the plant and absorb water from the soil

Parts of a buttercup

Roots spread out in all directions. 'Spreading out' increases the surface area of the roots, anchoring the plant into the soil. Fine **root hairs** fringe the tips of the roots and increase the surface area even more.

The **stem** not only supports leaves and flowers – it also connects them to the roots. Tubes of tissue called **xylem vessels** run from the tips of the roots, through the stem and out into every leaf of the plant. The xylem vessels help to support the plant.

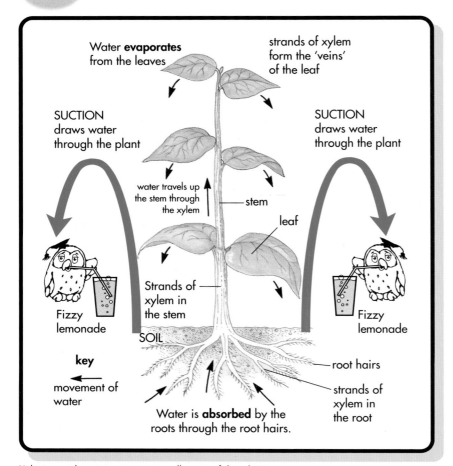

The roots also absorb minerals in solution

SOLUTIONS
Page 19.

Water **evaporates** from the leaves

strands of xylem form the 'veins' of the leaf

SUCTION draws water through the plant

SUCTION draws water through the plant

water travels up the stem through the xylem

stem

leaf

Fizzy lemonade

key

movement of water

Strands of xylem in the stem

SOIL

Fizzy lemonade

root hairs

strands of xylem in the root

Water is **absorbed** by the roots through the root hairs.

Xylem vessels transport water to all parts of the plant

Transporting water

'Spread-out' roots do not only anchor plants firmly in the soil. Their large surface area also helps plants to obtain water. In the figure you can see that water enters the plant through the root hairs and passes into the xylem vessels. Once in the xylem vessels, water forms unbroken columns from the roots, through the stem and into the leaves. Water evaporates from the leaves, mainly through the tiny gaps, called **stomata**, on the underside of leaves.

As water evaporates from the leaves, more is drawn up the xylem, rather like the way you draw drink into your mouth when you suck on a straw. Suction draws water from the roots, which replaces the water lost by absorbing more water into the plant.

3.2 Light, life and photosynthesis

preview

At the end of this section you will:

- **know that plants need carbon dioxide, water and light for photosynthesis**

- **be able to summarise the chemical reactions of photosynthesis in a word equation**

- **understand how the leaf is adapted for photosynthesis**

- **know that plants need sugars and minerals to grow properly**

- **understand why plants are at the beginning of food chains.**

Plant cells use sunlight to help them to make food by photosynthesis. They contain the green substance

chlorophyll, which is packaged in tiny structures called **chloroplasts**. Chlorophyll traps the energy of sunlight. The energy is used to convert carbon dioxide and water into sugars. The chemical reactions of photosynthesis take place inside the chloroplasts. The figure shows you what happens.

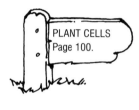

PLANT CELLS
Page 100.

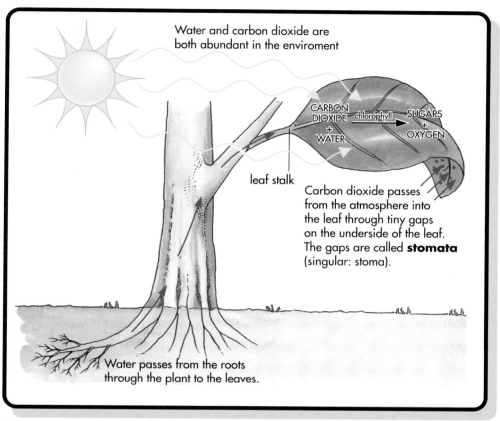

Water and carbon dioxide are both abundant in the enviroment

CARBON DIOXIDE + WATER → chlorophyll → SUGARS + OXYGEN

leaf stalk

Carbon dioxide passes from the atmosphere into the leaf through tiny gaps on the underside of the leaf. The gaps are called **stomata** (singular: stoma).

Water passes from the roots through the plant to the leaves.

The leaf and photosynthesis

A leaf is a food-making factory. It is adapted for photosynthesis:

★ Each leaf is **thin and flat**, exposing a large surface area for the absorption of light.
★ Carbon dioxide and water vapour **circulate** through air spaces within the leaf and are absorbed by the cells of the leaf.
★ Palisade cells near the upper surface of the leaf are **packed** with chloroplasts containing chlorophyll.

The figure opposite shows you inside a leaf.

Photosynthesis produces oxygen as well as sugars. Plants release oxygen into the environment. Oxygen is part of the air that we (and all other living things including plants) breathe. Cells use oxygen to release energy from the breakdown of sugars. The process is called aerobic respiration.

AEROBIC RESPIRATION
Page 104.

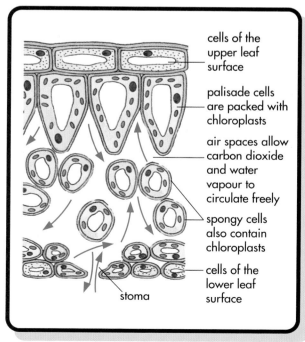

cells of the upper leaf surface

palisade cells are packed with chloroplasts

air spaces allow carbon dioxide and water vapour to circulate freely

spongy cells also contain chloroplasts

cells of the lower leaf surface

stoma

Inside a leaf

Growth

Sugars are food for plants. They help the plant to grow. Growing means producing more biomass. All living things need food to increase their biomass. The figure shows how plants use food (sugars) to produce more biomass and grow.

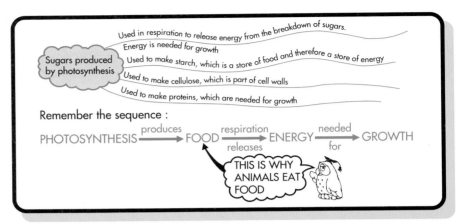

Sugars produced by photosynthesis

Used in respiration to release energy from the breakdown of sugars.

Energy is needed for growth

Used to make starch, which is a store of food and therefore a store of energy

Used to make cellulose, which is part of cell walls

Used to make proteins, which are needed for growth

Remember the sequence :

PHOTOSYNTHESIS —produces→ FOOD —respiration releases→ ENERGY —needed for→ GROWTH

THIS IS WHY ANIMALS EAT FOOD

Using food for growth

Plants begin food chains

Because plants *produce* food by photosynthesis they are at the beginning of food chains. Other living things *consume* (eat) food and therefore depend on plants and photosynthesis for their existence. All the plants need are sunlight, carbon dioxide and water.

ENVY

It's food for free

Cheapo!

FOOD CHAINS Page 113.

3.3 Reproduction

preview

At the end of this section you will:
- **know that flowers are shoots which are specialised for sexual reproduction**
- **understand that pollination is the transfer of pollen from the male sex organs to the female sex organs**
- **understand that fertilisation is the fusion of a male sex nucleus with the female egg nucleus**
- **know that seed is formed from the fertilised egg.**

Although flowers come in different shapes and sizes they are all made up of similar parts: sepals, petals, stamens and carpels. The parts of a flower and what each part is for are shown in the figure on page 123.

Notice that the male sex cell is inside the pollen grain and that the female egg cell is inside the ovule.

Remember

Fertilisation occurs when the male sex nucleus fuses with the female egg nucleus.

How does the male sex nucleus reach the female egg nucleus?

Answer

★ Pollination is the process that brings pollen grains from the anthers to the stigma of a carpel. Insects are very important as pollen carriers.

Keep studying the diagram of the flower.

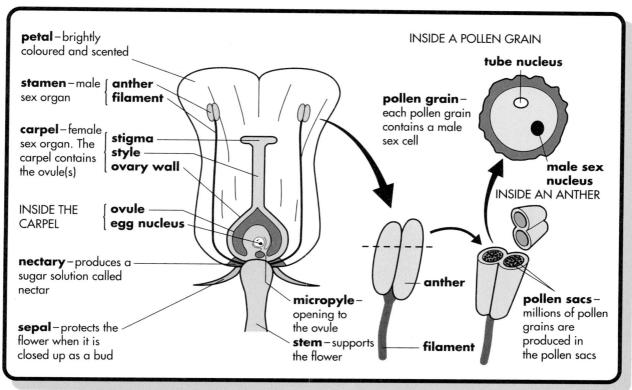

petal – brightly coloured and scented

stamen – male sex organ { **anther** / **filament** }

carpel – female sex organ. The carpel contains the ovule(s) { **stigma** / **style** / **ovary wall** }

INSIDE THE CARPEL { **ovule** / **egg nucleus** }

nectary – produces a sugar solution called nectar

sepal – protects the flower when it is closed up as a bud

micropyle – opening to the ovule

stem – supports the flower

INSIDE A POLLEN GRAIN

tube nucleus

pollen grain – each pollen grain contains a male sex cell

male sex nucleus

INSIDE AN ANTHER

anther

filament

pollen sacs – millions of pollen grains are produced in the pollen sacs

Parts of a flower

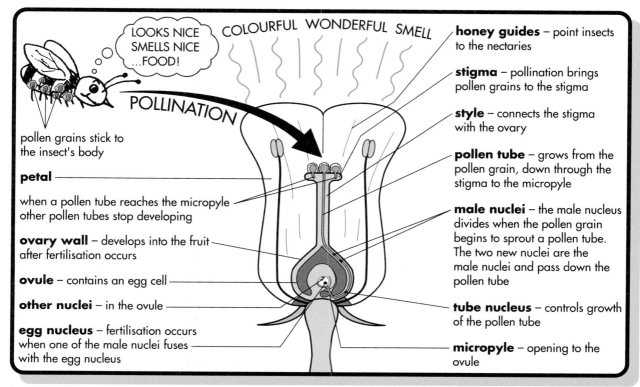

LOOKS NICE SMELLS NICE ...FOOD!

COLOURFUL WONDERFUL SMELL

POLLINATION

pollen grains stick to the insect's body

petal

when a pollen tube reaches the micropyle other pollen tubes stop developing

ovary wall – develops into the fruit after fertilisation occurs

ovule – contains an egg cell

other nuclei – in the ovule

egg nucleus – fertilisation occurs when one of the male nuclei fuses with the egg nucleus

honey guides – point insects to the nectaries

stigma – pollination brings pollen grains to the stigma

style – connects the stigma with the ovary

pollen tube – grows from the pollen grain, down through the stigma to the micropyle

male nuclei – the male nucleus divides when the pollen grain begins to sprout a pollen tube. The two new nuclei are the male nuclei and pass down the pollen tube

tube nucleus – controls growth of the pollen tube

micropyle – opening to the ovule

Fertilisation follows pollination

★ Each pollen grain sprouts a **pollen tube**, which grows through the style of the carpel to the opening to the ovule. Find the opening on the figure. The opening is called the **micropyle**.

★ The male sex nuclei pass through the micropyle into the ovule.

★ One of the male sex nuclei fuses with the female egg nucleus.

Now you know how fertilisation takes place in flowering plants. The figure shows you the process.

And the other pollen tube nuclei?

At the end of its journey the tube nucleus dies, its job of controlling the growth of the pollen tube done. The male sex nucleus that does not fuse with the female egg nucleus fuses with other cell nuclei in the ovule.

More about pollination

Why do you notice flowers? Probably because they are brightly coloured and have a pleasant smell. Insects notice flowers too (see the figure). They are attracted to

★ the **sweet smell** of many flowers
★ the **bright colours** of large petals
★ marks on the petals, called **honey guides**

★ **nectar**, which is a sugar solution produced by the nectaries at the base of the petals. Nectar is an important food source for many types of insect. The honey guides point insects in the direction of the nectaries.

All of these features of flowers attract insects (especially bees).

When visiting flowers, insects pick up a load of pollen, which is carried to the next flower they visit. Some of the pollen rubs off onto the stigma(s) of the carpel(s) and pollination takes place (see the figure on page 123 to remind yourself how this happens).

Some flowers don't depend on insects for pollination. Instead they take advantage of the **wind** to scatter pollen far and wide (see the table below).

Cross-pollination and self-pollination

When insects or wind transport pollen from the anthers of the flower of one plant to the stigma(s) of the flower of another similar plant, **cross-pollination** has taken place. Pollen is transferred *between* plants of the same type.

If pollen is transferred from the anthers to the stigma(s) of the *same* flower or to the stigma(s) of another flower on the *same* plant, then **self-pollination** has taken place. Cross-pollination increases **genetic variation**.

VARIATION Page 146.

Part of flower	Insect-pollinated plants	Wind-pollinated plants
Petals	• Brightly coloured • Usually scented • Most have nectaries	• If present, green or dull colour • No scent • No nectaries
Anthers	• In a position where insects are likely to brush against them	• Hang loosely so that they shake easily in the wind
Stigma	• In a position where insects are likely to brush against them • Sticky	• Feathery branches catch wind-blown pollen grains
Pollen	• Small amounts produced • Large grains • Rough or sticky surface, which catches on the insects' bodies	• Large amounts produced • Small light grains • Smooth surface, which easily catches the wind

Comparing insect-pollinated flowers and wind-pollinated flowers

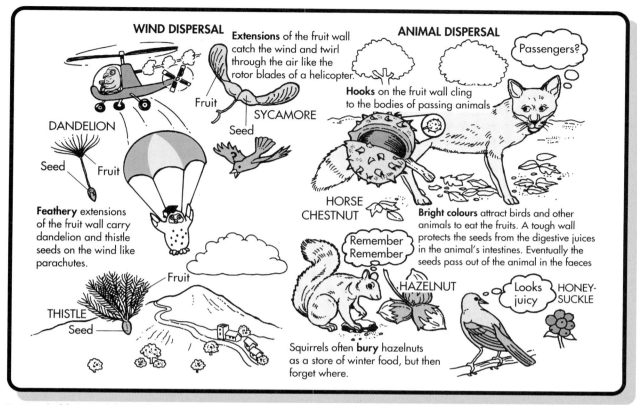

Dispersal of fruits and the seeds they contain

Seeds

A **seed** forms from the fertilised egg. It contains the embryo plant. The tissue that develops from fusion of the male sex nucleus with other cell nuclei in the ovule (see page 123) forms a food store. The embryo plant uses the stored food as a source of energy during its germination and growth into a new plant.

Fruits

After fertilisation, a **fruit** develops from the wall of the **ovary**. The fruit contains the seed. It helps scatter the seed far and wide. The scattering of seed is called **dispersal**.

Question

Why does seed dispersal help plants survive?

So that the plants which grow from the seeds are not overcrowded.

Answers

Methods of seed dispersal

After fertilisation, fruits develop in different ways for different methods of dispersal. The two main ways of dispersal are by **wind** and **animals**. In the figure you can see how a variety of fruits are suited (adapted) for different methods of dispersal.

Coconuts are fruits which contain the seeds of the coconut tree. They float and are dispersed by **water**.

Asexual reproduction

New plants can be reproduced without a male nucleus fusing with a female egg nucleus. Instead, different parts of a *single* plant can develop into new individuals. The parts, called **vegetative** parts, are formed from the **root, leaf** or **stem**. Reproduction from vegetative parts is a form of **asexual reproduction**. New plants come from a single parent and are identical to each other and the parent plant.

Gardeners and farmers depend on plants that can reproduce asexually. Fresh stocks of plants are free of disease and inherit the parent's desirable characteristics such as disease resistance, colour of fruit and/or shape of flower.

Words to remember

You have read some important words in this chapter. Here's a list to remind you what the words in red mean.

Adapted	suited for a particular job or to a particular way of life in a particular environment
Aerobic respiration	uses oxygen to release energy from food
Biomass	describes the mass of living things
Embryo	the early stages of development after fertilisation
Germination	the stages of growth from the embryo plant to the time when the growing plant no longer depends on stored food
Photosynthesis	the chemical reactions that use the light energy trapped by chlorophyll to convert carbon dioxide and water into sugars and oxygen
Tissue	a group of similar cells that are adapted to perform a particular biological task

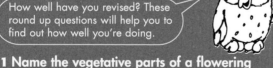

How well have you revised? These round up questions will help you to find out how well you're doing.

1 Name the vegetative parts of a flowering plant. [3]
2 What are the advantages to growers of reproducing crops asexually? [3]
3 The equation summarises the reactions of photosynthesis. Identify gas X and briefly explain what the cells of living things use gas X for. [3]
 Carbon dioxide + water → Sugars + X
4 Briefly explain why most chloroplasts are found in the palisade cells lying just beneath the upper surface of the leaf. [3]

5 Why do plants need the minerals nitrogen, magnesium and iron to grow properly? [2]
6 Water passes through the different parts of a plant. Arrange the parts listed below in the order that correctly describes the passage of water through a plant. [4]
 stem, root hairs, leaves, root

How well did you do? You might want to answer the Test yourself questions again so that you can measure your improvement compared with your first try.

Humans as organisms

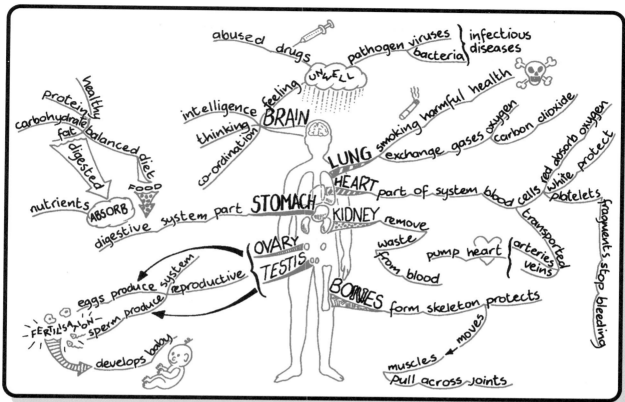

abused drugs pathogen viruses bacteria } infectious diseases

UNWELL feeling

intelligence thinking co-ordination BRAIN

healthy protein carbohydrate fat balanced diet digested FOOD nutrients ABSORB

smoking harmful health

LUNG exchange gases oxygen carbon dioxide

HEART part of system blood cells red absorb oxygen white protect platelets transported fragments stop bleeding

digestive system part STOMACH KIDNEY remove waste from blood pump heart { arteries veins

OVARY TESTIS reproductive system eggs produce sperm produce

FERTILISATION

develops baby

BONES form skeleton protects muscles ← moves pull across joints

How much do you know already? The Mind Map will help you to organise your thoughts and answer the questions below.

Test yourself

1 What is meant by a 'balanced diet'? [3]
2 Why is milk particularly important for strong bones and teeth in babies? [3]
3 The different parts of the intestine are listed below. Re-arrange the words below in the order in which food passes from mouth to anus. [5]
   mouth, rectum, stomach, large intestine, oesophagus, small intestine, anus
4 Explain the relationship between **(a)** lungs and alveoli **(b)** bronchi and bronchioles **(c)** breathing and gaseous exchange. [7]
5 In the table, the different components of blood are listed in column A. Match each component with its correct description in column B. [4]

A	B
Plasma	Absorbs oxygen
Red blood cell	Contains wastes, which are removed by the kidneys
White blood cell	Helps stop bleeding
Platelet	Helps protect the body from disease

6 Complete the following paragraph using the words below. Each word may be used once, more than once or not at all. [6]
   protect, joint, bones, support, contract, shape, muscles
   The _____ of the skeleton _____ and _____ the tissues of the body. The limb bones move because _____ attached to them _____. Where bones meet a _____ is formed.

127

4.1 Diet and digestion

preview

At the end of this section you will:

- **know what makes up a balanced diet**
- **be able to identify the different foods in the diet**
- **know that enzymes help to digest food**
- **understand that the products of digestion are absorbed into the body and that wastes are removed from the body.**

Nutrients are the raw materials which food provides to keep our bodies working properly. The Mind Map opposite summarises the different nutrients needed for healthy living, the role of water and fibre in the diet and some of the substances we add to our diet.

Different foods contain nutrients, water and fibre in different proportions.

A healthy diet is a mixture of foods which together provide enough nutrients, water and fibre for the body to work properly. If all of the components of a diet are eaten in the correct amounts and proportions, then we say that the diet is **balanced**. The figure below gives you the idea. By choosing different foods from each of the food groups you will have a healthy, balanced diet.

Remember the sequence:

nutrient + water + fibre $\xrightarrow{\text{components of}}$ food $\xrightarrow{\text{eaten}}$ diet

Taking in and digesting food

The **intestine** (gut) is a muscular tube through which food moves. Food is taken into the body through the mouth (**ingestion**) and processed as it moves through the intestine. The liver and pancreas also play important parts in processing food.

The intestine, liver and pancreas together make up the **digestive system**. Digestion involves mechanical and chemical processes.

Question

Why must food be digested?

Answer

The molecules of most types of food are too large and insoluble for the body to absorb. **Digestion** breaks down food molecules into smaller molecules which are soluble so that the body can absorb them.

- meat and alternatives to meat such as soya
- milk and products like cheese and yoghurt which are made from milk
- bread and cereals
- fruit and vegetables

VARIETY IS BEST!

The 'basic four' food groups help us to choose a balanced diet. Eat at least one helping from each group daily. Choose different foods from each group for variety

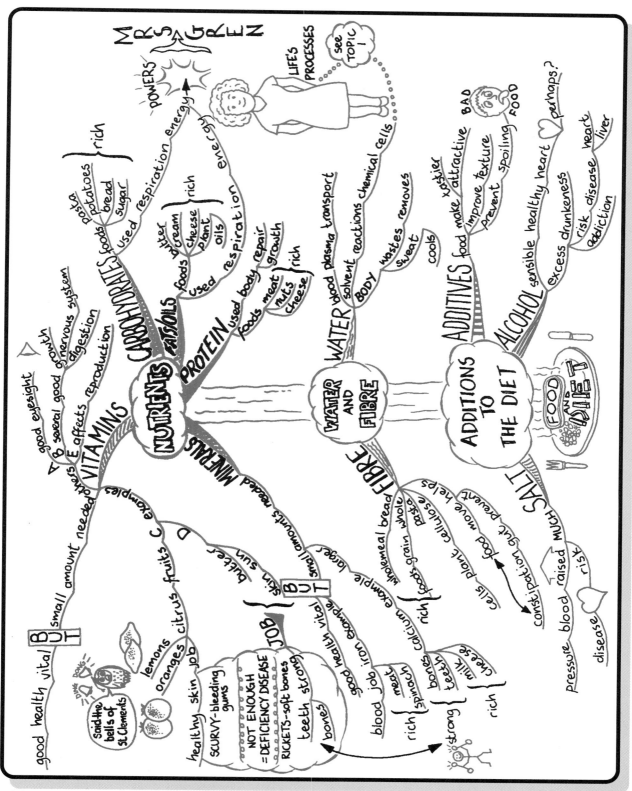

What we eat

Mechanical processes	Chemical processes
Teeth chew food, breaking it into small pieces Contractions of the muscles of the wall of the intestine mix food with digestive juices	Enzymes in digestive juices help break down the large insoluble molecules of food into soluble molecules, which can be absorbed

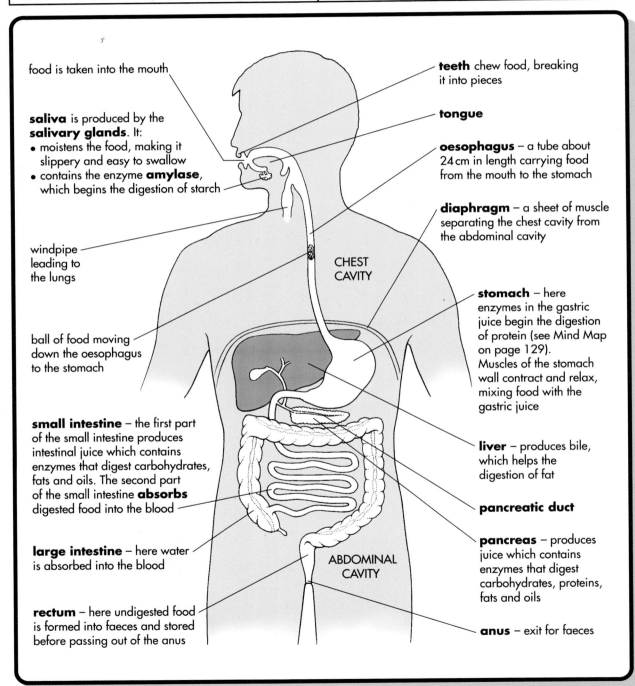

food is taken into the mouth

saliva is produced by the **salivary glands**. It:
• moistens the food, making it slippery and easy to swallow
• contains the enzyme **amylase**, which begins the digestion of starch

windpipe leading to the lungs

ball of food moving down the oesophagus to the stomach

small intestine – the first part of the small intestine produces intestinal juice which contains enzymes that digest carbohydrates, fats and oils. The second part of the small intestine **absorbs** digested food into the blood

large intestine – here water is absorbed into the blood

rectum – here undigested food is formed into faeces and stored before passing out of the anus

teeth chew food, breaking it into pieces

tongue

oesophagus – a tube about 24 cm in length carrying food from the mouth to the stomach

diaphragm – a sheet of muscle separating the chest cavity from the abdominal cavity

CHEST CAVITY

stomach – here enzymes in the gastric juice begin the digestion of protein (see Mind Map on page 129). Muscles of the stomach wall contract and relax, mixing food with the gastric juice

liver – produces bile, which helps the digestion of fat

pancreatic duct

pancreas – produces juice which contains enzymes that digest carbohydrates, proteins, fats and oils

ABDOMINAL CAVITY

anus – exit for faeces

Processing food through the digestive system

Remember the sequence that processes food through the digestive system:

ingestion $\longrightarrow$ **digestion** $\longrightarrow$ **absorption** $\longrightarrow$ **egestion**

food is taken into the mouth / large molecules of food are broken down into smaller molecules / the small molecules of digested food pass into the bloodstream / undigested food is removed from the body through the anus

Absorbing food and removing wastes

The figure below shows that the small intestine is not only where food is digested but also where the digested food is absorbed into the blood. The area available for the absorption of food is increased by:

★ **coiling**, which packs as much small intestine as is possible into the abdominal cavity
★ **folding** of the lining of part of the small intestine.

Undigested food passes to the large intestine (see the figure), where faeces are formed. The faeces are removed from the body through the **anus** – a process called **egestion** (or **defaecation**).

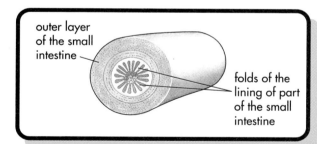

outer layer of the small intestine

folds of the lining of part of the small intestine

Helping absorption of digested food

What does 'absorbed' mean?

Answer

Molecules of digested food pass through the wall of the intestine into the bloodstream.

4.2 Blood

preview

At the end of this section you will:
● **understand that blood carries (transports) different substances to and from the tissues and organs of the body**
● **know that the heart pumps blood through a system of blood vessels called arteries and veins**
● **understand that the substances carried in blood are exchanged between the blood and tissues at the capillaries.**

Blood is a liquid tissue which contains different types of cell. The cells are suspended in a solution called **plasma** (see the figure on page 101).

★ **Red blood cells** contain the red pigment called **haemoglobin**, which absorbs oxygen.
★ **White blood cells** protect the body from disease.
★ **Platelets** help stop bleeding by starting to form a clot.
★ **Plasma** is 90% water with 10% of materials dissolved in it. These include:
  ● foods, vitamins and enzymes
  ● wastes, which are removed by the kidneys (excretion).

Blood carries oxygen, digested food and other substances to the parts of the body that need them. Blood also carries carbon dioxide and other waste substances produced by the activities of cells (see Topic 1) away from the tissues and organs of the body.

In other words – blood **transports** substances around the body.

★ The walls of capillary blood vessels are very thin. Substances therefore easily pass between blood in the capillaries and the surrounding tissues.
★ Lots of capillaries form **networks** in the tissues of the body. Cells therefore are never very far away from a capillary.
★ The blood in capillaries supplies nearby cells with oxygen, food and other substances. It also carries away carbon dioxide and other wastes produced by the activities of cells.

The capillaries are where blood does its work. Arteries carry blood *from* the heart to capillaries; veins carry blood from capillaries *to* the heart.

Moving blood

The heart pumps blood around the body through a system of tubes called **arteries** and **veins**. Capillaries join arteries to veins.

Capillaries are tiny.

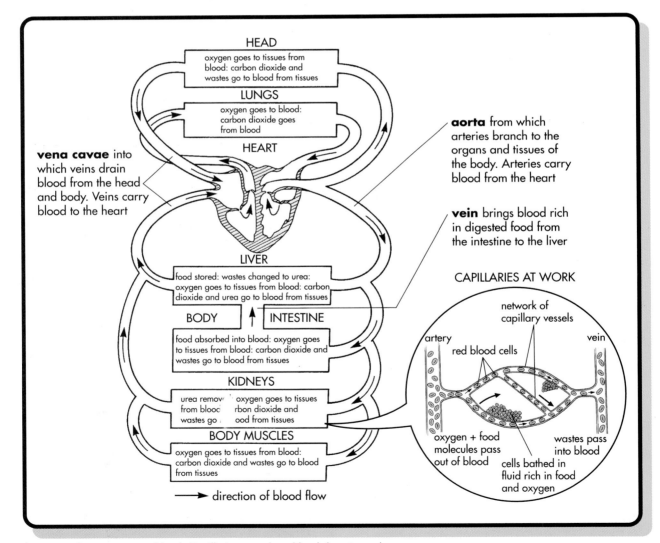

Arteries and veins transport blood. Capillaries are where blood does its work

4.3 Let's move it!

preview

At the end of this section you will:
- **know the relationship between the skeleton, joints and muscles**
- **understand the idea of pairs of antagonistic muscles.**

The human skeleton is made of bones. It **supports** the body and gives it **shape**. It also provides surfaces to which muscles can **attach**. When muscles **contract** (shorten) they pull on the skeleton, moving it.

Remember the sequence:

$$\text{muscles contract} \xrightarrow{\text{pull}} \text{skeleton} \longrightarrow \text{moves}$$

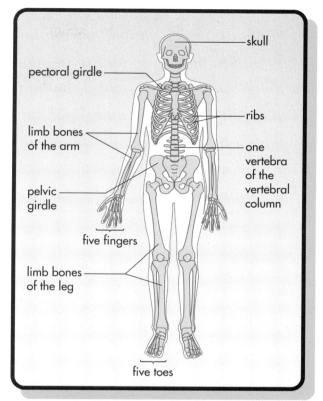

The human skeleton

The top figure shows the human skeleton. Notice that the skull, vertebral column (backbone), ribs and girdles form a central framework which

★ **protects** delicate tissues and organs
★ has **attached** to it the limb bones of the arms and legs.

Joints are formed where the bones of the skeleton connect to one another.

★ **Sutures** are fixed joints, for example the bones of the skull.
★ **Synovial joints** allow considerable freedom of movement:
  • ball and socket joints are formed where the upper limb bones meet their respective girdles
  • hinge joints are formed at the elbow and knee.

You can see the structure of the elbow joint in the bottom figure. Notice that friction in the joint is reduced to a minimum. Also notice that strap-like **ligaments** hold the bones of a joint together.

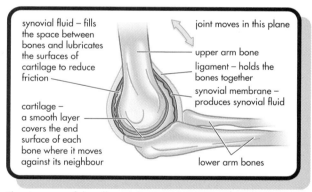

The structure of the elbow joint

Muscles in action

Contracting muscles pull on bones. One muscle will pull a bone in one direction; another muscle will pull the same bone in the opposite direction. In other words, muscles work in pairs, where one muscle of the pair has the opposite effect to its partner. These opposing muscles are called **antagonistic pairs**. The figure on the next page shows you the idea.

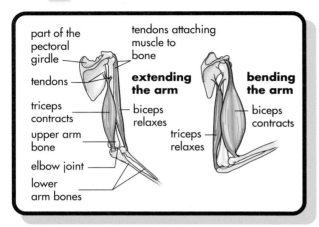

The biceps muscle and triceps muscle stretch across the joint. They work as an antagonistic pair of muscles moving the lower arm by bringing about rotation around the elbow joint

4.4 Having a baby

preview

At the end of this section you will:

- **know that physical and emotional changes take place as you grow up**
- **be able to identify the different parts of the human reproductive system**
- **understand how a baby develops inside its mother.**

The time line below shows the stages signposting human growth and development. The onset of adolescence is marked by the development of **secondary sexual characteristics**, which are the physical features that help us tell the difference between boys and girls. Different types of hormones help to develop and maintain the secondary sexual characteristics, which are summarised in the table.

Adolescence (including the teenage years) is a period of physical change. Feelings of sexual attraction to other people may also produce emotional turmoil. Many adolescents have sexual feelings at some time in their growing up. Talking about sexual feelings with someone you trust often helps keep a sense of balance in relationships.

The human reproductive system

A man and woman together produce a baby by **sexual reproduction**. Their reproductive systems are shown on the next page.

During sexual intercourse the man's erect **penis** is placed inside the woman's **vagina**. Movement stimulates the penis and results in **ejaculation**. Sperm enter the **uterus** and swim along the tubes

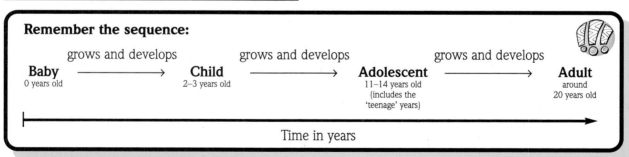

Remember the sequence:

Baby 0 years old — grows and develops → Child 2–3 years old — grows and develops → Adolescent 11–14 years old (includes the 'teenage' years) — grows and develops → Adult around 20 years old

Time in years

Boys	Girls
Pubic hair develops around the penis and testes	Pubic hair develops around the opening to the vagina
Penis becomes larger	Breasts develop and fat is laid down around the thighs
Voice breaks and develops a deeper (lower) sound	Menstruation ('periods') starts, usually with the release of an egg from one of the ovaries every 28 days
Hair grows under the arms and on the chest, face and legs	Hair grows under the arms

Developing secondary sexual characteristics

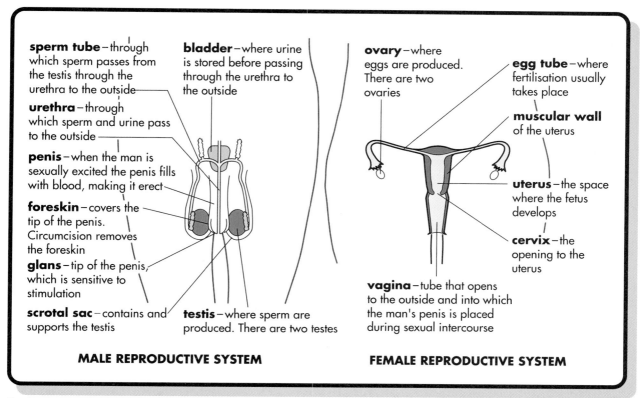

sperm tube – through which sperm passes from the testis through the urethra to the outside

urethra – through which sperm and urine pass to the outside

penis – when the man is sexually excited the penis fills with blood, making it erect

foreskin – covers the tip of the penis. Circumcision removes the foreskin

glans – tip of the penis, which is sensitive to stimulation

scrotal sac – contains and supports the testis

bladder – where urine is stored before passing through the urethra to the outside

testis – where sperm are produced. There are two testes

MALE REPRODUCTIVE SYSTEM

ovary – where eggs are produced. There are two ovaries

egg tube – where fertilisation usually takes place

muscular wall of the uterus

uterus – the space where the fetus develops

cervix – the opening to the uterus

vagina – tube that opens to the outside and into which the man's penis is placed during sexual intercourse

FEMALE REPRODUCTIVE SYSTEM

The human reproductive system

that connect the ovaries to the uterus. If an egg is present then one of the sperm may enter the egg and **fertilise** it. This is the moment of **conception**, and the woman is now **pregnant**. The figure below shows you what happens next.

The fetus develops *inside* the uterus. Oxygen, food and wastes are exchanged between the mother and the fetus through the **placenta**. The **umbilical cord** attaches the fetus to the placenta.

SPERM AND EGGS Page 100.

Being born

Birth usually occurs about 9 months after conception, when development is complete and the baby is fully grown. Babies born before 9 months are said to be **premature**. Providing birth doesn't happen too early, premature babies have a good chance of survival.

At birth the bag of watery liquid surrounding the baby bursts. Powerful contractions of the muscles of the wall of the uterus propel the baby, usually head first, through the vagina.

Being born is quite a shock, and stimulates the baby to start breathing. The placenta comes away from the uterus wall and passes out through the vagina as the **afterbirth**. The umbilical cord is clamped and cut near to the point where it joins the baby. Cutting the umbilical cord does not hurt the baby.

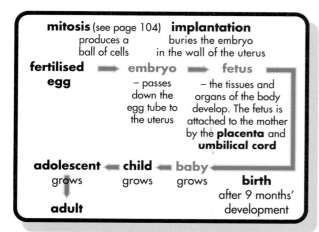

mitosis (see page 104) produces a ball of cells

implantation buries the embryo in the wall of the uterus

fertilised egg ➡ embryo – passes down the egg tube to the uterus ➡ fetus – the tissues and organs of the body develop. The fetus is attached to the mother by the **placenta** and **umbilical cord**

adolescent grows ⬅ child grows ⬅ baby grows ⬅ birth after 9 months' development

adult

Development of the fertilised egg

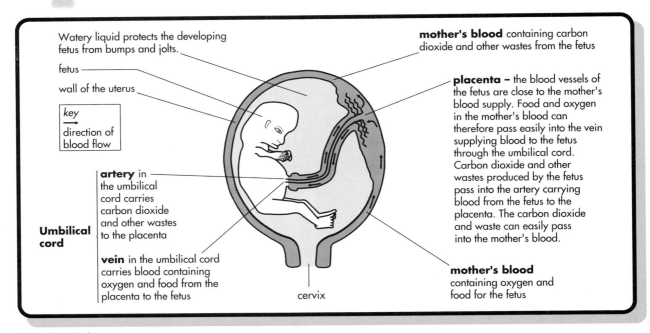

Watery liquid protects the developing fetus from bumps and jolts.

fetus

wall of the uterus

key
→
direction of blood flow

artery in the umbilical cord carries carbon dioxide and other wastes to the placenta

Umbilical cord

vein in the umbilical cord carries blood containing oxygen and food from the placenta to the fetus

cervix

mother's blood containing carbon dioxide and other wastes from the fetus

placenta – the blood vessels of the fetus are close to the mother's blood supply. Food and oxygen in the mother's blood can therefore pass easily into the vein supplying blood to the fetus through the umbilical cord. Carbon dioxide and other wastes produced by the fetus pass into the artery carrying blood from the fetus to the placenta. The carbon dioxide and waste can easily pass into the mother's blood.

mother's blood containing oxygen and food for the fetus

Caring for the fetus

4.5 The air we breathe

preview

At the end of this section you will:
- **know how the exchange of gases takes place in the lungs**
- **understand how smoking affects the lungs.**

Breathing in (**inhalation**) takes the gases of the atmosphere into the lungs. Breathing out (**exhalation**) removes gases from the lungs. The table shows you that there is less oxygen and more carbon dioxide in exhaled air than in inhaled air. Why? The figure explains the reasons and shows that oxygen and carbon dioxide are exchanged between the lungs and the blood. It also shows that aerobic respiration is responsible for the changed proportions of gases in inhaled and exhaled air.

Taking in oxygen for aerobic respiration and removing carbon dioxide produced by aerobic respiration is called **gaseous exchange**. The figure on page 137 shows you how gaseous exchange takes place in the lungs.

Gas	Amount in inhaled air (%)	Amount in exhaled air (%)
Nitrogen	78	78
Oxygen	21	16
Noble gases	1	1
Carbon dioxide	0.03	3
Water vapour	0	1

Differences between inhaled and exhaled air

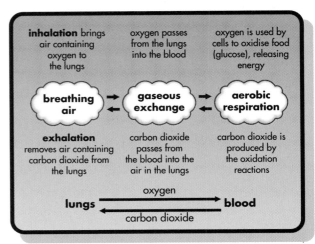

inhalation brings air containing oxygen to the lungs

oxygen passes from the lungs into the blood

oxygen is used by cells to oxidise food (glucose), releasing energy

breathing air → gaseous exchange → aerobic respiration

exhalation removes air containing carbon dioxide from the lungs

carbon dioxide passes from the blood into the air in the lungs

carbon dioxide is produced by the oxidation reactions

oxygen
lungs ⟶ blood
carbon dioxide

Relationship between breathing, gaseous exchange and aerobic respiration

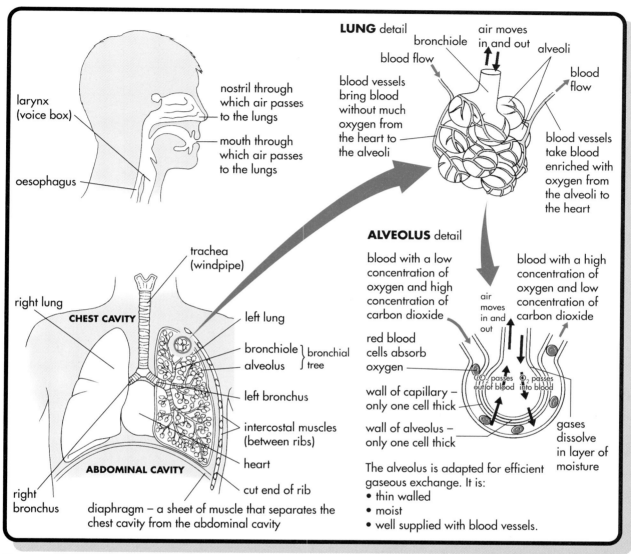

Gaseous exchange in the lungs

Smoking

Cigarette smoking is a major cause of disease, especially **lung cancer, heart disease** and **emphysema**. The damage is done by various substances in cigarette smoke.

★ **nicotine** is a powerful drug which increases the heart rate and blood pressure

> **Risk factor** – nicotine increases the risk of heart disease.

★ **carbon monoxide** is a gas which combines with the haemoglobin (see page 131) in red blood cells much more readily than with oxygen. As a result the heart has to work harder to supply the tissues and organs of the body with oxygen

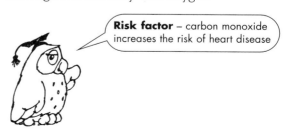

> **Risk factor** – carbon monoxide increases the risk of heart disease

★ **tar** is a mixture of substances, some of which cause cancer

Risk factor – tar increases the risk of developing lung cancer and other types of cancer

Emphysema is caused by repeated coughing, which destroys the walls of the alveoli. As a result the absorption of oxygen into the body is reduced and the person becomes breathless trying to make up for the loss.

Question

Why do many smokers cough?

Answer

Substances in cigarette smoke stop the cells lining the trachea from working properly. As a result mucus (**phlegm**) builds up and smokers cough in an attempt to remove it.

Today there are fewer smokers than non-smokers in the United Kingdom. However, of the people who do smoke there are many young people (especially girls).

Smoking is a mug's game – don't start!

If you do smoke, you can give it up – advice and help are available.

4.6 Drug facts

preview

At the end of this section you will:
● **know that the abuse of alcohol, solvents and other drugs affects health.**

Doctors provide different drugs to help people fight disease and control pain (see page 139). However, some drugs are highly addictive and may be abused.

Alcohol

Ethanol (the alcohol in alcoholic drinks) affects the brain. Small amounts of alcohol may increase confidence and reduce inhibitions but alcohol slows the speed of reactions, making the drinker clumsier. Vision and behaviour are also affected. All this makes drinking and driving particularly dangerous. The law imposes limits on the amount of alcohol that a driver can have before being 'over the limit'.

The amount of alcohol people drink is measured in units, which are shown in the figure below. But deciding the 'safe' limits for the number of units a person can drink is difficult because each person's body uses up alcohol at different rates. However, everyone agrees that drinking alcohol affects driving ability.

Units of alcohol

Solvents

Glue, paints, nail varnish and cleaning fluids (dry cleaners) contain **solvents** (see page 11), which readily produce a vapour at room temperature. Breathing them in gives a warm sense of well-being but also makes people act in completely irrational ways – for example, jumping out of windows or running into a stream of traffic. Long-term solvent abuse can damage the brain, kidneys and liver.

Other drugs

Depressants slow down a person's reactions. Alcohol and heroin are examples. **Heroin** is made from a chemical substance found in poppy plants.

Stimulants are drugs that speed up a person's reactions. The nicotine in tobacco (see page 137) is an example; cocaine is another. **Cocaine** is made from the leaves of the coca shrub, which grows in South America.

Hallucinogens are drugs that produce sensations of false reality (**hallucinations**). Solvents are hallucinogens, so is **cannabis** (marijuana). Cannabis is made from the leaves of the cannabis plant.

Like smoking, doing drugs is a mug's game – don't start!

4.7 Feeling unwell

preview

At the end of this section you will:
- **know that bacteria and viruses can affect health**
- **understand how immunisation and medicines help the body to fight disease.**

Many infectious diseases are caused by **microorganisms**. For example:

★ **bacteria** – different types cause cholera, typhoid fever, tuberculosis, syphilis, gonorrhoea.
★ **viruses** – different types cause AIDS, 'flu', poliomyelitis, German measles.

Organisms that cause disease are called **pathogens**.

Viruses are very small structures that can't reproduce unless they infect cells. Bacteria are also very small but not as small as viruses. They can live and grow outside cells. Because viruses and bacteria are so small, they are called microorganisms.

People infected with pathogenic microorganisms feel unwell because the pathogens rapidly reproduce and release large amounts of poisonous substances (**toxins**) into the body. The toxins cause the signs (**symptoms**) of the disease.

Fighting disease

The figure shows the body's natural defences against disease. Physical and chemical barriers keep us healthy for most of our lives.

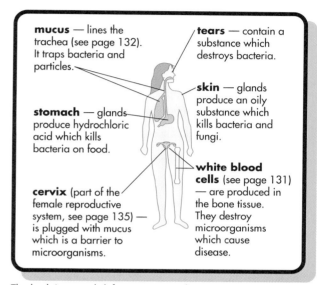

The body's natural defences against disease

Sometimes the body needs help to fight pathogens. **Chemotherapy** means that doctors provide drugs to help people combat the pathogens that make them unwell. For example, **antibiotic** drugs attack bacteria that cause disease:

★ **penicillin** is an antibiotic that kills bacteria
★ **tetracycline** is an antibiotic that prevents bacteria from multiplying.

Unfortunately, antibiotics do not affect viruses. Few drugs do, but there are exciting developments. For example, zidovudine (AZT) prevents the **human immunodeficiency virus** (**HIV**), which causes **AIDS**, from reproducing.

The action of white blood cells against pathogens is called an **immune reaction**. The responses give the infected person an **active immunity**. **Immunisation** (or **vaccination**) boosts a person's active immunity against a particular infection by means of an injection, or a substance to swallow. The substance injected or swallowed is a **vaccine**.

Words to remember

You have read some important words in this chapter. Here's a list to remind you what the words in red mean.

Absorption of food	molecules of food pass through the wall of the intestine into the bloodstream
Addiction to drugs	a person's craving for particular drugs without caring about the damage the drugs may cause
Aerobic respiration	uses oxygen to release energy from food
Baby	a fully developed fetus ready to be born
Diet	what we eat and drink
Drug abuse	the non-medical use of drugs
Embryo	the early stages of development after fertilisation. After a few weeks it develops into the fetus
Enzymes	catalysts made by living cells. Different enzymes help to speed up the digestion of food
Faeces	the semi-solid undigested remains of food from which water has been reabsorbed into the body from the large intestine
Fetus	the stage of development during which the tissues and organs of the body are formed
Hormones	chemicals produced and released by different tissues into the bloodstream
Infectious	pathogens that can be passed from one person to another
Tissue	a group of similar cells that are adapted to perform a particular biological task

round-up

How much can you remember? Check out your score on page 152.

1 Different components of the diet are listed below:
carbohydrate, protein, fibre, additive
Study the list and answer the following questions. **(a)** Which component helps move food through the intestine? **(b)** Which component is a major source of energy? **(c)** Which component is important for the repair and growth of the body? **(d)** Which component helps to make food tastier? **[4]**

2 Match the process in column A with its correct description in column B. **[4]**

A	B
Ingestion	The removal of undigested food through the anus
Digestion	Food is taken into the mouth
Absorption	Food is broken down into soluble substances
Egestion	Digested food passes into the bloodstream

3 Match each item of food in column A with its correct description in column B. **[4]**

A	B
Fruit	Source of fibre
Bread	Source of vitamin C
Meat	Source of calcium
Milk	Source of protein

round-up

4 Match each structure in column A with its correct description in column B. [3]

A	B
Intercostal muscle	One of two tubes that branch from the trachea
Diaphragm	Attached to the ribs
Bronchus	Sheet of muscle that separates the chest cavity from the abdominal cavity

5 The parts of the body through which air passes to the alveoli of the lungs are listed below. The sequence begins with the nose and ends at the alveoli. Arrange the other parts in their correct sequence. [3]
nose, bronchioles, trachea, bronchi, alveoli

6 Drugs that are abused have different effects on the body. Match the type of drug listed in column A with its effect on the body in column B. [3]

A	B
Stimulants	Slow down a person's reactions
Hallucinogens	Speed up a person's reactions
Depressants	Give a false sense of reality

7 The diagram shows the reproductive system of a man. **(a)** In which part are sperm produced? **(b)** Which part fills with blood, making the penis erect? **(c)** Name the parts labelled A–E. [7]

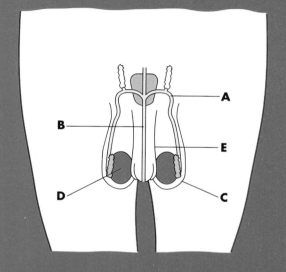

How did you do? Don't worry too much if you couldn't remember everything. Take a break and try again.

Living things vary

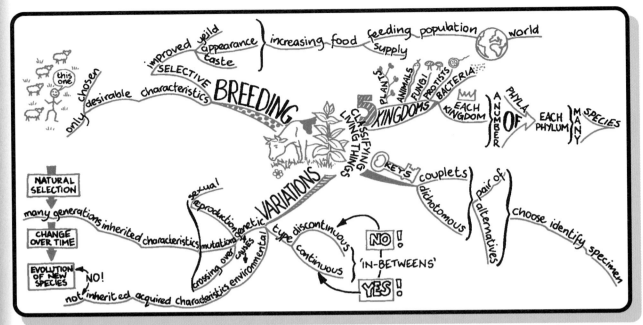

How much do you know already? The Mind Map will help you to organise your thoughts and answer the questions below.

Test yourself

1 Complete the paragraph below using the words provided. Each word may be used once, more than once or not at all. [6]

jointed, ten, exoskeleton, two, wings, three

The body of an insect is divided into _____ parts. The body of a spider is divided into _____ parts. Insects and spiders have _____ legs for walking. Insects also have _____ to help them move from place to place. Spiders do not have _____. An _____ surrounds the body of insects and spiders.

2 What does the word 'dichotomous' mean? [1]

3 Look at the different fruits in the figure in the next column. Using their appearances, make a key written in couplets. [6]

4 List the characteristics that make an apple different from a strawberry. [2]

5.1 Classifying the variety of life

preview

At the end of this section you will:

- **know that Earth is home to millions of different types of living things**

- **be able to put living things into groups according to the features they have in common**

- **understand the words species, phylum and kingdom**

- **be able to identify living things using a key.**

The word species is used to describe a particular type of living thing. About 5 million species have been described so far – but scientists estimate that millions more have yet to be discovered.

LIVING THINGS IN THEIR ENVIRONMENT Page 107.

You and I might be different in some ways, but we also have similar features.

Classification

Owl seems to be very different from you and me – for example, Owl is covered with feathers; we are hairy. However, we also have features in common. One feature is a **backbone**, which supports the body.

Living things that have features in common are grouped together. For example, animals with backbones are called **vertebrates**. The word **phylum** is used to describe a group of living things that share a feature as important as a backbone. Organising things into groups is called **classification**. Different phyla (plural of phylum) come together into a still larger grouping called a **kingdom**. There are five kingdoms. Living things in each kingdom obtain food in different ways. Each kingdom therefore represents a way of life which all its members share. The figure on pages 144–145 shows the major phyla in the Animal kingdom and Plant kingdom.

The other kingdoms are

Kingdom Fungi – living things made up of thread-like cells.

FUNGI AND DECOMPOSITION Page 110.

Kingdom Protista – single-celled living things.

Kingdom Bacteria – single-celled living things. The cell body is simple in structure compared with the cell body of protists.

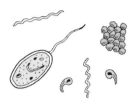

Keys

A **key** is a route to giving a name to something you want to identify. Practice in using keys makes the job of identifying **specimens** easier. Looking at the figure on page 142 will help you.

The descriptions of the fruit in the drawings opposite are clues to identifying the different fruits whose external features are illustrated. Each set of clues makes up the key. Each pair of statements is called a **couplet**. Choose one statement from the couplet. Then follow the description to the next couplet. By working through the key in this way you arrive at a statement that identifies the specimen. Here is a simple key for identifying different fruits:

1 Hairy skin? – GOOSEBERRY
   Non-hairy skin? – Go to 2

2 Pips on the fruit's surface? – STRAWBERRY
   No pips on the fruit's surface? – Go to 3

3 Nearly spherical in shape? – Go to 4
   Other shape? – BANANA

4 Smooth surface? – APPLE
   Rough surface? – Go to 5

5 Fruit made up of sub-units? – BLACKBERRY
   Fruit made up of one unit? – ORANGE

Alternative statements may also be presented as a **chart**. In the figure on page 146, the chart branches into two statements – the chart is **dichotomous**.

5

The body is surrounded by an armour-like **exoskeleton**. Jointed legs are used for walking, swimming, gathering food and other activities

Spiders: the body is made up of two parts. There are 8 legs.

Crustacea: the body is made up of two parts. Woodlice are crustaceans, they have 14 legs.

Insects: the body is made up of three parts. Flies are insects. Each fly has 6 legs and wings.

Worms
The body is long and thin. It is made up of many segments.

Cnidarians
The body has no front or rear. Its parts are arranged evenly in the round. Tentacles catch food.

Fish
The body is covered with scales. Fins control the position of the body in water. Gills are used for 'breathing'.

Birds
The body is covered with feathers which make flying possible, keep in heat and keep out water. Birds lay eggs, protected by a hard shell.

Amphibians
Live on land but breed in water. The young are swimming tadpoles. Development of young into the adult is called a **metamorphosis**. The soft skin loses water easily in dry air.

Reptiles
The skin is dry and covered with scales that restrict water loss from the body. Reptiles lay eggs, each protected by a hard shell.

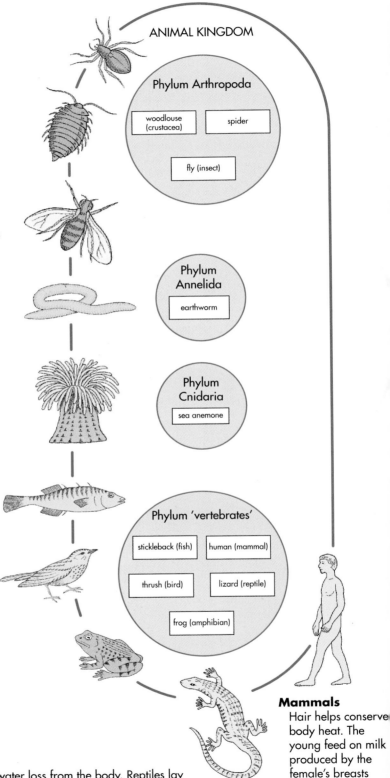

ANIMAL KINGDOM

Phylum Arthropoda
- woodlouse (crustacea)
- spider
- fly (insect)

Phylum Annelida
- earthworm

Phylum Cnidaria
- sea anemone

Phylum 'vertebrates'
- stickleback (fish)
- human (mammal)
- thrush (bird)
- lizard (reptile)
- frog (amphibian)

Mammals
Hair helps conserve body heat. The young feed on milk produced by the female's breasts (mammary glands).

The major groups of the Animal kingdom and the Plant kingdom, with an example of each. Each major group of plants is called a division rather than a phylum.

Mosses

Mosses live in damp places because they quickly lose water in dry air. Each plant is short and grows from a **spore**. There are no roots and water is soaked up the plant by the leaves. Underground extensions called **rhizoids** anchor the moss plant.

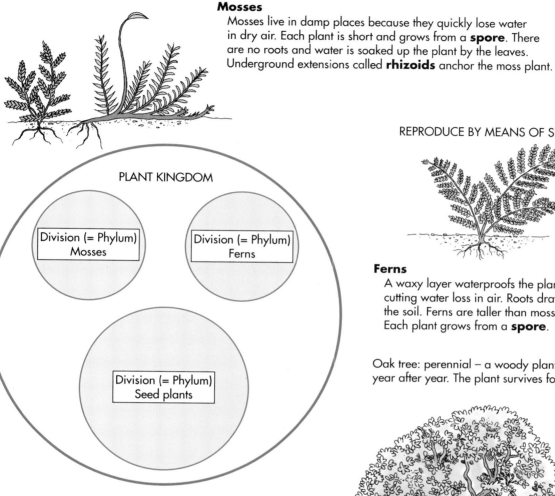

PLANT KINGDOM

Division (= Phylum)
Mosses

Division (= Phylum)
Ferns

Division (= Phylum)
Seed plants

REPRODUCE BY MEANS OF SPORES

Ferns

A waxy layer waterproofs the plant's surfaces, cutting water loss in air. Roots draw water from the soil. Ferns are taller than mosses. Each plant grows from a **spore**.

Oak tree: perennial – a woody plant that seeds year after year. The plant survives for many years.

REPRODUCE BY MEANS OF SEEDS

Forget-me-not: a non-woody plant that flowers and produces seed in one growing season. The plant then dies.

Flowering plants

A waxy layer waterproofs the plant's surfaces, cutting water loss in dry air. Roots draw water from the soil. Each plant grows from a **seed** contained in a **fruit**. Seeds and fruits are produced by **flowers**, which carry the male and female sex organs (Section 3.3). Trees are flowering plants and may be tall because wood supports the stem, forming a stout trunk.

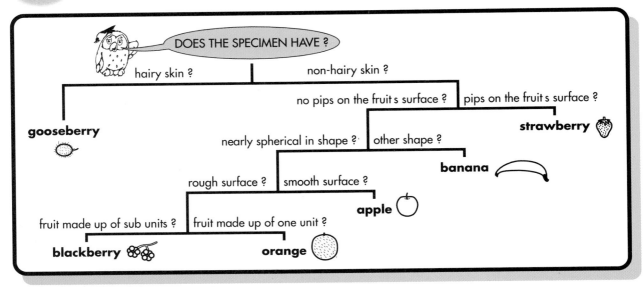

Key chart for identifying fruits

5.2 Variation

preview

At the end of this section you will:
- **know that there is variation between individuals of the same species and between individuals of different species**
- **understand the difference between continuous and discontinuous variation**
- **know that variation between different species is the result of natural selection and evolution.**

When next you are in a crowd, look closely at the people near to you. Notice the different colours of skin, hair and eyes and the differently shaped faces. Everyone (except identical twins) differs in the features that make up our physical appearance.

Even though people vary, humans all belong to one species. It's the same with owls. My friend flying the helicopter on page 125 may have a slightly longer beak and 'browner' feathers than I have but we belong to the same species.

Variation between individuals of the same species

Some variations may arise from **genetic** causes, others arise from environmental causes.

Genetic causes

★ **Sexual reproduction** involves the fusion of the nucleus of a sperm with the nucleus of an egg. The process, called **fertilisation** (see pages 122 and 135), recombines the genetic material from each parent in new ways.

Remember that the **genetic code** (carried by the genetic material) contains the information that cells need to do their job properly.

GENETIC CODE
Page 104.

★ **Mutations** arise from mistakes in the replication of chromosomes and their genes. A mutation changes the information that cells are given to do their job. The wrong message may cause the cell to work abnormally or even kill it.

★ **Crossing over** sometimes occurs between chromosomes. Each chromosome swaps a length of genetic material with another chromosome.

Environmental causes

★ The amount of **food** we eat affects our height and weight. Generally people are taller and heavier than people were 50 years ago.
★ **Drugs** may affect development of a baby, causing abnormalities.
★ **Temperature** increase may improve the rate of growth of plants.
★ **Physical training** helps to develop muscles.

Inherited and acquired variations

Variations that arise from genetic causes are inherited by offspring from their parents. Variations that arise from environmental causes are not inherited and so do not affect the offspring. These variations are **acquired**. For example, a weightlifter may have bulging muscles but his or her children will not be born with bulging muscles. When the child grows up, training with weights to develop ('acquire') a muscular body will be just as important as it was for their parent.

Continuous and discontinuous variation

The variation shown by some characteristics is spread over a range of values. We say that the characteristic shows **continuous variation**. The height of people is an example. A few people are either very short or very tall and there is a full range of 'in-betweens'. In other words, people cannot be put into 'height groups' that are distinctly different from one another – there is a full range of heights possible from one extreme (short) to the other (tall).

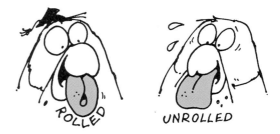

Variation in the height of the adult human population – an example of continuous variation

Try to roll your tongue. Are you a tongue roller like Owl or can't you manage the trick, even though you try and try? Tongue rolling is a characteristic that

shows **discontinuous variation**. There are no 'in-betweens'. You can either roll your tongue or you can't – there are no half-rollers!

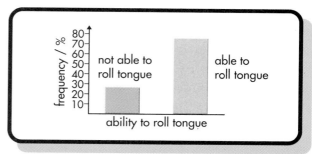

Ability to roll the tongue is an example of discontinuous variation

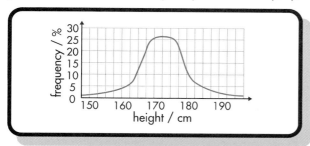

Variation between different species

Owl and Seagull are both birds but they belong to separate species. The variation between Owl and Seagull is much more obvious than differences in height or the ability to roll your tongue. How is it that Owl and Seagull are so different?

About 155 million years ago early types of bird were flying the skies of Earth, which was dominated by dinosaurs and other types of reptile. The different features of these early birds varied. Some features suited birds to follow a particular way of life, such as pouncing on prey. Other features suited birds to another way of life – for example, tapping plant stems for insects. Successful variations of features helped individuals to survive and reproduce. The process is called natural selection. The genes controlling the successful variations of features were therefore inherited by offspring ... and so on for many generations. Features gradually changed. For example, some birds became more and more suited to catching fish. Seagulls are their modern-day descendants. Other birds became more and more suited to catching mice. Owls are their modern-day descendants.

Question

Is there a word to describe 'best suited to survive'?

Answer

Yes! The word is **adapted**.

The natural selection of favourable variations over many generations produces change. The process of change is called **evolution**. It means that present-day living things are descended from ancestors that were different from them.

Although the figure opposite shows that different species of birds are different from one another as a result of natural selection and evolution, they are related because of their descent from a **common ancestor**.

5.3 Selective breeding

preview

At the end of this section you will:

- **understand how humans have used the variation in plants and animals to improve the production and quality of food**
- **know that selective breeding produces improvements over a number of generations.**

Ever since people began farming (around 10,000 years ago), we have taken advantage of the large amount of variation in the characteristics of food plants and animals. By choosing the characteristics they want to be passed on to the next generation, farmers have produced more grain, sweeter fruit, more meat and milk, more of … everything to feed a growing human population.

Owl and Seagull are suited to different ways of life

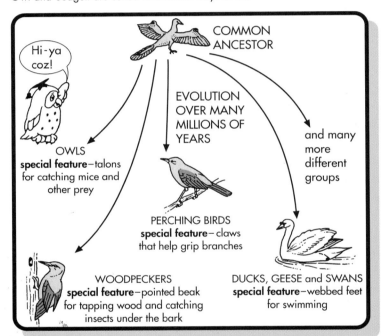

Different groups of birds, each adapted to a particular way of life, have evolved from a common ancestor which lived millions of years ago

Question

How have farmers produced more food?

Answer

The plants and animals which are 'super yielders' have been chosen by humans to breed new generations of 'super yielders'.

Selective breeding (or **artificial selection**) is the process of choosing 'super yielders' and breeding from them to produce new generations of 'super yielders'.

Selective breeding of a variety of apple for eating

Because of selective breeding we have a range of different types of food selected for sweetness, leanness, appearance, crunchiness and all of the other characteristics of food that we enjoy eating.

Words to remember

You have read some important words in this chapter. Here's a list to remind you what the words in red mean.

Adapted suited for a particular job or to a particular way of life in a particular environment

Natural selection the process that favours the individuals in a group with the features that best suit them to survive. Less well-suited individuals leave fewer offspring or die before they can reproduce

Species a group of individuals able to mate to reproduce offspring, which themselves are able to mate and reproduce

Variation the word used to describe the differences

In choosing the individuals that are to produce the next generation, humans are choosing the genes (see page 104) controlling the desired characteristics to be passed on to the offspring. The figure shows you the idea.

Apples have other desirable characteristics which have been ignored in the figure. The diagram only tracks the process of selecting apples that are good for eating. For example, medium-sweet apples may be 'good' for cooking, sour apples 'good' for making jam … and so on. By choosing different characteristics that make for 'good' eating (or cooking or jamming), different types of apple have been developed to suit different tastes.

Farmers have also selected animals with desirable characteristics through selective breeding over many generations – for example, cattle that provide large amounts of milk, pigs that produce lean (low fat)

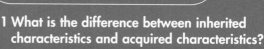

How well have you revised? You may want to look at the Test yourself questions again so that you can measure how you've improved.

1 What is the difference between inherited characteristics and acquired characteristics? [2]

2 Match the kingdom in column A with the correct description of its members in column B. [3]

A	B
Fungi	Single-celled living things
Plants	Made up of thread-like cells
Bacteria	Grow from seeds

3 What is the difference between continuous variation and discontinuous variation? [5]

4 What is the difference between natural selection and artificial selection? [5]

Answers

Topic 1 Life's processes and cells

Test yourself
1

Cell structure	Plant cell	Animal cell
Cell membrane	✓	✓
Cell wall	✓	
Cytoplasm	✓	✓
Nucleus	✓	✓
Chloroplast	✓	
Mitochondrion	✓	✓
Large vacuole	✓	

(7✓)

2 The cilia of ciliated cells are fine hairs which sway to and fro (✓), moving mucus and other substances along (✓). A sperm cell has a tail which lashes from side to side (✓), enabling it to swim (✓). The extension of the root hair cell increases the surface area (✓) available for the absorption of water (✓).

3 Membrane, cytoplasm, nucleus, mitochondria, chloroplasts, vacuole. (6✓)

4 All living things are made of cells (✓). The functions of an organism (the way it works) depend on the functions of its cells (allow tissues/organs) (✓). The more you know about the structure and function of cells (allow tissues/organs), the more you can know about the whole living thing (allow organism) (✓).

Total = 22 marks

Round-up
1

A	B
Mitochondrion	Where energy is released from the oxidation of glucose
Cell membrane	Allows substances to pass into and out of the cell
Chloroplast	Where light energy is captured
Cell wall	Made of a substance called cellulose
Nucleus	Controls the cell at work

(5✓)

2

Animal cells and plant cells	Plant cells only
Nucleus	Cell wall
Cell membrane	Large vacuole
Mitochondria	Chloroplasts
Cytoplasm	

(7✓)

3 Cells, tissues, organs, organ systems, living things. (5✓)

4 **a)** Photosynthesis (✓), chloroplasts (✓). **b)** Aerobic respiration (✓), occurs in mitochondria (✓). **c)** Photosynthesis releases oxygen into the environment (✓). Aerobic respiration uses the oxygen to oxidise sugar (✓), releasing energy (✓).

Total = 24 marks

Topic 2 Living things in their environment

Test yourself
1

A	B
Habitat	The place where a group of organisms lives in the community
Community	All of the organisms that live in a particular environment
Population	A group of individuals of the same species

(3✓)

2 Prey are eaten (✓) by predators (✓). Dead prey and predators are eaten by scavengers (✓).

3 Most animals eat more than one type of plant or other animal (✓). A food web shows the range of different foods eaten (✓).

4 Plants produce food by photosynthesis (✓). Animals consume this food directly when they eat plants (✓) or indirectly when they eat other animals (✓) that depend on plants for food (✓).

5 Each tree is large and can meet the food needs of many organisms (✓). However, the pyramid of numbers does not take the size of a tree into account (✓).

6 **a)** Grasses (✓). Their shallow roots do not reach the water table (✓) when the soil dries out in the dry season (✓). **b)** Plants are able to tolerate high levels of water loss during the dry season (✓) and revive in the wet season (✓) (e.g. the Resurrection plant). Plants survive as seeds during the dry season (✓). The seeds germinate and grow into new plants during the wet season (✓). **c)** Acacia tree (✓). Its deep roots (✓) reach the layer of soil that is saturated with water all of the time (✓).

7 A: few individuals (✓), population growth is slow (✓); B: more individuals (✓), population growth is proportional to numbers (accept exponential) (✓); C: limiting factors (✓) slow down population growth (✓); D: population stable (✓).

Total = 31 marks

Round-up

1 **a)** The non-living part of an environment (✓). **b)** The amount of light affects the rate of photosynthesis (✓) and therefore the amount of plant growth under the canopy (✓). This in turn affects the animals that depend on plants for food and shelter (✓) – and so on along the food chain (✓).

2 **a)** Three (✓). **b)** Water weed (✓), which makes food by photosynthesis (✓). **c)** Tadpoles (✓). Tadpoles eat water weed (accept plants) (✓). **d)** Minnow eats tadpoles and perch eats minnow (accept meat) (3✓).

3 See figure on page 113 (2✓).

4 The Sun. (✓)

5 When the different organisms in the community show an approximation (accept 'are roughly the same') in size. (✓)

6 **a)** Correct axes (numbers: Y axis; years: X axis) (2✓); correctly plotted (6✓ = 12 × ½ mark for each correct co-ordinate). **b)** 1840–1880 (2✓) (allow ±5 years). **c)** 1900 (✓); 1930 (✓). **d)** Population numbers were stable (✓). (Allow: population numbers fluctuated around a mean (average) number.)

Total = 30 marks

Topic 3 Green plants

Test yourself

1 Light energy (✓) absorbed by chlorophyll (✓) is used to combine carbon dioxide and water (✓), making glucose (a sugar) (✓). Oxygen is released (✓).

2 The leaf is flat (exposing a large surface area for the absorption of light) (✓) and thin (✓).

3 More water is drawn up the xylem (✓), suction draws water from the roots (✓); water lost is replaced by the roots absorbing more water (✓).

4

A	B
Nectary	Produces a sugar solution
Stigma	Structure to which pollen grains attach
Fruit	Develops from the ovary after fertilisation
Ovule	Contains the egg nucleus
Seed	A fertilised ovule

(5✓)

5 **a)** Insects are attracted to flowers (✓) and pick up a load of pollen (✓). Wind blows pollen (✓) from flower to flower (✓). **b)** Pollination brings pollen grains from the anthers (✓) to the stigma of a carpel (✓). Fertilisation occurs when one of the male sex nuclei from a pollen grain (✓) fuses with the female egg nucleus in the ovule (✓).

Total = 23 marks

Round-up

1 Root (✓), leaf (✓) and stem (✓).

2 Plants are healthy (✓), the same (✓) and inherit all the parent's desirable characteristics (✓).

3 Gas X is oxygen (✓). Cells use oxygen to oxidise sugars (✓), with the release of energy (✓).

4 Maximum light reaches the palisade cells (✓), which are packed with chloroplasts (✓). Photosynthesis therefore occurs at a maximum rate (✓).

5 Nitrogen is used to make protein (✓), magnesium and iron are needed to make chlorophyll (✓).

6 Root hairs, root, stem, leaves. (4✓)

Total = 18 marks

Topic 4 Humans as organisms

Test yourself

1 A balanced diet is a mixture of foods (✓) which together provide sufficient nutrients (✓) for healthy living (✓).

2 Milk is a source of calcium (✓), which is an important part of bones and teeth (✓). Babies need a lot of calcium for the development of strong bones and teeth (✓).

3 Mouth, oesophagus, stomach, small intestine, large intestine, rectum, anus. (5✓)

4 **a)** A person has two lungs. Within each lung bronchioles sub-divide into even smaller tubes (✓), which end in clusters of small sacs called alveoli (✓). **b)** Two bronchi each branch left or right into the lungs (✓). Each bronchus branches many times into small tubes called bronchioles (✓). **c)** Breathing takes in (inhaling) (✓) and removes (exhaling) (✓) air. Gaseous exchange occurs across the surfaces of the alveoli (✓).

5

A	B
Plasma	Contains wastes which are removed by the kidneys
Red blood cells	Absorb oxygen
White blood cells	Help protect the body from disease
Platelets	Help stop bleeding

(4✓)

6 Bones, protect (or support), support (or protect), muscles, contract, joint. (6✓)

Total = 28 marks

Round-up

1 **a)** Fibre. **b)** Carbohydrate. **c)** Protein. **d)** Additive. (4✓)

2

A	B
Ingestion	Food is taken into the mouth
Digestion	Food is broken down into soluble substances
Absorption	Digested food passes into the bloodstream
Egestion	The removal of undigested food through the anus

(4✓)

3

A	B
Fruit	Source of vitamin C
Bread	Source of fibre
Meat	Source of protein
Milk	Source of calcium

(4✓)

4

A	B
Intercostal muscles	Attached to the ribs
Diaphragm	Sheet of muscle that separates the chest cavity from the abdominal cavity
Bronchus	One of two tubes that branch from the trachea

(3✓)

5 Nose, trachea, bronchi, bronchioles, alveoli. (3✓)

6

A	B
Stimulants	Speed up a person's reactions
Hallucinogens	Give a false sense of reality
Depressants	Slow down a person's reactions

(3✓)

7 **a)** D (✓). **b)** E (✓). **c)** A = sperm tube (✓) B = urethra (✓) C = scrotal sac (✓) D = testis (✓) E = penis (✓).

Total = 28 marks

Topic 5 Living things vary

Test yourself

1 Three, two, jointed, wings, wings, exoskeleton. (6✓)
2 Branching into two. (✓)
3 1: Hairy skin – gooseberry (✓); Non-hairy skin – go to 2. 2: Pips on the fruit's surface – strawberry (✓); No pips on the fruit's surface – go to 3. 3: Nearly spherical in shape – go to 4; Other shape – banana (✓). 4: Smooth surface – apple (✓); Rough surface - go to 5. 5: Fruit made up of sub-units – blackberry (✓); Fruit made up of one unit – orange (✓).
4 Pips on the fruit's surface – strawberry (✓); Smooth surface – apple (✓).

Total = 15 marks

Round-up

1 Inherited characteristics arise from genetic causes (✓). Acquired characteristics arise from environmental causes (✓).
2

(3✓)

A	B
Fungi	Made up of thread-like cells
Plants	Grow from seeds
Bacteria	Single-celled living things

3 Continuous variation describes the variation of a characteristic (✓) which is spread over a range of values (✓). Discontinuous variation describes the variation of a characteristic (✓) which exists in one form or another (✓). There are no intermediates (accept 'in-betweens') (✓).
4 Natural selection favours individual living things with the features (✓) that best suit them to survive (✓). Artificial selection occurs when humans choose living things (✓) with desirable characteristics (✓) and allow only these individuals to produce offspring (✓).

Total = 15 marks

Index

BUZAN TRAINING COURSES